Tom was born in North Wales in 1977,
much to the dismay of his parents.

The destiny written upon his forehead was that he should
tirelessly pursue the elusive Free Lunch
or go hungry in the attempt.

He plays rhythm-less guitar, clarinet melodies that defy the
laws of acoustics and dances in a style that will surely one
day win him all expenses paid entrance to the nearest
institution for the deranged.

tom@tomthumb.org

GW00707858

Tom - November 1999
(photo - Mal Burns)

This edition published in the UK in June 2000 by:
Alchemy Books,
261 Portobello Road,
London W11 1LR
Tel 020 7792 0166
email: openmind@fsbdial.co.uk
www.leeharris.co.uk/alchemy

Originally published in India by:
Starving Freak Publications UnLimited 1999
Tom Thumb © 1998

Distributed by Turnaround Publisher Services Ltd.
Unit 3, Olympia Trading Estate, Coburg Road,
London N22 6TZ

ISBN 0-9508487-2-7

A catalogue record for this book is available from
The British Library

Printed and bound in the United Kingdom by:
Biddles Ltd. Guildford, England.

Hand to Mouth to India

by Tom Thumb

For Ali

I only wish that the book was as good as the cover!

With love + respect,

Tom

Alchemy
BOOKS

Acknowledgments

In chronological order, I must first thank Robin Brown (author of the profound "Deccan Tamasha" and "Further Up the Road") without whose inspiration, wisdom and wit - not to mention donation of paper and pens - I would neither have attempted the journey nor written the book when I arrived!

Paul Eagle was also of immense help in the course of this book. Not only did he let me swear at his Apple Mac for the month it took me to type the thing up, he then also took on his shoulders the unenviable task of typesetting and coordinating the first edition of 500 copies in Goa, 1999. Without him it might just have remained the fodder for cows which it nearly became when I left it unattended under a palm tree on the beach. I'm indebted also to the fruit lady who chased the bull off with a vicious machete.

The book was further rescued from obscurity half a year later by the present publisher, Lee Harris. The winds of chance blew me into his shop - Alchemy - on Portobello Road and he happened to catch a glance at a road-worn first edition. It was one of the last of 70 remaining books that I'd lugged on my back as I hitchhiked through Turkey, Syria, Jordan and Israel. Lee had the heart not to take me at face value and envisioned a greater potential for my ragged tale. With unstoppable enthusiasm and loving motivation he took on the daunting mission of delivering the book unto the market. Where would the world be without these men who bring dreams into reality?

Thanks to the dedicated artwork of Alistair, it is to be hoped that people will judge this book by its cover. The quality and professional touch of his work is only matched by his easy-going charm, which eased the project along in the best of spirits.

I couldn't begin to list the people who have helped me out over the last few years. But the journey itself was made much happier by the faith and kindness of Meriana, the Guptas, Naresh and Mustafa. And I cannot complete this section without acknowledging the continued, unconditional support of David Pearce.

Dedicated to my first gurus
Andy, Patti and Woody

Map of Tom's
"Thumbing Blues"

Contents

Contents

"The man who sleeps on the floor
will never fall out of bed."
(old Turkish proverb)

Chapter 1

Free-Wheeling
(England, France, Luxembourg)

I walked out one midsummer's morning to hitchhike to India with no money at all. I had with me my clarinet, a sleeping bag, a ticket for the boat to France and a couple of loaves of date bread so as to be sure of not starving to death within the first day or two. I paused beneath a giant billboard poster of Tony Blair smooching the street with his smarmy, sinister smile and then walked on to exchange grey cities for palm tree beaches, politicians for snake charmers. A stranger in my hometown, I walked down to the coastal road with little but my freedom on my back.

Already a memory were the touching farewells of heartfelt friends and bosom buddies I never knew I had, who had sprung out into my path around town to suffocate me in tight emotional embraces. Not many thought I'd get very far, or even survive and with tearful reluctance they crossed me off their Christmas card lists.

But all camaraderie dies when you hit the road alone and prepare for the vessels of Fate to bear down upon you in screeching metal boxes on wheels. Standing as an exposed and anonymous figure with an aching thumb, it's an old journeying adage that there's a fine line between hitchhiking and waiting by the side of the road like an idiot.

My first lift pulled up within minutes and I jumped in without a glance back.

"I'm going to India!" I told the driver smugly, as I strapped on my seat-belt.

"Well, I can take you as far as the university…" he told me doubtfully.

A couple of rides later, I was sitting on the pebbles of Hastings Beach, eating a farewell meal of English *haute cuisine* fish 'n' chips. The sea was smothered in a miserable gloom and refused to yield any hint of what might lie ahead. But during the previous winter in Goa, I had sat at the feet of various hobo gurus and learnt that if you have eaten this day then you are successful. Period. Providence had already provided well for me in a penniless tour of springtime Europe. But fear has the habit of mushrooming back up at even the thought of rain and so I flicked open the pages of Kahil Gibran's "The Prophet", to seek some confirmation. I read:

"Is not the fear of being thirsty when your well is full, the very thirst that is unquenchable? And what is fear of need but need itself?"

Things were going to be fine. More or less. I disposed of the grease-soaked wrapper of my chips and, turning from the moody waves, I stomped back through the stones to the road, large and weighty doors of the past slamming shut behind me.

Towards the end of daylight, I arrived at Dover, having survived some fairly uninspiring conversations and found at the dregs of Britain's roadways, a skaggle of hitchhikers attempting to leave this tiny island and rejoin the greater potential of the Continent. We were all experts at travelling light but none of the drivers seemed to care as no one was getting any luck–possibly due to the ticket restrictions on how many people could travel in each car. I caught the boat and made my bed on the tiled floor of Calais port, pretty much at the feet of the other people waiting on the plastic seats and was quite content–sleeping inside is always a bonus in this mode of travel, even if it is punctuated with piercing loudspeaker announcements every ten minutes for the departing ferries.

Some hours later, I dragged myself out of the feverish horrors of half-sleep, and heaved my bleary body out into the chilly morning to make an early start and avoid competition. Outside, I discovered that the same notion had occurred to many others and we threw etiquette out of the window, as we all tried to flag down and solicit truck drivers with no sense of order or queuing–the equivalent of cutting each other up when driving. Hitchhiking is hardly a communal activity as no group larger than two is going to get any lifts–unless an exceptionally beautiful girl is present. So hitchers don't like to hang around talking with other *gratis* voyagers.

There seemed to be no real chance of moving out with so many people waiting, so I chose to walk a few miles in search of a better spot, leaving behind a die-hard French couple who told me:

"We'll sleep here if we have to—we don't care!" They were off to India in the autumn and we speculated that we might meet again in more serene surroundings than this murky slip road. Wishing them luck, I sweated my way up the road and caught a chance lift with an Englishman, winging his way out of town after a bistro breakfast.

Relieved not to be forced into my inadequate French, I set to navigating our way out of the confusion of roundabouts, whilst sizing up my benefactor of the hour out of the corner of my eye. He was a fat and bearded Geordie, called Jeff. He wore the image of an itinerant cowboy who waddled into the saloons of every town and hitting the whiskey; a rolling stone entertainer, paving his way through the towns of Europe. He had been a professional busker for the best part of ten years and within minutes, we were exchanging stories and anecdotes of playing music on the street—his far more rich and prolific than mine and so I let him do most of the talking, whilst I concentrated on a map of North-West France.

"Some days luck is with you and other days it's not—simple as that!" He told me, "I was playing in a duo on the trams in Switzerland last year and me and my partner, Mike, we were playing an amazing set—all of our solos were bang on time, we were making up hilarious verses and we improvised a completely new finale! Then Mike went around the tram to collect money in his hat. And I watched him as he set off all confident like and slowly, he became more and more depressed until he came back with the lowest face you ever saw—no one gave us a single coin!" Jeff stroked his beard in remembrance. "But then a week or two later, we were playing together again on the trams and we were both really hungover, I forgot the chords to the song we were playing and two of Mike's strings snapped—and before we could even attempt to finish, people were coming over and stuffing our hat full with all they had in their wallets!"

We avoided the incredibly expensive *peage* pay roads that dominate the signs at each junction and hit the 'A' roads that ran almost parallel to the motorways in elegant straight lines that rose and dipped over graceful hills through the countryside. The road intersected every small town on the route and each approaching settlement was heralded by the beautiful visage of a proud and lonely white church, towers and spires aspiring high above the Christian buildings that all possessed refined and individual character. With haystacked meadows and grazing sheep, the route was sweetly picturesque and these rural charms reconciled my doubtful heart to the prospect of a great voyage—here at last was real travelling! And I wouldn't have traded this life for all the splendour of a sultan's palace... unless he possessed a particularly fine harem!

Unhappily enough, Jeff turned out to be a born-again Christian, though thankfully not of the evangelical 'now listen up' variety. However, he limited his sermon to a brief warning about the risks of Eastern wisdom:

"You see, many of the Eastern religions talk about making the mind empty—but that's actually very dangerous!" And he'd pause to allow my understanding to catch up. "Because when the mind is empty, evil spirits can come in and start to take control!" Jeff was a good guy though and we settled down into a trusting repartee where neither of us needed to say too much.

We drove all day and came to rest in a small town with a pleasant, drifting river that carried bubbles and pieces of straw along no faster than need be. Jeff went off into town on the pretext of changing money, whilst I sat on the soft grass and played provincial blues on my harmonica. He came strolling back an hour and a half later with a happy, drunken swagger and we spoke wistfully about the strangeness of existence; two misfits sitting with their legs dangling over the riverbank, staring into the folds of twilight that closed the day about us.

My German army sleeping bag and waterproof poncho of the same issue, proved effective against the cold, dew and damp that are ever present in Northern Europe even at the height of summer, whilst Jeff also struggled for comfort in the back of his van.

The next morning, we got ourselves together to pull out of town only to break down after two miles. Cursing, Jeff went off in search of a telephone but it began to rain before he'd gone a hundred metres. I sat patiently in the car, wondering if that was his karma for not sharing his beer session with me the night before. I looked to the drops of rain rolling down the windscreen for an answer. What the fuck am I doing here? I asked myself, as I do twenty times a day on the road. I just reclined the seat a bit and let the patter of falling water call the shots; strangely pleasant to be in some stranger's car near a little red dot on the map.

With the help of some local mechanics, we got moving again and by mid-afternoon came rolling into Luxembourg City, where Jeff proposed that we raise some funds with his music in the public squares. He was looking for a gold-mine where he could work for a week or two and then use the earnings to steadfastly vegetate on a beach in Portugal. And man,was this the right place! We struggled to find what name to call the people of Luxembourg–the Luxemese? The Luxish? The answer became rapidly clear–the Luxurious! For everywhere we looked were lush BMW's and smooth Mercedes cruising around in the nonchalant manner of the very rich. This tiny country measuring about 60 miles long by 50 miles wide lies as a select watering hole for the wealthy hippos of Europe. Jeff licked his lips in anticipation.

In addition, Luxembourg receives massive amounts of tourism from holidaying Europeans and Americans, whose guidebooks on how to survive on $300 a day, specifically recommend them to come and spend as much money as possible on the authentic local cuisine of tacos and re-fried beans, in the traditional grandeur of the main square where a large brass orchestra played Abba tunes twice a day.

There was no shortage of street performers, either, as fire jugglers, New York break dancers, concert flute players and didgeridoo dudes, all competed to empty the bulging purses of the visitors who clearly had more than they knew what to do with.

Jeff swaggered down to the Square in his cowboy hat and leather boots and began to set up his backing equipment and electric guitar. This was to be the first time that I saw busking being really profitable; I had busted my ass howling 1930's Mississippi Blues on the streets of France and Austria, whipping out razor-sharp riffs that sliced the air, with a slide on my little finger producing a groove to reduce any cultured and sensitive soul to tears–but it's well-known that most of society is made up of Philistines who were bottle-fed on mediocrity from day one. At least that was my conclusion on the days when I didn't earn enough to even buy a cup of coffee, let alone a pint of whiskey!

Playing music on the street is great when things are going well. You can feel yourself bringing life and vitality to the city; a colourful bard of the urban scene, you can laugh and joke with the locals in true minstrel style. But on a bad day the street becomes the most heartless place in the world as the police move you on with unnecessary aggression, passers-by seem almost offended by your daring to break the monotony and when the few coins that you placed in your hat (as 'bait' to lure further additions) sit as lonely as only metal money can be.

On those dire occasions, you feel like laying down in the gutter and allowing the tarmac to swallow you up for all that anyone would care. Performing is a creation that must be resurrected every time you start anew. The maestro act of yesterday means little in the bleak and hungover face of the new morning.

Jeff shared this feeling as he admitted to me that:

"Sometimes I push myself too far–playing every day without enough breaks. Then all the fun goes out of it and I become kinda drained and depressed. And I have to say to myself 'Hey, Jeff! Take it easy, will you?'" It was for this reason that I'd grown tired of busking and was now giving it a rest.

I'd achieved my personal target in Vienna, two months before when, poor and bored, I really began to feel the full measure of the low-down, empty-belly, so-lonesome, rambling blues that groan in your gut and squeeze your heart until there's nothing else you can do except howl it to the world–and let them be damned if they don't like it! Because everyone knows it and there ain't no place to hide from it–so let's play it, by God!

To those passing by, a sudden transformation could be seen in the shabbily-dressed, unshaven Englishman, who sat sunken into his guitar–a sudden dirt-gravel growl broke into his voice that interrupted all conversations and his head began to rock with a moaning passion; his fingers began to dance of their own accord across the fretboard, hammering the strings to the edge of breaking-point as he screamed:

"And the blu-ues, is just a low down shaking chill.
Yes, I'm telling you that the blu-oo-hoo-ues, is nothing but a
low down shaking chill,
You ain't never had them. Hope you never will."

("Preaching Blues" 1935, by Robert Johnson)

People were compelled to stop, stare and dig in their pockets for the coins and notes that started to flood the hat. But then a bored Austrian policeman decided that Delta Blues hollers didn't really cut the ice in bourgeois Vienna and so he stopped the show. The whole episode was recorded by the many tourists armed with hand-held video cameras, collecting items for their home movies–but *they* never gave a schilling.

ॐ

Meanwhile, back in Luxembourg, Jeff had his routine pretty well worked out, sounding quite professional with his electric guitar and formulaic backing tapes. These laid down the percussion and bass lines for the five or six songs from which he never varied. His sparrow-like Geordie voice vanished when he sang, to be replaced by the cliched American twang that can be heard in most modern music. His vocals were clear and bold though and the overall sound could be heard from fifty feet away, extending our target audience.

The arrangement was that he played opposite the cafe terraces to win the favour of the well-dressed businessmen and families as they dined on pasta and wine, filling the space between songs with the well-practised comments of 'Thank you for that wonderful round of indifference' or 'No dancing on the tables'! My job was to do the 'bottle', a name deriving, Jeff claimed, from the original Punch n' Judy shows, when a pretty girl used to hit up the crowds after the act, collecting the money in a glass bottle that contained a fly–the trick being that if she took her thumb off the top for too long, the fly would escape and then the puppeteers would know that she'd been trying to syphon the money for herself.

After about three or four songs, Jeff would give me the nod and I'd go into full hustle mode. I walked from table to table, shaking the hat to give the coins an expectant jingle and accosted the punters in the middle of their meals, persuading them to dip their soup-stained fingers in their wallets, as I cried out:

"*Un peu d'argent pour les musiciens, s'il vous plait!* **Ein bischen geld, bitte, mein herr?** Spare a bit of cash for the music, mate, so that we can eat?" Depending on what tongue was appropriate in this conflux of linguistic drifts.

With a bit of coaching from Jeff, I soon learned the various tricks to bring in more money: no one could be hurried into bringing out their purses, as it was far more effective to introduce the idea to them slowly by mulling about in a relaxed saunter, to give everyone the idea that they were supposed to contribute. The first point of attack was always the table that gave most applause. From there I'd plan the rest of my route to gain the maximum possible attention. As long as I was loud and funny, polite and insincere, the hat I carried gained in weight rapidly and I couldn't pretend we were so poor any more. We moved from terrace to terrace, Jeff playing the same set each time to the new cafe crew and, by the end of the evening, we'd got about $100 together.

As I was pretty inexperienced at plying the 'bottle', Jeff proposed that I take 25% of the take. I reckoned I was doing more than okay at the job but didn't press the point as, after all, I was hardly trying to swell my pension funds! So I took an easy-come easy-go attitude about it and just got into the fun of new experience. That's why I came on the road in the first place.

At the last cafe of our evening's tour, a bunch of Brazilian businessmen implored us to share a drink with them. Beer always tastes good after hard work and it was only after the first sip that we looked up and realised that we were sitting with a group of sallow-faced, shifty-looking men, with all the sly vibe of reptilian schoolboys as they wisecracked and competed for status amongst themselves.

"These men are all very rich men!" Our translator told us in a reverent tone. Looking from each screwed-up face to the next and, studying each pair of troubled eyes behind a worried mist of alcohol, it was clear that these were also very unhappy men. Maybe they weren't praying hard enough to the Greenback Dollar God who promises to bring everlasting delight to his most successful devotees.

Below where we'd parked the van was a deep valley where a public park lay. I trotted down to find a shady place to sleep away from the main path and the harsh glare of the streetlights. Under the scrutiny of the many CCTV cameras that dotted the park, I tried to look like a casual late-night stroller, arm-in-arm with my sweetheart-sleeping-bag. But was there really anyone watching on the other end who gave a damn? No one came along to evict me but I spent an uncomfortable night being frequently awoken by the drunken antics of late-night clubbers, on the path some 20 metres away.

The morning didn't start off too well, as a persistent itch alerted me to the sadly undeniable fact that I was now host to invisible park fleas–'What to do?' as they say in India with a fatalistic waggle of the head. Then I managed to get into a full yelling row with the Dutch woman who ran the public toilets. She took exception to me washing my armpits in the sink and I only just about managed to clean up in a petty struggle of power, whereby the old hag kept turning off the water for a minute or so in petulant demonstration of her authority, whilst I bent under the taps trying to salvage enough of the leftover drips.

As I left, a guy looking like a security guard passed me on the steps. I counted it as a close escape and went off in search of some breakfast with jingling francs in my pocket as a result of the previous night's endeavours.

I stood in the supermarket, staring bleakly at the prices of fruit per kilo to see what I could afford–and so hapless did I look, that a middle-aged lady stopped and asked me in concerned German:

"Do you have enough money to eat?" And before I could effectively protest she handed me 200 francs (about $10) with the apology that it was not much and departed before I could find the appropriate words in her language to express my stunned gratitude. Kindness is like water and will find you no matter how low you stand. Even here in the heartland of capitalist Europe, there were angels who took my well-being upon themselves. Travelling hand-to-mouth restored my faith in the essential goodness of human nature and frequently left my hardened cynicism agape, soaked in the melting sunshine of the care and warmth that was almost always given to me when I was in real need.

I was getting hungry for the road again but Jeff persuaded me to stay and work for another night so that my journey would be better greased by my share of the evening's take. We relieved the tourists of their spending money again and I became heartily sick of hearing the same poppy tunes of which Jeff never seemed to tire:

"And your smile, is just a big disguise,
For now, as you realise,
There ain't no way to hide those lying eyes!"

Sleeping in the park was even worse that night, as party-goers stumbled upon my resting-place no less than three times. They were more freaked out than I though and I called out good-day to them in German and French from my reclining position in their path of reckless exuberance.

"Aaaargh! Un habite!" ('a dweller!') One of them called out in alarm and distaste, that there could be such people who slept out under bushes and trees.

My mood was greatly improved in the morning by the ridiculous bouncing form of a young American guy. He came scampering and bounding through the park and accosted me:

"Could you take a picture of me please?" Placing the camera in my hand before I could respond. He then darted away to pose by trees and hillocks with both arms splayed open wide. I particularly liked the surety with which he assumed everyone that he approached would be able to speak fluent English—well, these people are educated , aren't they?

Despite our differences in character, I'd gotten along well with my road-buddy, Jeff—he was a good sort and a seasoned freak in his own right, bravely making his way on the fringes of society. I gave him my European map book, ripping out the pages I'd need and gathered the $50 or so that I'd made from the bottle. Small coins and shrapnel galore, the bane of all buskers, I managed to get them changed up into higher denominations before Jeff gave me a starting lift to a petrol pump on the edge of town.

It's always useful to get dropped off at gas stations as then you can take hitchhiking onto the offensive, by hitting up the drivers as they stand around with petrol hoses in their hands, nervously watching the display rack up the litres and escalating cost. In this scenario, you get the chance to approach them personally and make a verbal contact that they can't just ignore, as some humanity is injected into the relationship between hitcher and driver; a warmth that is somehow absent when separated by a windscreen and a projectile speed of 8okmph, their rejection exhaust smoke leaving you coughing and black in the face. The personal approach also gives them the chance to see that you're probably not a crazed axe murderer. Once they realise that you're not a threat it becomes a lot harder for them to say 'no'.

In some ways, though, I prefer the romance of standing by the side of the road, inviting the pot-shots of chance to sweep me away from my lonely mooring, my fate thus out of my hands. Also, the grace of the slowing car tends to produce more charming encounters, as these drivers are those who voluntarily have an affection for the free travelling spirit and make for much better company.

But if you want to get anywhere fast, then it's best to be as pushy and bold as can be, soliciting every driver you can with cheerful and courteous turn of speech so that they consent before they have time to even think about it. The downside is that when very few drivers are actually going your way, you end up with a lot of polite rejections that really tax your energy and enthusiasm–as happened on this day and I became increasingly dejected, jaded and desperate. Walking in the mid-day heat amongst the intoxicating petrol fumes, I ended up weaving around like an alcoholic fresh in from the desert.

I was trying in vain to decipher the destinations of the cars by the tell-tale initials on their number plates, when I overheard an approaching couple of businessmen talking in cockney English. I approached them in my salt-of-the-earth accent and asked: "Excuse me, mate–you wouldn't happen to be going towards Saarbrucken, at all, would you?" With brilled blonde hair, one of them gave a sneering laugh and replied: "Nah, mate! We're going to work !" The implications were pretty clear and I was only consoled by remembering the story an old college tutor of mine had told me: he'd decided to hitchhike back from a conference he'd attended that weekend and had been waiting for a couple of hours in a lay-by when a van stopped. He ran quickly up and a head popped out of the window:

"Do you want a job?" The driver asked him.

"No!" he replied, with all the pride of a professional man, wondering where this was leading.

"Thought so!" came the retort and the driver sped off with a triumphant cackle.

Chapter 2

Round the Bend to Vienna
(Germany, Austria)

I eventually got my rides into Germany and I told, rather than asked, the drivers that I was going to sleep and that they could forget any ideas about stimulating conversation. I often get picked up by people who need someone to talk to so that they don't doze off at the wheel, or else just to break up the monotony of pursuing the ugly concrete motorway–thus it doesn't generally go down well when the stray wanderer they've picked up passes out within minutes in the front seat, snoring loudly. But sometimes there are just no two ways about it and I was in no mood to try and fight the rocking lull of a car's motion that pulls the eyelids inexorably together. On the road you need every bit of shut-eye that comes your way.

I got stuck again at a petrol station inside Germany and ended up approaching a tall, bald guy in my best German as he rummaged in the boot of his car. He responded in perfect English. He didn't believe me when I told him my destination was India but he relented and let me in, allowing me the satisfaction of proof when I flashed the Irani and Pakistani visa pages of my passport at him.

"Wow, man! You've got a long journey ahead of you!" Too true.

This turned out to be one of the best rides of my hitchhiking career so far. This large and lanky guy's name was Jan and he drove his Mercedes at a silent 200 kmph down the no-speed-limit German autobahn. The transformation of setting is one of the reasons I love this mode of travel. Five minutes before I was choking on the fumes and frustration of petrol pumps going nowhere fast, but now I was turning my hand to sophisticated conversation in a well-oiled machine of flying motion and everything seemed groovy.

It emerged that Jan was something of a hi-tech prophet of the first order; a designer of future state-of-the-art computers, he was working on contracts with very wealthy German businesses and Austrian banks and it was clear that some serious money was involved.

Once he sensed that my mind was open to the other-than-normal, he began to outline his whole project, growing in enthusiasm and eloquence as he went on. Jan was becoming the architect of computers that would possess souls–giving independent life to the byte-biting hardware recently formed into one being with the generation of the internet. This visionary who sat beside me with one hand on the wheel and both eyes trailing off into a grandiose distance, foresaw a near future when computers would be endowed with belief systems and values. He stood at the threshold of a revolutionary New Age that smacked of scary Bladerunner scenarios.

It was not all easy street for his notions however, as he had to do daily battle with the dinosaur-like minds of the directors and 'experts' of the companies who hired him but were as yet too cautious to let him take the full reins of progress between his gnashing teeth. He ran himself blue in the face attempting to persuade these fat cats that computers would soon become something astronomically more than fancy calculators that can keep the score on the stock markets and produce nice little graphics for souped-up space invader games.

Not only this but Jan was keenly aware of the potential dangers of computers gaining partial or full autonomy and considered that the whole process would have to be handled with the utmost care and aforethought. He considered that there were many malevolent influences who sought to contaminate or dominate this amazing potential for power that would soon emerge in the forthcoming computer epoch. In this sense, he saw himself as a figure of light engaged in a struggle for good against evil. Already he and his like-minded associates were taking steps to forestall the dastardly, Lex Lutherish designs of the more sinister players in this particular game.

I began to spin off this warped conversational tack with relish and speculated on how the megalithic oppression of the multinational companies (who are, of course, the immediate source and cause of 95% of economic and social evil in the world) might be left behind as toppling giants with their minds stuck in the past, unable to cope and adapt to the new organic macro-intelligence that would run rings around them. Thus, I reasoned, such enormous firms would soon sorely be in need of techno-warriors and strategists of Jan's calibre to undertake uprooting of posture and operation crucial to their survival.

Soon at the top of the innovation and logistics departments of multi-billion dollar firms would be weird and warped techno-prophet minds right at the heart of the beast. With their intrinsically alternative nature and designs they might revolutionise the whole nature of these institutions from the inside!

"Now you might laugh, Tom but I envision the whole drive towards advanced computer technology as mankind's instinctive and unconscious flight from the hazards of the physical world–where we as humans are threatened by climatic, ecological and social chaos! So we're perhaps retreating towards the internal kingdoms of cyber-space!

"And there will be infinite realms of wonder, magic and beauty–places where we can write the laws of physics ourselves and where the only limits to the nature of existence will be our imaginations. Once we learn how to fully connect the neural pathways of the human brain to silicon routes in… cyber-valleys, we can actually *fully invest* our consciousness into the machine!" Right! *Then* we could truly liberate ourselves from the chains of individuality, with the arrival of the potential for internet-telepathy and merging of minds, possible once all cerebral constructs become compatible.

"So what do you think of the weirdos you met on the German autobahn, Tom?" Jan asked me with a wry smile, bringing my wandering mind back down to Earth for a minute. I laughed as I realised that as usual, I had been swept away with the force of another person's passion and platform, willing as I am to believe the dreams of the wild and the free. But really, what would

Buddha have said at the prospect of such a vision? Perhaps this was an example of the other realms of heaven and hell that the Tibetan Buddhists are always talking about–and surely we're meant to achieve enlightenment in this physical world, no?

I sensed, however, that these doubts were probably symptomatic of a mind that would be left behind in the next era and that my future children would have no difficulty in assimilating the cyber-dimension at all! Would I really come to lose the love and support of my offspring to a cortical shunt plug in the side of their heads? It couldn't be, could it? I swallowed nervously as I considered that if someone went back 100 years and told the people of that time, that in the future you could talk to a special kind of box called a computer and that it could give answers to sums and equations beyond our calculation–he'd have been sent away to the loony bin. Jan confirmed my reasoning by reminding me that before the future is born, it is conceived in the dreams of those who can float above the reality of current times and plot a course to the islands of the impossible.

Back in the three-dimensional world, it turned out that Jan would be driving to Vienna the next day and as the sky began to grow dark, he offered to give me a bed for the night at his house in Stuttgart. It was what I'd been hoping for - he could hardly have left me to the mercy of the elements after a conversation like that, could he? So we went back to his oasis of strangeness in the midst of German suburbia. I rustled up some vegetarian fare from his cupboards, enjoying the trust and the marijuana of this unusual and likeable guy.

We headed off in the early morning, making ridiculously good time in his rather superior vehicle and not talking so much, content to follow our own respective thoughts to the background of fast-diminishing countryside and the psychedelic sounds of the Asian Underground; chants, tablas and sitars of ancient Indian ragas blending with the samples, drum patterns and effects of synthesizers invented within the last decade or so.

We arrived in Vienna in the mid-afternoon. I left Jan with my copy of Kahil Gibran's "The Prophet". He gave me the Asian

Underground tape, 60 schillings and of course, his E-mail address.

So I found myself wandering the streets of Vienna, again. It's a very cool and detached town, whose populace give new meaning to the word 'bourgeois'. They drift through long, cold winters and pleasant summers, posing and pouting but never really leaving second gear.

The nature of the people finds it's reflection in the Viennese architecture that draw huge amounts of tourism in the summers, as enormous cathedrals and stately buildings dominate the scene and the style is characterised by sharp, angular relief-work that mirrors the scornful expressions I'd seen a thousand times in the cruel expressions of the women of the city, as they made their way below past the opulent cake shops.

I hopped on what must be the smallest underground train system in the world and as such is a monument to the languid take-it-as-it-comes attitude of the Viennese. As is the case in much of Europe it's no problem to ride without a ticket, for there are no machines or officials to routinely check that you've paid as you enter–you just have to deal with the occasional hazard of the thoroughly unpleasant ticket police who shunt around the network all day, (dressed as hippies or businessmen) making sudden and aggressive raids on the carriages.

This arrangement suited my friends who lived here as okay, it was unpleasant but they simply took it as their due that every now and then they would be caught and shouted out by these fascistic minor officials with walkie-talkies and fined lots of schillings. It worked out cheaper in the long-run than buying a ticket every day and why walk when you can ride?

Easy for me, of course, as I just needed to flubber around in confused and apologetic English and they'd eventually get frustrated and leave me alone, perhaps with my false address written down in their notebooks.

I stepped out into the Jewish quarter of town by the sullen canal and passed various kosher food stores, between which strode Hassidic Jewish men in black suits, caps and long beards, with earnest and purposeful expressions, doubtlessly wrestling with some Biblical contradiction that was teasing their minds. Police could be seen hanging around to offer the synagogues a constant protective presence against the legacy of persecution that has seemed to follow them wherever and whenever for the last five thousand years.

I climbed the steps of the apartment building, ignoring the elevator and rang the bell of the friends I was hoping to stay with. They were pretty surprised to see me–a little freaked would be closer to the truth. The first question they asked me with nervous and fearful eyes was:

"How long are you going to stay?" Having met two of them first in Goa, I'd already taken up their ill-considered invitation to come and visit in the May of that year and had managed to pretty successfully outstay my welcome–to which there is something of an art.

There were four girls living in the flat and they all possessed minds of sharp and destructive honesty that reduced any insincerity to dust. O beware, innocent and vulnerable wayfarer! These were women to reckon with and woe become anyone caught in vain or narcissistic speech–four more earnest and acute souls you could not hope to find and their impeccable integrity hunted down with a vengeance any signs of pandering to the ego. The result was that they gave themselves (and everyone else!) as hard a time as their strength could bare!

But for all their mental toughness their debates often centred around the eternal issue of whether there was any such thing as true love, sides being chosen on the basis of recent experience!

We'd eventually muddled together some kind of living pattern and, after the initial annoyance and incomprehension, they found my sideline presence amusing:

"You just sit around all day *doing* nothing!" They cried. Which was not true. I wrote at least one song every few days and I rarely missed my morning session of yoga–an island of peace amidst the helter-skelter emotional melodrama of their day-to-day lives.

They had effectively watched me starve in the two weeks that
I'd stayed with them. I had sat around almost empty-handed in a
fiercely competitive and possessive kitchen where they wrote
their names on their bottles of soya sauce and jars of honey, lest
their supplies be usurped by one of the others. To be fair, they had
shown me some ways of making money, including the racket of
picking up 5 schillings per empty bottle left behind at the local
alternative nightclub–but I had rejected this as sleazy–and so,
with occasional lapses of charity, they ate huge meals before me
while I attempted to survive on three bowls of porridge and a kiwi
every day (the fruit, not the bird!)

But then after a hungry week of cooking oats, I spied a poster
on the tunnels of the underground advertising that the dance and
rhythm performance extraordinaire, "Stomp", would be playing
the next day. With a smile like the Cheshire Cat, I remembered
that the sound engineer of the show was a friend of mine from
Brighton.

"Tom! What are you doing in Vienna?" My friend, Mike, asked
me in amazement.

"Starving, mainly." I informed him.

I came down the next night, watched the stunning show from
a choice seat and was afterwards taken along to the opening night
party–where were gathered all the top socialites, personages and
papparazzi of Vienna, milling and mulling in polite conversation.

I headed straight for the buffet where on a pristine scarlet red
cloth, covering the tables that ran across three sides of the room,
was laid a spread of at least a hundred dishes. I piled my plate
with the smoked salmon, the olives, the mango, the chocolate
gateaux and the French cheese. Upon returning to the free bar to
claim *gratis* beer and wine, Mike took a photograph of me leaning
against the counter, with my absurdly-filled plate in one hand and
a glass of Bordeaux in the other–the spoken caption was:

"Tom joins the bourgeoisie."

After boozing with the crew of Stomp, whose capacity for
making rhythms out of anything from newspapers to lighters, was
matched only by their ability to consume incredible amounts of

alcohol and other such stuff; I stumbled back home, leaving their little bubble of London-streetwise on-the-case accents behind me. On the way, I had fancied a little more excitement in my inebriated state and stumbled into an open-air nightclub. Seeking a good place to piss, I walked through to the darker parts of the beer gardens. I saw a choice looking spot by a tree, just across a black shiny path. Two moments later, I discovered that it was not a black shiny path.

"Hmm, " I thought, "Someone's walking in the pond...it's me."

That was May and a lot of water had passed under the bridge since then, without me falling into it. Now August heat soaked all of Europe and left sultry evenings in the wake of the sweaty days. I walked down by the canal where the sunset lay on the silent drift and crossed the town to visit Meriana: a Bulgarian lady who had just secured Austrian citizenship with her marriage that day. She's a bubbly, bouncy girl with flames licking about her. We had first met on a Goan dancefloor where our mutually exuberant kinetics found affinity and she had recognised me on my last visit to Vienna by virtue of my twirling arms in the darkness of the Flex nightclub.

She was a true Punetic—a regular character of the Osho Ashram in Pune in West India. She was a perfect fit for the archetypal model of wild and creative promiscuity in incessant and hot pursuit of sensual realms of passion. Her eyes twinkled with feline mischief and her rampant demeanour meant that she had trouble to even sit at the dinner table for more than five minutes, before something else would snatch her attention.

She spent half the evening on the telephone listening with guilty unease to the sobbings of a guy who'd fallen in love with her and was now realising that she was an eternal free agent of the night. We've never gotten involved and I seriously doubt if I could keep up with her 100 kmph pace—but we had a strange and touching supper together and at the end of it, she booned me 500 schillings to "spread good vibes with…"

The following morning, before I left for Hungary, I walked up to her apartment and left a note outside her front door. It read: "Meriana, you are beautiful."

Chapter 3

Bound for Budapest

"Let there be wine, women, mirth and laughter,
Sermons and soda water the day after"
(Lord Byron)
(Hungary)

As usual, it was a complete bitch attempting to hitch out of Vienna, as traffic-jammed streets seemed to merge into snarling motorways without any graceful interlude. It was hot and Western Europe seemed reluctant to let me go. But I couldn't return to the mocking laughter of those Austrian females who were both impressed and sceptical as to my voyaging ambitions:

"I hope you don't get killed!" They had sung as I left their apartment.

I sang songs to myself and tried to prevent any curses for the passing cars from surfacing, as I always feel you then enter on a downward spiral–According to the Zen school of hitching, if you swear at a car after it fails to stop for you, then you've also sworn at it before it stops for you–and what driver is going to help someone who's hurling abuse at him.

But sometimes...

"Fucking bourgeois self-centred middle-class mundane shits!" I yelled, with a headache coming on from the heat. Almost immediately however, someone pulled over and took me out of town to a lazy, hazy hill where I sat on my bags and stared out across a sweeping silence of wheatfields and cottages.

One hour later, I was in a van with two Germans who were off to see the Hungarian Grand Prix. The border was straight-forward and I waited eagerly to see what changes the ex-communist lands would bring. The Germans swopped bundles of schillings for even larger amounts of Hungarian Forint at the Bureau de Change. The single note that I took to the counter seemed rather paltry in comparison–but it all counts, no? As long as I can buy my raw beef stroganoff and pilsner beer at the end of day, alright,

Jack? I mean, Olveg?

I had an address for a girl I'd never met before who lived a little way outside the capital. I dreamed of some provincial romance with an autumn-haired Balkan beauty; gathering fresh eggs in the morning from the unlikely laying places of the hopelessly errant chickens; long evenings playing with the spriteful children of the sprawling village family, three cats and two dogs in the yard–something smells good in mama's cookpot! And look! Young Jan is whittling away psychotically at the foundations of the house, whilst I and my love lounge around on an old wooden swing in the soft summer twilight. Ah.

Concrete. An ugly word for an ugly thing. Big fuck-off lumps of concrete posing as places of human residence, rising from the towns that we passed en route to Budapest. Okay, now concrete is everywhere but the communists actually seemed proud of these grey monstrosities–strong and symbolic constructions of proleteriat sweat I guess but in that case who'd want to be a prole? The high-rises stood as some irreverent moon at the gods and as a blot on the artistic vision of mankind. The totalitarian regimes quickly realised that the surest way to stifle originality of thought and creativity–things directly challenging to the monotone model of society dominant in the communist countries–was to create a depressing and vulgar immediate environment, yielding the barest of the grace and poetry of life and replacing it with a stagnant and grim bureaucracy, that choked the colour out of the world.

Our visions extend as far as the nearest horizon but for those living in the cities of Eastern Europe, the next concrete high-rise was about as far as their eye could take them. Where could the dreams and inspiration of a William Blake-visionary arise in Hungary? Communist philosophy has very little time for anyone who sees any end other than the glory of the Common Good and try getting the word metaphysics out of your mouth before a sneering Lenin-like laugh spits out in scorn. Anyone for a military polka march? It's sure that they'd have shot the birds who sing in the morning too, if they could have afforded the bullets.

Budapest was big and bustling and I jumped out of the van to start walking purposefully in no particular direction at all, in the same kind of bleary haze that accompanies most people in the early morning hours. The signs of frontier Western commerce were evident with flashing neon Kentucky Fried Chicken signs and suchlike–but they lacked the almost regal status they command in the shopping centres of the West. They seemed almost pitiful token symbols in the obscurity of these grey lanes. Outside the supermarkets sat darker-skinned women and men, selling apples and peaches from their portable set-up stands, reminding me of Asia.

It was getting towards dark and I wasted half an hour hesitating between stepping onto the stage for an unlikely romance in the nearby village, or heading on East. Somehow it was hard to maintain the dreams of rural love in the congestion of Budapest. I let my shyness get the better of me and hustled my way out onto the highway.

I had intended to stay and dig Budapest but the horse-trap 19th century cultural capital of my imaginings disappeared in the smog of the late 20th century reality. Big cities are not always such great places for the ragged traveller who has no way to pay for a hotel room–yeah, avenues can open up if you find the right kind of scene where musicians and dope-smokers hang around. But in an unknown metropolis, it's just as likely that you'll walk into the wrong part of town, where the twilight is not so pleasant and naive and tired hitchhikers who don't speak the local lingo can meet with heavy situations if they stumble into ghettoes of soul-dead heroin depravity.

With more luck than usual, I managed to find the right place to stand and a car skidded to a halt within minutes, even though it was now dark. My driver was headed to Debrecen, which was near the Romanian border and so I sat tight and made polite conversation. He was a young, self-employed guy with his own business and he drove fast and neatly, intent on reaching his hometown where his girlfriend was waiting for him, before she could fall asleep. He seemed pretty impressed with my resolve to get to India and I allowed his spoken compliments to my bravery to fill the gaps inside where my courage ought to have been.

Jeez, I wasn't even sure if the route was even possible; I didn't know if anyone would feed me and I half-expected to be ambushed and beaten up by a bunch of gypsies, who'd rob me of my clarinet, my good looks and my passport containing all the visas I'd painstakingly obtained–making it impossible for me to make the overland route–Courage? Come on! Foolish? Maybe. Naive? Most definitely. But God is supposed to love drunkards and fools and I counted myself as one of the favoured.

As I was sort of hoping that this nice young guy might give me a bed for the night at his Debrecen home, I accepted his offer to recline my seat so that I could sleep, hoping that my apparent fatigue might evoke his charity. As we came near his town, he switched on the radio to wake me up and he pulled over by a garage–no warm bed was awaiting me but he did give me a handful of coins. At my gratitude said:

"Wait, I have paper also." Which seemed to sum up the whole money thing–these green and blue survival tickets that won't keep you warm and certainly don't taste good. He was more than generous and now, after leaving England with nothing my fortune had swelled to around $80, largely thanks to the kindness of strangers.

I wasn't going to spend any of that on a place to stay, of course–I mean, what kind of self-respecting freak am I? Money is a thing reserved for the tasty cakes in the windows, the spare parts for my instruments and the drinks at the bar to win the hearts (and the bodies) of dark and sultry gypsy maidens. Sweet tastes and fun times are the things that keep you going on the road, for nothing will lower your spirits more than standing by the highway for hours with an empty belly, or staggering through some drizzly town where everyone is supping croissants and coffee behind the windows of warm and friendly cafes where you can't afford anything on the menu. So, true to my principles, I walked into the garage restaurant and ordered three pieces of cherry strudel and a mint tea.

Europe seemed to be going past quickly as after a week, I had come 1500 miles to the heart of the Continent and fate had been so kind in lining my pockets that I felt almost fraudulent in carrying so much money. Alright, I wasn't loaded by most people's standards but for a bread and soya margarine hippy I was doing pretty well. I figured, that if the hitching got really bad, I'd at least be able to buy some train tickets further East and then be obliged to continue the journey by hook or by crook–probably ending up facing the hook, if the legends of traditional Islamic justice bore any truth. I imagined myself being caught pilfering apples form a market-stand: "I'm innocent!" I'd cry–or rather: "I'm English! Doesn't that count for something?" With hands chopped at the wrist, how would I ever play my clarinet again? (Or indeed thumb a lift?)

Catching myself as I almost fell off my stool in a half-dream, I grabbed the counter for support and drew half-a dozen glares–How much of that had I spoken aloud? Time to leave.

The night was cool and the ground already wet with dew–that moist curse of all outdoor sleepers and the forerunner of creeping tuberculosis and consumption. There was no way I was going to try to hitch on to Romania that night, as the dark hours are never advisable hours to cross borders, especially in dodgy police-states.

I walked away from the revealing street lamps and strode over an area of redundant wasteland until I found a bush I could sleep behind, out of the view of anyone who might happen to be walking nearby. I laid down my waterproof poncho on the ground as thin insulation and curled up with my passport, cash and clarinet buried at the bottom of my sleeping bag. I settled down to the lullabies of honking huge trunks 100 yards away but I passed out okay, as sleep is always the time when I feel safest–as I found out to my cost in Prague three months before.

I had been led to a little park by a once-beautiful Russian lady, her features now stretched by her smack habit. She assured me we would have the security of her friend, who worked as night watchman for the museum there. I slept on a wooden bench whilst she roamed the park in her heroin introversion, maybe discovering more reasons to hide from the world.

I dreamt of theft and strange, shifting figures. At one point I awoke and saw two young guys walking past, carrying something heavy. When I fully came to at dawn, I realised what that 'something' was. My guitar no longer rested against the bench as meal-ticket and friend.

I then had to hitch on with just my wits back to England via Amsterdam, without the instrument of my soul; together with 20,000 words of a novel I'd been writing and some crucial addresses–all of which had all been stashed in the pockets of the guitar-case. Of course, that gave me less to carry and was a good sob-story for my benefactors that day, plus giving me the inspiration to get a new instrument–But no way was I going to lose my jazz blowpipe now!

The minute you start to sleep rough in Europe, you step outside the area of accepted social conventions into a shady zone of chance where nice people don't go. There is nowhere really set aside for those sleeping out: no free public shelters to provide some cover, warmth and safety–the idea presumably being that such a facility would be abused–whatever that means. So when I turn up in an unknown town I have to search around in streets and parks, prospecting the comfort of climbing frames and bushes–Look, Mummy! What's that strange man doing lying down there? How many people do you know who sleep outside each night? Millions of people do, in countries all across the world but most people would rather not know how or why–I mean, it's just not savoury, is it? Just imagine laying down in the dust and dirt to sleep!

Most of society is far too squeamish for that kind of thing and the average person's survival kit would consist of a collection of visa cards and cheque books. If the crunch ever comes to modern civilisation and all the infrastructures fall apart, then my money is on the hitchhiking types to be foremost among those left standing. These will be the people who know how to make a fire and cook on it; people who won't wilt at the thought of using water instead of toilet paper. Anyhow, these are the kind of thoughts I end up with to salvage some feelings of pride and worth after a cold and lonely bed.

I got through to the morning without being robbed, beaten-up or run-over by a ten-ton truck. I gathered my things and stumbled away into town with the strange injuries in the joints one seems to pick up during the night. Impervious to the funny looks coming my direction from the early-morning commuters, I decided to sit down on a grassy corner and make a breakfast of tinned tuna, bread and garlic. Like a panda eating bamboo, it cost me almost as much calories to open the tin with my fake, little Swiss Army knife than anything I could possibly have gotten from the contents.

Then I spent three hours watching cars slowly turn my mucous membranes black with their exhaust smoke. No rides. It was the road to Romania and from what I'd been told, the two countries didn't get on too well. Apparently, the Hungarians tend to take a rather superior social and cultural eye to the 'thieving, hitchhiking, gypsy-cousin Romanians'–and no doubt I looked the part.

But waiting is all part of the deal, nowadays, as the world grows more paranoid and fearful about the unknown. In the old days, hitchhikers could be seen on every main road and it was simply a matter of common good spirit to pick them up and help them along their way. My grandpa used to tell me of the wartime days when young servicemen could be seen by the hundreds by the sides of the roads, trying to get back to their stations after the excesses of their drunken weekend leaves with their family and sweethearts.

He told me that he could always count on drivers to save his neck from the fury of his commanding officer, by going out of their way to get him back on time.

"Don't worry, son," They'd say, "We'll get you back fighting Hitler before dinnertime!"

He'd have had a hard time nowadays, if he had been alive to

try it because wearing a uniform or any suspicious outfit is enough to automatically disqualify you as a potential passenger in the eyes of most people. I learnt this a couple of years ago when it took me and my friend, Tony, two and a half days to hitchhike to Scotland. I was proudly wearing a kilt, sunglasses and a towel wrapped around my neck which wouldn't fit into my bags. Tony has never quite forgiven me.

No longer is a hitchhiker a helpless stranded soul but rather a likely mugger, rapist or crazed crackpot with a mind as random as his method of travel. Of course, some people do stop–often those who have hitched before themselves. But it becomes harder and harder as the Press feed a never-ending stream of hysteria to the neurotic public–urging them to remain behind the safety of a locked and bolted door, opening it only to selected family members and only then if they can provide at least three valid forms of identification.

In England, a single incident of a nasty murder or abduction has the power to change laws affecting the lives of the rest of the 55 million people living there, such is the frenzy that can be whipped up by the unscrupulous mercenaries of the media. And in America, a bloody film entitled unfunnily enough, "The Hitchhiker", hugely regressed the tradition. Anyone who saw the movie was paralysed with the image of the psychotic repaying the kindness of the driver who stopped for him with the most savage and maniacal of violence. It's your worse nightmare, folks!

I dreamed of the days of the 60's when VW vans full of marijuana smoke were said to pull over like a shot to rescue anyone flagging a ride, a time when hoboing around was an understood and approved thing to do, if a little eccentric. But as times grow harder and money grows scarce, so too does the general spirit become miserly and suspicious and no one dares risk a dream of romance and adventure–'We've all got bills to pay–why should we pick up some tree-hugging freeloader?'

And so we wait and we wait and we wait. In some countries longer than others, in a direct ratio to the level of paranoia in the area which usually corresponds to the general wealth of the place–Switzerland is widely reputed to be the worst country in Europe for catching rides and credit cards grow on trees there. Of course, national character has a lot to do with it and no one but a single beautiful girl moves swiftly across France and Spain.

Despite this, I must admit that I had it pretty good on the road. I was young enough (20) to seem fairly unthreatening and so thin that many people felt I needed a good meal. On top of this, Israelis are always telling me that my name means 'innocence' in Hebrew (though *'naievete'* might be closer to the truth!) and I have the general lost, dreamy manner of someone who really needs to be helped along his way! What else for this brief self portrait–Oh yeah, I'm damn good-looking too!

On this occasion I'd had enough of waiting and didn't want to die as a pointless martyr to the virtue of Patience. I began walking back to the train station to see if I could get some transport over the border and into the Dracula country of Transylvania. As I strolled, I made a few half-hearted attempts to thumb the oncoming cars and one of them actually pulled over.

A red-faced, grey-haired man opened the passenger door and asked me something in Hungarian (A very strange tongue that I never made the slightest effort to learn). In response, I whipped out my map page and tried to point out to him the name of a town that I couldn't pronounce.

"Do you speak English?" He asked me in classic stage manner. I threw back a hip and answered with stature and elegance:

"I am English!"

"Well, come on, then!" He replied with a laugh. I climbed in and began chatting easily and quickly with this wild-haired guy who told me he was originally from Poland but had spent the last ten years or so living in Amsterdam.

"Well, how about this then, Tom–An Englishman and a Pole driving an East German car in Hungary!" And of course everything was wonderful, as it always is with the happily-drunk. Though he wasn't going very far, he invited me for a drink which he bought at the local petrol station. He was friends with the petrol attendant–in fact he seemed to know everyone–and in the general good atmosphere it was decided that I should stay and rest for a day or two, share stories and of course, get very drunk on the excellent Hungarian beer.

Naturally, my new Polish friend, Bishek, had to hide his can between his knees whilst driving and I accompanied him on the rest of his morning's work, as he delivered spare engine parts to the shops in the area. Our adventures included an episode taking a stray dog to the vet. Bishek frightened the sensibilities of all the respectable cat owners with our 'illegal' rogue mongrel. A dog without papers, he had dark grey hair that was unruly and proud and he bounced alongside Bishek in the happy knowledge that he had an ally. As I died of fatigue in the sun-baked car, a quick glance back at my approaching friends could not tell the difference between the pair.

Ah yes, it was all good laughs and jokes until that is, we reached home where his girlfriend was waiting with in absorbed melancholy. Bishek whispered to me that she had only discovered a few days before that she was pregnant.

Our raucous cackles fell flat as chapattis on the silent atmosphere of the apartment and I immediately got the feeling that my timing as wandering guest was not so good. But Zsoka, as she was called, did her best to mask the fact that she had been crying for much of the morning and began to prepare a lunch that I dared not refuse–though it was the first meat I had eaten in three years. Now on holiday for the weekend, Bishek tried to gloss over the awkwardness by sloshing more and more 'brown water' and soon began to dominate the conversation with anecdotes from his time in Nepal–which were interesting from what sense I could make of them.

He had been walking near his flat in Amsterdam, when he ran across a German girl he knew, called Lotti. She was involved in the Tibetan resistance movement and was someone, Bishek told us, who had 'gods with her'.

"Hey Bishek!" She had called, "Do you want to come to Tibet to make a documentary programme about the injustices there?" Three days later they were all on a plane to Nepal, due to sneak into Tibet without visas or permission. Bishek was scouting ahead to make arrangements in the next villages, joyfully throwing back the local booze whilst everyone else was crippled with altitude-sickness.

"You bastard!"Lotti had growled at him.

The expedition failed but the drama wasn't about to stop for my friend, because back in Kathmandu he'd seen a young Tibetan guy being beaten and kicked on the ground by a bunch of Nepalese police.

"Stop! Stop! I'm a doctor!" He had cried, the soldiers parting to let this wild grey-haired lunatic through. "This man must go to hospital now!" He shouted with authoritative madness and then bundled the youth into a taxi and escaped, leaving behind a very confused gaggle of officers who had the growing feeling that the joke may have been on them. After that, Bishek told us, he couldn't pay for anything in the town again as he was plied with food and drink wherever he went, the many Tibetan friends and relatives of the boy insisting on repaying him for his brave deed.

I gratefully accepted the invitation to sleep and was given a cool double-bed in a large and shady room–Maybe *now* they'd have the opportunity to talk. Though Bishek seemed to have sabotaged the chance for dialogue with his speedy inebriation. I felt for Zsoka, as sometimes a flurry of drunken laughter and smiles just won't do.

I woke again in the late afternoon. Bishek was out so I took the opportunity to get talking to Zsoka. She turned out to be a delightful and intelligent woman, who struggled daily with the alcoholic passions of her boyfriend.

She was midway through describing the beautiful towns and countryside of Hungary when Bishek burst in wild and incoherent as a Dean Moriarty, declaring that I had to come with him at once. He was so plastered and excited that it took a while for me to realise that there was a taxi waiting for us in the street. I felt bad for the embarrassment and hurt that this was visibly causing Zsoka but I was a guest in the hands of my host and so I allowed myself to be pulled away, though I acted like a moral drag on the

Pole for the rest of the evening.

We went down to the Jazz Cafe and a really pleasant bunch of people was gathered in this bohemian hang-out spot, where artists and musicians sat at long tables beneath poster portraits of Charlie Parker, John Coltrane and Miles Davis, hanging from the walls that glowed purple and orange in the light of the mounted side lamps. Bishek would not let me pay for any drinks and seemed almost offended at the suggestion. However he was generally uplifted by our meeting.

"Ah, Tom! With you, I am travelling once again, you know? In my mind!" He confided, in between spells of introducing himself (and me) to every pretty girl in the club. Several times I had to prevent him from making ostentatious showman announcements that the whole cafe must stop to hear me playing the harmonica. Hard work, actually.

But for all of the guilty role that he wrote for himself at home, Bishek was a bold and generous guy, possessed of more spirit and zest for life than ten people wagging their fingers put together. I like to dig people for their qualities and relax about their failings; I end up sympathizing with Jerry Garcia, when he sang:

"I'll set out running but I'll take my time
A friend of the devil is a friend of mine"

It was getting late and I was trying to cajole and blackmail Bishek into leaving–a near impossible task–when I found my efforts impeded by the compulsion to talk to a pretty and *petite* woman who had been with us at the table and who now stood in front of me by the exit.

"I will be here tomorrow, too." She told me and that seemed to be a fairly clear hint. Her name was Marianne and she was visiting Debrecen for the weekend, due to return to Budapest on the Monday. Through my drunken stupor, I tried to gather the implications of this. I promised to meet her the next evening.

I pulled Bishek into a taxi and we came back to a dark apartment. I quickly excused myself to lay down for bed. For the next hour I heard shouts and tears that would have served for an anti-alcohol advertisement, as the demon of liquor spread its strife in age-old style.

The next morning, whilst Bishek slept soundly, I attended a classical music concert with Zsoka. We were overwhelmed with the intricate beauty of the flute performances of two young girls. The first was the less proficient and more nervous but somehow more charming for the anxious modesty that gave her solo a sweet and soulful tone. Zsoka took me for lunch and we ate real Hungarian salads and soups, strange and salty–a clear sign that the 'cook was in love', according to my hostess.

In her, I saw some of the less celebrated aspects of the heart: in the patience she exerted in her domestic struggle and I learnt something about inner strength. She spoke with a soft tenderness and it was touching how automatically she had accepted me as witness to their drama, I, a passing wayfarer that her husband had brought home with a 'look what I found' merriness.

"He *has* changed, Tom–when I first met him five years ago, he was much worse! But now I'm thinking that maybe it is not enough change after all this time."

When we returned, she and the hung-over Bishek, just out of bed, went on a bicycle ride to the country and left me alone in the flat.

I spent all day sitting around, playing clarinet, reading the odd English book that was lying around and thinking about my evening rendezvous with Marianne. The day grew older and older until I watched the sun sink, spraying rich juice on the flowers and window-boxes that adorned the exterior of the towerblocks–their one saving grace.

Bishek and Zsoka did not return until dark, after 9pm. It seemed as though things were more settled between them but it had obviously been a heavy day. It seemed an inappropriate time to suggest going out to the jazz club.

Early the next day, Bishek woke me to join him making deliveries on his Monday morning shift. He would put me on the bus for Romania at 10am and I'd resigned myself to forgetting about my darkhaired beauty from Budapest. But then as we stopped for petrol at the local service station, we met our friend,

Janski, who worked there. He told me that Marianne had waited
sadly for me all night and was now pissed off. He gave me her
phone number and bade me call her.

Bishek at once grasped that I had stood her up in sympathy to
the events of the previous day and went out of his way to arrange
a meeting with Marianne for me, though he counselled caution:

"Ah, Tom, maybe you should get to Romania if you want to
reach India, after all, Budapest is West from here."

"But Bishek, she has the most soft and tender of brown eyes!"

"Ha, ha–Beware the eyes of Hungarian women, I can tell you!
But I don't know how to advise you here,"

After a morning and an afternoon of several false starts,
missed phone calls and train deadlines that existed in our mis-
informed imagination, Bishek finally got to speak to Marianne
herself on the phone. At 3:30pm, we pulled up at the rendezvous
by a famous statue. She was already waiting and gave us a
nervous wave as we drifted past to find a parking spot. She was
far more shapely than my drunken recollections and whilst Bishek
discreetly hung back to attend a non-existent engine problem, it
took just two minutes conversation to settle that I was going with
her to Budapest on the 4:30 train. She ran to collect her bags from
her mother's apartment upstairs and didn't quite understand the
immediate reluctance of Bishek or I to come with her. She
disappeared to grab her luggage and my comrade and I agreed
with schoolboy humour:

"Always avoid the mother!" I was definitely not into any
character assessment by any girlfriend's parent, for I was unre-
pentantly poor marriage material and made no bones about it!

Bishek made me promise to let him know what happened in
the 'next part of the story', as we'd been referring to the day as a
strange comic drama in which we were the dizzy protagonists. We
parted with a wink, a laugh and an unspoken bond of mischief
between us.

Chapter 4

Heart Breaking

(Hungary)

Within an hour, Marianne and I were on the train to Budapest. We sat close for the whole of the two and a half hour journey, slowly uncovering the secrets of each other's souls. As usual, it was a complete surprise to find myself sitting next to a beautiful woman with the hint of intimacy in the air and everything about her nervous, pouting features suggested that she also yearned for some company.

I was returning to the capital with a guide this time and I had to concede that the magnets of Fate will always pull you back to a place or a person until they are quite ready to let you go–by no other device than that circumstances will fall so sweetly as to make you choose to follow the path laid down before you.

It was a romantic evening with sunset goldness kissing the streets. A sweet breeze caressed our necks and Marianne told me how she thought that I might be the most important person to turn up in her life. Gulp. We didn't touch though due to a timidity and shyness that seemed strange in a woman nine years older than me.

We had not been in her flat on the third floor for more than fifteen minutes, before there was a knock at the door that sounded familiar even to my ear. It was her ex-boyfriend.

Later I found out that he had been in the habit of coming to see her every day, even though they had broken up a year before and the way they spoke to each other yielded a closeness that was yet estranged by embedded and unresolved issues. I felt like a cartoon character stepping into a Shakespearean script; a new player stepping into an old story with a bold new iambic cadence and foreign wit, that threatened to invent an entirely new sub-plot of a digressory nature to challenge the integrity of the original story. Communications were strained as they were obliged to talk in English for the sake of politeness and, despite some amicable chat about my journey, there were some pretty awkward silences. We were all relieved when he eventually left.

"I would feel strange, too." Marianne told me. "if I went to his house and saw him with a girl there!"

He didn't call around again for the week that I stayed there–but he was friendly enough when I bumped into him in the street.

Marianne was small; her delicate head reaching my shoulders and her short, tidy hair, roasted almond eyes and cheeks puffed with hope, all suggested the innocence of someone who wanted life to be above all, *nice.* That things weren't consistently pleasant bothered her a great deal and she harboured a 'sad-eyed lady of the lowlands' anxiety that all her ships might be about to sink and such pretty ones too!

However, at the age of 29, she was the manager of a popular cinema and maintained a small and attractive apartment, laid out and adorned with her natural good taste and sense of order. The double futon lay in the corner; the sprawling square draped with a flowery batik and a sophisticated library of classic authors lined the far wall (alas, all the titles in Hungarian). The window to the courtyard let in light upon a writing desk by the stereo on the floor and I immersed myself in the selection of CD's.

Marianne prepared a dinner that she served with home-made pickles, chutneys and relishes. I was hungry for only one thing but felt a little like someone surveying the terms of a new contract. She was clearly not happy alone and her homely nature suggested someone keen to make a family in the near future. This was my first reason for holding back.

Secondly, I generally prefer to wait for women to seduce me. I've spent so much time alone that I'm always nervous about intruding upon another person's space. I was also only 20 years old and had spent too much time caressing harmonic minor scales to know much about seduction. With Marianne as coy as me it seemed we might have to wait a while longer yet!

"Do you want to sleep in the bed or shall I make a place on the floor?" she asked, avoiding my eyes.

"Oh, I'm happy in the bed!" I assured her, placing my pillow where I assumed was the head-rest.

"Oh! Are you going to sleep at that end?" She cried in disappointment. After a bit of confusion, careful co-ordination enabled us to fall asleep that night with our faces just a few inches apart, still with no clear statement about our relationship. In the early hours of the morning the storm broke as a series of tentative nose proddings broke the humid tension and the rain of love came tumbling down. We clung to each other for support in Passion's overwhelming flood.

From the beginning, I knew I'd bitten deep into soft clay and I swallowed events with a lumpy unease. No way was I staying for the full romantic trip and so I made every effort to preserve her heart intact.

"I'm going to leave you, you know." I told her at the first.

"I'm a travelling man."

I could not help but think of Leonard Cohen's "Stranger Song":

" And then, taking from his pocket, an old schedule of trains,
He'll say 'I told you when I came I was a stranger.'"

I was following in the time-old footsteps of the itinerant minstrels who would drift into a town and win themselves tender company and free accommodation by virtue of the legend that curled up in smoke from their heels. For, as a travelling man, you sometimes become the symbol for the missing piece in the emotional jigsaws of the women you meet. Confusing all kinds of dreamy notions about Destiny and magic bells, they project their hopes and desires unto you as a long-awaited romantic saviour, sculpted by the winds. Yearning to grasp the ethereal in their hands they find only air in the morning.

Five times around Europe that year, girls became convinced that I was some magical seed with whom they would wake each day to find fresh flowers. But with my emotional immaturity, I couldn't pretend to be anyone's hero and by the time they fully opened their eyes, I was gone.

We lived together in a strange pattern, where we would lie in bed all morning and she'd teach me Hungarian folk songs that I'd play on the clarinet. We'd struggle to translate the lyrics and bridge the linguistic gaps of imagery that were the metaphorical canyons between us. Then she'd be at work from 4pm until 11pm (I watched a lot of films that week) and I would spend a lonely sunset by the Danube, before returning to the flat to await her key in the lock a few hours later.

Marianne was quite open to the novelty of taking in such a ragged vagrant as I, though she took exception to some of the habits I picked up in Asia. She scowled each time I let loose a satisfyingly large piece of throat phlegm into the gutter:

"This isn't India!" She'd scold.

"But my dear," I'd rejoin, "I carry India in my heart!"

The days were hot and I enjoyed hanging around the market. The main streets were bustling with colour and I could usually find adventure of some kind. On one day, whilst waiting for a film to start, I saw a strange old guy walking up and down with a placard reading:

"Jesus is the Messiah!" And on the other side: "What do you think of the Lord your God?" And that was the weird part—that I could read it—the poor fool was walking around with a sign printed in English in a country where the second language was Russian. Seeing me smile, he recognized that I was probably the first person all day to understand his message and he came over to chat. He was a sweet old soul, if a touch lost in the head and for the whole half-hour that we talked, he didn't mention religion once—he could just as well have been trying to sell cherry cakes for all it seemed to matter.

It turned out he'd been to India a few months before and that seemed to fit the picture perfectly. If something or someone is beyond explanation then you're more than likely to find them on the Indian sub-continent sooner or later, where everyone has a place. Maybe that's why *I* was going.

Then, with this new revelation, I strolled home after the movie and met an old hobo who, after finding that I didn't speak any Hungarian, addressed me in the universal tongue to indicate his need:

"Coca-Cola? Cigarettes? Hamburger?" As we were essentially

on the same plateau, though I happened to be in Fortune's good books at the time, I gave him the contents of my pockets and tried to communicate by means of hand gestures that it was all just part of the Great Cosmic Cycle of Giving and Taking. I knew that before long I'd be on the street level again myself and I smiled inside at the poetry of things, deciding that I dug the wheels of the world and that I could ride the horses of fortune in good enough style the world over.

I was a long way off being killed just at the moment, my Austrian friends would have been glad to know and I wished certain people in England could have seen me now. I felt the kind of smug pride that comes when things are going invincibly well and which ought to have suggested the approaching comedown lesson. It struck me in a way I was totally unprepared for and it hit me deep and low, coming a few days later on the weekend as I got ready to be on my way and make some new tracks.

I hadn't been doing much more than hanging around and all the time I felt like getting back on the road again. Various hellhounds were on my trail and the discontentment blues stared back at me every which way I turned, churning deep inside with a howling and a growling that just left me plain old unsatisfied. Them restless blues that do a man no good and even worse to the woman he's with–for they make him unreliable, shiftless and unsteady, so that the only thing he knows how to do is to rock and to roll and to reel around with awful mean things upon his mind.

Marianne wanted me to come with her to a wedding party in the countryside but the romance was becoming sticky and I felt it was time to leave. When Saturday afternoon arrived however, I started to move my bags out of the door to the inner courtyard on our third floor level and ominous peals of commanding thunder suddenly broke out, causing the windows to rattle. We exchanged glances and laughed only to be drowned out once more by the resounding claps of great hands in the sky.

"Maybe the gods are telling you not to go!" Marianne suggested hopefully, wanting to show me off to her friends at the party. I could not but submit to the poetry of the occasion and consented to come along to this wedding thing, which was at least in the right direction towards Romania.

But pretty much from that moment our relationship ended in any meaningful sense. I began to drift away into my travelling dream world where none save the wind can find me. On the train journey, I stood in the corridor, gazing out the window at the diminishing Hungarian countryside, leaving Marianne to talk with her gaggle of friends in the cabin. The clack-a-clack of the carriages told me I was being unfair but it was none of their business. I stared obstinately out into the fields and forests, so far from the sea.

They all elected to hit the village pub before arriving at the country-house of the newly-weds and again I left them to booze it up indoors, whilst I went to sit on the grass and dig the August evening. I mooched with the melancholy meditation of getting back on the road and was already beginning to miss the comforts of the settled life in which I had indulged this past week–tomorrow morning there would be no pair of nipples to nibble at and no fresh cakes baked for me in the afternoon!

Changes, changes, I told myself and decided to centre my mind with some Tai Chi movements on the lawn. Pretty soon, the attention of the locals was aroused and they wanted to know if I was completely loco or what–quite understandable, considering that even practising yoga got people into trouble in the communist times, thus all of the esoteric arts were strange and new to them. Three young men came up to me and uttered some throaty greeting. I stood on a stone to reply (for Hungarian yokels are *all* enormous):

"Anglezi!" I told them with that half-crazed, self-excusing smile, common to all English abroad–Ahem! Which way is it to the beach? Do you speak English? You people just don't *try*, do you?

The youngest of my new friends moved forward, wanting me to teach him how to make the movements, so I grabbed his beer bottle and began to raise it to my lips with an exaggerated slow-motion concentration. That convinced them that even if I was a weirdo, I was also a good sport and they left me alone.

The country-home of the newly-weds was large and impressive with wide, lounging gardens and pear and plum trees amongst the casting shade. Very few people seemed to speak English and I couldn't really be bothered trying to make conversation, despite Marianne's attempts to introduce me to various groups. The only two that I knew did speak my language were a beautiful blonde Estonian girl, whom I carefully avoided and a New Zealand guy who had learnt to speak fluent Hungarian from his girlfriend in Budapest. He was as much of a social oaf as I and once he was sure that I wasn't the kind of self-righteous 'spiritualist' that he couldn't stand, we got on famously. Our mutual appetite for gluttony bringing us together as we devoured beef, beer and cakes throughout the evening.

I was saved from having to participate in smalltalk by the dancing frolics of two small girls, who pranced about in carefree fun to the music playing from the large speakers. In no time, I joined them and found playmates far more on my level of sophistication than the society of the adults who sat in small groups with large wine glasses.

Dinner was traditional cow and it sat heavy in my usually herbivore stomach. Everything was going fine until after the dessert, when the Estonian chick sauntered by the opposite side of the grand banquet table and flashed me a quick, inviting glance. A minute later I found myself talking to her at the far end, making use of the obscuring shadows there.

Her name was Ciscelia and she was a 19 year-old studying to be an architect. She was on a seven-year university course in her home town in Estonia, a country bordering the icy Baltic Sea. She was in Hungary for the summer holidays and was not having such a great time, as her host was a languid bore who tired her with his sticky *amor*. He clung on past all conceivable hope–I'd heard him say to her in English earlier:

"The only thing I seem to be a master at is annoying you!"
That kind of hopeful playtalk shows real desperation and he must have been fuming as he saw me with this pristine goddess who

was telling me:

"I don't mind telling you that I think you're very handsome!" She spoke quickly and with a bold blush that endeared her to me straight away. I almost turned around to see if she was addressing someone standing behind me. Her eyes were wide and new-morning blue, her skin dripped with melting butter and her hair draped in fine golden threads across an elegant, slender neck and bronze shoulders that ought to have been the subject for every sculptor in Europe. Though graceful and long, her legs were oddly muscular and I wondered if she lived at the top of a hill–I'd climb it

She spoke with sharp intelligence and perception, yet with the purity and innocence of a child as if she were about fifteen seconds old. Our hearts leapt into each other's mouths at once and our eyes met constantly, seeking reassurance that the feeling was mutual. I boasted about my travelling exploits to milk all the admiration I could get from this angel who fixed me with an adoring gaze I could scarcely have deserved.

I tried to understand the significance of our meeting at this time–Surely someone had misplaced the pages of the script! I was in the middle of the Character-Making Epic Voyage movie–This was no time for the Irresistible Girl Of My Dreams theme to come along!

Cis told me about her family back home and the affection with which she spoke about them and her life there, made me want to throw my plans up in the air and go to huddle close with her throughout the pneumonic darkness of the Baltic winter.

"My mum would have made you a big packed lunch!" She said with hot pride.

I'm still not sure that I shouldn't have gone with her and if I had the money, I'd go and try to find her now, though it's too many months later and it occurs to me that I only know her first name and type of university course! These are the moments when the drifts of lives are determined and I could just as easily now be trudging through snow as I am presently sitting in the shade of a palm tree.

The whole evening was made more complicated by the fact that I was still together with Marianne–you remember Marianne? And also by the jealous sulks of Cis' host who hunched moodily over a growing pile of emptied beer bottles. I allowed the haze of the celebrations to blur my nagging guilt that we were walking on the wrong side of the fence but then as I was trying to persuade Cis to come to Romania with me, Marianne mooched over and tried to drag me off to dance with her. No way.

"But you were dancing with the children, before!" She protested in a slurred voice.

"Yeah but I don't dance with adults–especially drunk ones!" I told her, my sympathies now captured elsewhere. I tried not to feel the looks that Marianne was throwing at Cis and it was a relief when she gave up, allowing me to feel like a hero again in the eyes of my newly-found beloved.

"Hitchhiker in action!" Ciscelia declared as we watched Marianne walk sadly away. That seemed to be about the face of it and maybe that meant I was a bastard but gold is gold and only a fool would stay hanging onto the silver. I reached for her hand under the table and she braced herself for a kiss–but that would have caused Marianne too much pain and so we just sat talking until the early hours, trying to make the most of the time we had been given together. Fatigue eventually overtook us and we separated for sleep with both of us longing for what was not-to-be.

Marianne left early in the morning and I stumbled up to see her off, hoping to leave a good last impression to smother the grief that she must have felt the night before. Thankfully, she didn't cry and I did my best to say all of the right things before falling guiltily back on my mattress. I've not written to her since and I only hope she managed to round the whole thing off okay in her mind. Where did all my shining armour go?

After a few hours, everyone who had tried to sleep roused themselves from unconscious, drunken catatonia to join the mentally-absent hard-core of partyers who had stayed awake throughout the mosquito-swarming night. Cis and I could hardly look each other in the eye that morning, as our dreams could no longer hide under the sweet deceit of night. The light of day left the situation bare and bleak. The obvious and depressing truth was that she would not be coming with me to Romania, as she had to rejoin her college in Estonia within ten days. It was clear also that I could not abandon *my* journey. I was signed up on a contract to blunder on East with no ticket to ride.

The awkward atmosphere began to ease as the morning wore on and we realised that this would be a test of our maturity–To understand that in the true alchemy of love, the perfect will always keep its essence and find its place and meaning through changing tides of fortune–only that of transient worth could fade. But what did we know? We were just kids.

"We should never have met!" She complained and I was careful not to drink in her expression too deep, lest I might never again emerge.

I appeased her jealous host with some charming morning conversation and managed to arrange a lift with him and Cis into the next main town where I could hitchhike on. I clambered into the back seats on the 20 minute drive whilst he and Cis sat in the front. I continued to maintain amicable chat with him, whilst my real focus of communication went into my right hand, exploring the soft nape of Ciscelia's neck on his blind side. My fingers contained the entirety of my soul as they probed her shoulder, smoothed the lobe of her ear and squeezed her free hand. All the while, my voice rattled on cheerfully, hollow of any attention or being.

Finally, we came to a road where I could start to thumb lifts and the farewells were made. I managed to plant a soft kiss on her neck as we embraced but we pulled apart to maintain the illusion to her host that nothing was going on. The car drove off and I was left to stand alone by the side of the road in the heat of noon. Two bags for company and feeling very sad, I watched as my last chance pulled away.

"Fuck! Fuck this! Why?" I shouted to no one in particular. A few mothers waiting for buses drew their children closer to them protectively. I didn't care. I stuck out my thumb with an expression that would have deterred all but a blind man. I held my head in my hands and looked up at the sky for answers. But there was no escape there either and nothing could change the basic story: She was going North and I was going South.

Chapter 5

Curtains of Iron
(Romania)

After two hours of sweating miserably in the blinding sun, I walked to the train station only to discover that the train to Romania would cost me all the money that I had. With moody, dragging feet I lugged my heavy bags full of warmth for the night (the last thing you're concerned with when you're pissed off and hot), to the next main road junction some 5km away. Every step was like an act of penance and I got some kind of grim satisfaction from levelling my physical state to a sweaty degradation that matched the hell my heart was enduring.

After another scowling hour, a car stopped to ask me directions–not so ridiculous as it might sound because hitchers often carry maps. By sheer force of presence I hustled my way into the vehicle belonging to two middle-age tourists, with whom I had not a single word or thought in common.

They let me off some 20km from the Romanian border and a lift from a grey-haired lady speaking German took me even closer. She was very interested in how I managed to live my life without thought of tomorrow's budget but didn't offer to take me in.

Within two minutes of hanging around in this suburban area a young man in civilian clothes approached me, demanding to see my passport. I asked him for ID first, thank you very much and sure enough, it identified him as an agent of the 'Green Police'. Once it was established that I was not a runaway Romanian, he wished me luck with a smile and a firm handshake. Then moments after that, an old man came cycling slowly past and asked me in German where I was going.

"Don't go!" He advised me. "The Romanians are very bad people–all thieves!" I smiled at this peculiar neighbourliness that I would encounter time and time again on my trip.

I continued to try and hitch until the sun went down and as

there would be no moon until late in the night, I decided to establish my bed in a field while there was still some light. Dogs yapped at me as I passed the garden hedges of the houses on the side of the lane and a few hundred yards away from where I laid down my sleeping bag, a blazing fire raged. I wondered if it might be a gang of gypsies waiting to cut my throat in the night, which popular knowledge held as common behaviour for the Romani folk. With a heart that weighed heavier than anything I might have been carrying, I almost wished that they would. I closed my eyes to the image of a grim and scarred face of a murderous bandit, which would alternate with the pristine features of the girl I've never seen again.

What is it that Kahil Gibran wrote?

"Love will strip you like wheat from the field,
Then pound you into a flour, that you might be kneaded like
dough, and baked in the oven as the bread of God."

If the Lebanese poet was still alive, I'd have been the first to buy him a cup of goat's milk.

In the morning, I resurrected my spirit and washed the tear-stains from my face, before walking down to the road and rejoining the trail that took me East, ever East, into the glowing red that coughed and spluttered its way into the sky with hung-over bloodshot eyes and pock-marked clouds–Reality is a pretty subjective thing, no? In better spirits, I'm sure the sunrise would have been like the pages of a great tome splaying open, to reveal the truth of the world with shafts of light striking forth as the voices of angels–But right then, I was not in the greatest of form so just bear with me.

Before long, a car shuttled me along to the border and I braced myself to face the first difficult border-crossing of the journey. Romania is basically still a police state run by much the same gang as in the days of Caucescu's evil tyranny. I wasn't too happy to be arriving at the border on foot because that generally completely freaks out the border police who can then give you a hard time as they just know your type of weirdo must be a criminal of some kind!

49

This happened to me crossing from Italy to Austria in the Spring. A gruff German had picked me up and then not said a word for the entire 2 hour drive. He suddenly told me that I would have to walk across the border on my own and that he would pick me up on the other side. Of course, he just drove off and I had to stroll through as a pedestrian. An old policeman came running out of his office, angrily demanding that I should go back to the train station. Then a calmer, mustachioed Italian officer bade me come in to the clearance building and after making a phonecall for further instructions, he proceeded to search through all of my luggage. I could imagine what the guy on the telephone might have told him:

"A young guy with a guitar, hitchhiking through Europe? He must have pockets full of dope!" Very polite and thorough, the officer almost said 'Aha', when he came across my collection of herbs given to me by a young witch in France. He held each bag delicately before his sniffing nostril but could detect nothing other than sage, rosemary and thyme.

He eventually let me through but the delay meant that it was now evening time and I was in an Alpine village with snowy mountains all around, the nearest white stuff just a few hundred feet away. But then within a few minutes, I was rescued from an icy grave by a woman who pulled over for me–she gave me my first real insight into the former communist dimension and it was she came to mind now, as I stood by the Romanian sentry post.

She was an artist in her early forties, called Ute and she burnt with a ferocious creative fire, fuelled by massive reserves of anger and bitterness accumulated during her youth in East Germany. With hair that smouldered like autumn and a sharp, pale face, she possessed all of the formidable beauty of someone who will always be free. She had proved to be too volatile for the communist authorities who eventually threw her over the wall to the West, before her outspoken criticism of the regime could muster significant support.

Many of her friends and fellow dissidents had not been so fortunate and were consigned to rot away in tiny prison cells, half-filled with icy water that forced them to remain in standing position for days at a time. I seriously doubted if I would have had the strength of spirit and purpose to risk such a fate in the pursuit of freedom.

Ute had taken me into Austria until we reached that make-or-break sunset situation, when my evening's fate is decided. It's at this time, after hours of waiting that I sometimes receive a pity lift from someone, whose conscience prompts them to rescue this stranded soul. Or if I'm already in a car, the driver will often ask me:

"So where are you going to sleep tonight?"

"Oh, outside someplace, I guess–Are the nights cold in these parts?" A thoughtful silence often then follows, after which, if I'm lucky, they'll slowly say:

"Well, look–you could stay the night at my place..."

Ute didn't need any hints to be dropped and as a warrior of liberty, she understood the intrinsic value of a warm bed and a meal. She drove me back to her place in Salzburg and gave me the keys to an entire spare apartment, adjacent to hers: complete with double-bed, shower, balcony and mountain views. She had lease of the whole building as part of her current art contract.

Over wine and dinner, she had described to me how the communist reality intruded upon every aspect of the private and personal world. Even as a child she had landed her parents in grave trouble with the authorities. Watching West German TV was strictly prohibited but her parents did so regularly. One day at school, she was overheard saying to her friends how she liked the dog on West German TV who said 'goodnight', more than the puppets on local television. As a result of this slip, her parents had been severely interrogated and were kept under surveillance there after. Ute told me how her parents had shook her and shouted:

"Look! If you can't understand that there's a world in here with us–that is different from the world out there with them–Then you can't be part of our world!" she engaged me with a searing gaze and said:

"Imagine! You're seven years old and your parents–who are

your life, man! Tell you that you can't be part of their world any more!" I tried to feel what it would be like but knew that she and her people had undergone a suffering that I would never be able to understand.

Ute had channelled her anger and resentment into inspiration for her art, producing the most amazing and unfathomable sculptures and photographic arrays. However, her fury still escaped at times in gasps of scalding steam, particularly when she was driving.

"Fuck you!" She'd scream in the middle of a pleasant chat, slapping both hands against the wheel in frustration when cars pulled out too fast in front of her. Her entire life had been one of confrontation, defiance and survival situations; it seemed appropriate that when she took me to the train station to buy me a ticket to Vienna, we ended up racing for time, fighting traffic and ultimately running down the platform so I could board the already-moving train. I barely had time to yell 'Ciao', let alone embrace her and I was left only with a bag full of fruit and some sandwiches she'd given me for the journey.

Her heroic spirit accompanied me as I left Hungary and dealt with the lean and hungry Romanian officials who grabbed £15 for the unexpected visa fee. They wanted to know if I was going to walk through their country.

I exchanged all the schillings I'd been given in Vienna and quickly found myself to be a millionaire in Romanian lire. I stuffed the absurdly-large bundles of notes into various pockets and wondered why they didn't just lop four or five zeros all the prices across the board.

I walked away leaving the bemused border police behind me and turned the corner into the first country lane. The breeze of adventure tousled my hair and lit up my smile as I took a large step towards the culture of the East that was the driving force for my whole trip. The August sun trickled morning rays through a loose filter of foliage provided by the overhanging trees on each side and a lattice of shadow lay cool on the quiet road. Chickens flapped and squawked around in the street and even an occasional cow stood about, as free as in India, chawing the berries that grew wild at the side of the road. The people seemed smaller and sharper: belonging to some archaic image of the country peasant. The women dressed in various skirts of green, red and blue, complete with small headscarves tied with a knot beneath their chins. In the space of a few hundred yards, I had stepped back a hundred years and it felt good. The modern world was obviously too complicated for my simple soul and so I stepped forth into the past and didn't look back once...except for a couple of glances over my shoulder in search of an Estonian blonde.

I'd heard that hitching in Romania is a public institution that flourished under communist times. Drivers went out of their way to pick up travellers in order to collect special hitching coupons that they could then exchange for petrol. In modern times, passengers simply gave some cash to the cars that stop for them–something that's a bit tricky when dealing with unwieldy denominations of unfamiliar paper currency. To the first driver, I gave way too little and to the second so much, that he even gave me change–the Romanians have a well-developed sense of solidarity. It made sense, of course, as a social function to help share the costs of travel but it also stripped away a lot of the romance of hoboing around that actually relies upon a good division of rich and poor–for as long as there are the Haves and the Have-nots, the latter will be able to find at least a temporary way to Have for free. Either way, now that everyone and his dog could be seen hitching around, I didn't feel quite so special any more–which popped the myth that I was trying to identify with the poor of the world. My trip became less pretentious by the mile.

The main problem came when I arrived in the first big town, named Arad. After getting some cheap breakfast of olives and bread, I walked down to the main road out of town and found myself competing with about 20 other men, women and children, all looking to flag rides East. And I mean it when I say *compete*–every car that stopped would disappear under a stampede of sharp-nosed men, a whirl of flaying handbags and a tumult of streetwise kids who would negotiate and blackmail their way through. Being English, I still had some naive and dainty concepts about queuing and the etiquette of waiting one's turn. Forget it. The survival of the fittest had found its roadside niche and was not about to step aside and say ' No, really! After you, my dear!'

The result was that I spent two or three hours running after slowing cars, struggling under the weight of my bags and being pipped at the post by old women who would fly ahead of me, elbowing me in the ribs as they went past. After a few hours, I decided I was a fool to fuck around establishing a hernia in the heat, when I still had money left to catch a train.

The train station was dusty, confining and busy. I felt like I was home in India already. I eventually located the queue for tickets to Bucharest. I leant against the wall in the middle of the line that stood complaining and moaning as the vending window remained closed and we fought off the occasional pleas of tired-looking beggars; bearded old men who most probably had fascinating stories to tell, if they could only remember them; and the arche-typical struggling mothers with babes in their arms for emotional appeal.

The ticket window remained closed, happily oblivious to the ever-closer departure time for the Bucharest train and the line began to grow restless. Still clutching their beer cans, the beggars were just making their second rounds–quite unaware that it was still the same queue–when the office opened.

Thirty minutes later, I was moving through the countryside in a shunting, swinging carriage, just pleased to be moving and on my way and fuck any pride about hitching 100% each last drop of the way. Was I trying to prove something here? I was just attempting to get from point A to point B with whatever means and devices as the journey cared to provide me. I would find further backing later on in Islamic philosophy where, recognizing the divine origin and destination of all things, it's considered just as disrespectful to refuse to receive as it is not to give.

We passed through small towns that were guarded by swollen green hills and crowds of children laughed at the sight of my head stuck out of the window, balancing the absurdly droopy black hat that Bishek had given me in parting. I knew I should have hopped out at one of these hamlets and made a bed beneath the stars but it was somehow easier to stay with the momentum of the train and just hope that things would shape themselves.

At 9pm, the train pulled into Bucharest. It suddenly occurred to me that it was a damned stupid time to pull into a large and unknown city, with not enough money to get a room. I eyed a few 24 hour cafes and wondered if I could make a cup of coffee last until dawn, without completely collapsing on the tables. I didn't fancy my chances.

So on a hunch, I went up to a blonde guy working on the American Fast Food stall and asked if he could speak English. He could and he found my entire situation to be an amusing and welcome break from the languid monotony of his job. He took me over to an empty cafeteria seating area where I could wait all night in safety, chatting to the other guy that worked there.

They sorted me out with some soda water and popcorn and I heard their depressing stories of the paltry pay and about the self-destructing society in which they lived but wished they didn't. They all wanted to leave but assured me it was near-impossible to obtain a passport in this corrupt country. This I found especially depressing because they were deprived of even the *opportunity* to set off and realise their dreams like I was doing. I felt almost guilty for being so privileged.

I generally feel that anyone can empower themselves to do whatever they want without excuse. But I was taking for granted my birthright of a British passport, that absolute gem of good fortune that ensures me a minimum status most places in the world, regardless of my material position. In India, they would have called that the result of good karma in my last life. In Romania, they call it lucky.

Outside of my shelter windows, young orphans, only five or six years old, played around in their underwear through the chilly night. Their skin dark with grime and their faces wild with the scars of life; yet they bounced, leaped and chased each other around though their joy sounded a lot thinner than the usual mirth of a child.

I couldn't blame everyone for wanting to leave. That was my immediate feeling too–particularly when they kept asking me if I knew some secret as to how they could escape, legally or otherwise. They stared at me with an envy that was too large to conceal and wondered by what law I had been given the grace of freedom. Equally puzzling to them was by what perversion was I wasting my treasure to come to Bucharest, their personal hell. And why was I choosing poverty? I didn't know. I just wanted to sleep, sleep, sleep and forget about today until tomorrow. Sometimes there is nowhere you can avert your eyes from blatant injustice and there's nothing you can do about it. Man, what a place.

My blond friend came back around dawn and offered to take me to his house in the countryside, to rest and recuperate. We boarded some lump of metal on steel rails and sat opposite three peasant women, who crossed themselves each time the train started after each stop. I was pleased they were praying for all of us for I was too tired to raise my hands and make the appropriate gestures.

We went to the house of his grandfather in a really quiet village. To say that life was slow there would be more than generous, as even a motorcar attracted attention in the boredom that hung like humidity in the air. Maybe I'm being unfair but my head was too full of my personal Hungarian dreams to appreciate the peace and beauty there may have been here in the lowest ranking country in Europe.

I was something of a disappointment to my friend, because I did very little other than eat, sleep and fool around with my blues harp and clarinet. All this much to the bewilderment of his grandpa, who ambled around nailing things, sawing and generally fixing things in a continual regime of maintenance and improvement to his wooden house.

The young guy wanted to fix me up with a job at the fast food stand. 'Easy work' he promised but I was having none of it. I'm a

Piscean space cadet with an employment history of six days–four of them selling hammocks, one day as a garbage man and half a day each as a mail sorter and a nude art model.

I've sponged off the social security in England for months at a time, until I felt uncomfortable about receiving such will-sapping handouts. Otherwise, it's pretty fucking difficult to make your talents pay in an alienated, hostile society where we all watch the hands of the clock go round and round, round and round, all day long.

The whole money question had completely spun my head into claustrophobic no-way-out situations, until I managed to scam my way out for a meagre season in Goa. There an old freak told me:

"Ah, well, you're probably a sadhu-type, then." Referring to the robed renunciates that live around the temples, ashrams and mountain caves of India. So maybe there was hope yet? Then I read his inspiring book* about his penniless hitchhike from San Francisco to Argentina and I was raring to get back to England, just so that I could return to India by the hard way!

* *"Further up the Road" a genius work by Robin Brown.*

Chapter 6

Orient Express-ion
(Bulgaria, Turkey)

I didn't even try to explain all of this to my blonde Romanian friend, when he offered to find me work and just told him that I was too lazy to have a job–easier to say and probably closer to the truth, too.

Back in Bucharest, the next day, he gave me a doughnut from his stall and abruptly disappeared. I jumped on the train to Bulgaria and stood in the corridor, hoping that the ticket inspector wouldn't turn up. Hope again. A small and plump women in a blue uniform came along half-way through the 50km journey and demanded more money than I had left in local currency. I hesitated, argued, fumbled and generally flustered about until she just said:

"Dah!" With a wave of her hand that wiped the air like a flag flown for humanity over the poison of the machine. She let me just pay the little that I had left.

The land was changing outside and each ridge and hill revealed new yet forgotten plains; redundant scenes of history where stories hung in the hazy air, beckoning the train to dare the trail to a dry and timeless continent where dark ancient folk search unceasingly for that final elixir of juice to quench their parched and sandy souls; where the air is thick with moisture and a magic that is just beyond reach. For as long as the lips and the liquid are separated there shall always be thirst–our very desire for the end to suffering is the selfish prompting that's the prime mover in this circle of transience to which we're all chained.

Maybe the heat was beginning to do strange things to me and the recent green fields of Transylvania already seemed a distant memory. The ground outside was more cousin to the scorched skin of the Earth found further South.

I was sick of Communism already as the legacy of the Iron curtain seemed to have been like a funeral shroud draped across the Creative Voice from Trieste to the Adriatic. I longed for somewhere with some depth and texture of culture.

Bulgaria wasn't any better from first impressions. I stepped onto the station platform and was assailed by money-changers in shorts and T-shirts. Their moneybags were attached to the waist and their calculators rested in their hands like a primed weapon. It seemed that they made their day's wage by hoodwinking the newly-arrived, who are often unsure of the rates of exchange. In a place where religion and folk-art were wiped out as being incompatible with the broader aims of the People's Republic of Wherever-it-is, it looked like thirst for money had filled the spiritual vacuum after the stringent totalitarianism toppled over. Money existed here as an end and a means in one.

Hot, tired and disillusioned with the places my journey was taking me, I allowed the tales of others to influence me, to the extent that I believed the stories of the taxi drivers who warned me that I was certain to be robbed by bandits on the unpoliced roads. I was pretty hung-up with the fear of losing my clarinet and passport and so I found myself trudging back towards the station before I had walked half a mile through the town.

For a small payment, I ended up staying in the home of a taxi driver, eating with him and his family and watching moronic Turkish films on his satellite television. Outside, in the street, the local youth recreated the sounds of artillery fire with cheap and loud fireworks and I felt very pleased to be under a roof.

My friend Meriana in Vienna, had already put me off her home country of Bulgaria when she told me that the character of the people was embodied in the nature of their language. She found that whenever she tried to speak about something intimate or sexual in Bulgarian, she would always choke on the words as she uttered them, decapitating the meaning and expression. She was much more at home in German or English where she could scream 'fuck you' with free and vibrant lungs.

Just as the classic snootiness of the French is intimated by the nasal sound of their tongue, so I was prepared to accept that the Bulgarians themselves lacked spirit and fire, with such a sticky and enclosed language. Or maybe I'm just trying to cover myself for not being a real traveller and unearthing the ins and outs of every place I passed through.

The next day, I had to wait six or seven hours at the station to catch the train to Turkey–this time with a ticket, which meant that I had just $25 or so left. The whole place crawled with the ugliest of vibes. I almost got into a fight with some physically-obtrusive Turks, who insisted on sitting much too close to me and I had to walk away from some mean-looking guys who claimed to be 'Romanian Narcotics police', declaring that they wished to search my bags for cocaine of all things.

In the restaurant, where I spent the last of my Bulgarian money, young children hovered just outside, swooping down on each table as it was vacated, to scavenge what they could of the leftovers. I wanted out and fast. A few hours later, I got it and hustled onto the Istanbul Express while the money-changers broke into their regular 4pm frenzy that was the main substance of their day's earnings.

The train ride was uneventful and dull, other than the commotion caused when two hefty peasant women forced their way into the couple of empty seats which the sour-faced Bulgarians hoped to save for their own bulky comfort. I pulled Bishek's droopy black hat over my eyes and hid until the border rigmarole. I got through easily and then stayed on board until the guards threw me off a few stops later. My ticket had expired at the border.

The train pulled away, leaving me at a small little station in 4am darkness. The clatter of wheels and carriages faded away into the night and I was left to collect my thoughts on a wooden bench, a big smile on my face.

I hadn't been drowned in the English Channel; I hadn't been smashed to pulp on the German autobahn and my throat hadn't been cut by a bloodthirsty gypsy. Sometimes, it's nice to be thankful for the good things in life. There only remained to be slaughtered by Islamic fundamentalists, eaten by wild desert animals and to contract any one of the long list of Asian fatal diseases! So I had good reason to be cheerful. Even the police patrol that checked my passport couldn't dent my good spirits.

And then the night air parted to allow a loudspeaker to issue its vibrations through the sleeping town, in the same commanding way that had been heard here for over a thousand years. The call to prayer.

"Awake! Awake! God is great! Come to prayer! Prayer is better than sleep!" The pure revelation of heaven embodied in sound. The rippling wail of a wide-awake *muezzin*, urging the Muslim hearts to rise and rouse their faith for the pre-dawn prayer; to perform the ritual water ablutions and shake off the dirt of sleep; to join their brethren in kneeling worship and begin the day with the humble acknowledgement of their role as a servant and a believer in Allah almighty in His magnificent Creation. It sounded good and I closed my eyes to bathe in the sound that resonated all about as nearby mosques let fly other wailing summons to form a collage of chants to awaken all drowsy heads for the dawn.

In the time I spent in Muslim lands, I never got far enough out in the sticks to hear the actual call to prayer directly from a human throat at the crown of the mosque's minaret. Audio technology is undeniably more efficient but the force of the chant is diluted from the days of a primary rumble of the larynx of a blind man. A sightless singer was preferred because the elevated seat on the minaret offered an alarmingly privileged view on all of the local neighbourhood.

Before long, the red crayon of the approach of sunrise appeared on the horizon and I strolled off down the road, to see if hitchhiking was possible in Turkey. Everyone had been pretty sceptical about my chances of riding *gratis* across these lands and I was a little worried that the drivers might demand money for my passage. Almost immediately though, I saw a man on the other side of the road hail a car. It pulled over even though the dark of night had not yet departed and he was off on his way.

Thus cheered, I made my way down to the highway and grabbed a lift with a lorry after just a few minutes. I found myself hurtling towards the dawn as a fountain of light erupted in the

Eastern sky.

"Me Ingliz!"I explained with an idiot's smile.

"Me Turk." He replied with his hand to his heart and this was about as far as communication got. He turned on the radio and our metal compartment was suddenly filled with a flood of Turkish song. I sat back in drowsy contentment as we left long stretches of road for dust and I did my best not to fall asleep.

For it was still way too early for this sort of caper and I kept jolting out of daydreaming lapses until I was finally let out on the edge of a town halfway to Istanbul. I had to walk through a few streets to arrive at the next junction and I sang strange spontaneous songs to myself, on a hobo high of roaming free. Pistachio shells littered the ground and the fruit stalls were full of local melons. I was looking pretty ragged and unshaven but paid no attention to the derisory laughs that may or may not have been aimed in my direction.

After another half hour wait, a smart-looking car stopped and we were off at high speed towards the capital. From here on, it was clear that seatbelts were not for Real Men and I averted my attention from the swinging lurches of the car, by gazing out the window. The Marmara Sea glistened not so far away on our right: a shining and beautiful visage as thousands of diamonds of light danced a fine ballet on its swaying blue waters. I figured I'd get the chance to swim later. So I sat tight and contented myself by playing spot-the-mosque as we passed each town.

The mosques in West Turkey are generally kept in great condition and are numerous even in the small villages that surely couldn't contain enough believers to fill all these places of worship. Turkish style focused on the tall, slim minaret that pierced the sky with poignant elegance–Slicing through the hazy business of the day with a sharp reminder of the Grace in which we live as a straight finger pointing to the sky-abode of Heaven.

Once the roaming eye is impaled upon the minaret that dance upon the skyline, the searching spirit is then drawn closer to the rich embrace of Islam, immersed in the curvaceous plump of the accompanying dome, that is the shell of the daily worship in the mosque below.

Many of the mosques were of a brilliant white which reflected the sight back upon the impurity of the eye and produced the longing to unite with the original essence of the divine vision. Other mosques were adorned with spirals of green upon the eternally-scribing pencil minarets and others wore symmetrical curving patterns of red and yellow polka dots. All of the spectrums found place in the House of God.

It may be clear by now that I find Islamic imagery to be pretty groovy though I had the feeling that most Muslims wouldn't be so wild and I was damned sure that most of the Qur'an wasn't. At least it never seemed to be in the translations that I'd flicked through, my interest evaporating under the torrent of black and white commandments for pleasing Allah.

I had the idea that most of the Islamic world doesn't quite live up to the magic of the mosques spellbinding beauty, the transporting chant of the Qur'an and of some of the more obscure Islamic stories and poetry. In these it seemed that there were glimpses of the original source of spirit felt by the prophets themselves and which preceded the structure of religion.

This feeling is by no means unique to Islam but is supposed to be the single fountain of inspiration from which all holiness derives. It perhaaps has its Twentieth Century equivalent in the Beatnik eruption in Eisenhower America; Jack Kerouac named this feeling 'beat', referring to the Beatific visions of the Catholic mystics and in doing so, he coined a new concept to represent his '50's generation. They broke out of the doldrums of post-war America in a volcanic, frenzied search for It–the Inner, the True–All to be found directly within the heart of experience. This they achieved in long drives across the continent, in empassioned all-night jazz explorations, in the heat of sudden love-making and in total integration of all they sensed or knew as they moved though lonely deserts, stood on top of windy mountains and gave ear to the sounds of the night on empty prairies. They placed their entire faith in their own capacity to find all answers in the absolute presence of the moment as found in whatever was at hand: a rocking boxcar of a freight train, a marijuana spliff accompanied by a lonesome blues harmonica, or in my case, in the all-consuming wail of perfect Quranic sound glorifying the wonders of Creation.

It seems to be a human tendency to focus attention on the aspects of a subject that are disagreeable to them, at the expense of grasping the purity of essence that often lies at the heart of the subject. To criticize something is to make yourself superior to it and most people are very proud to be able to find fault. Thus they spare themselves the effort of attempting to assimilate and learn anything foreign and new.

This is the pattern of consumer society, though–swallow, swallow, swallow! And if it doesn't taste right straight off then spit it out. There are a lot of things about Islamic practice that are difficult to accept but then we must also concede that without really living for extended periods of time within a foreign culture, a lot of things about it aren't going to make sense. Without first-hand experience nothing can really be known, only guessed at.

So what did I know? Most of my impressions about Islam had be gleaned from books and it was my first time in a Muslim country (not counting India, where everything is so mixed up it's hard to distinguish the differences in religious life). I arrived with an open mind and heart to what this dimension had to offer and I hoped it might live up to my esoteric expectations.

I imagined that Istanbul might be a gateway to a world of awe-inspiring smells, sounds and spells, woven of a tapestry of Middle Eastern finesse, enriched with thousands of years of living under starry desert skies and threaded with the soft steps of camel caravans, carrying merchandise of silver, silk and spices swaying on patient humps.

I was also a bit nervous about my vulnerability as a lone traveller, as most of what I knew the first thing about the people or the lands was all second-hand information. I was not yet a travel-worn 'rogue' of the road but rather a naive young musician with Piscean dreams about the romance of the Lone Traveller. At this time, I was still easily influenced by the fears of others and had not yet learned that it's often locals who are least knowledge-able about conditions over the next hill, because they never have cause to climb it.

But I didn't know this then and I had unconsciously absorbed many of the tales and advice I'd been given again and again on the road about the dangers of muggings and robbery. This came to a head when, 25km before Istanbul, my driver took us off the main road and out on a desolate dirt track on a hill leading up to a small cabin by a rubbish heap. I was ushered inside where an old guy and his two sons lived. They at once set about making tea in a samovar.

The pot of leaves fitted on top of the urn of boiling water and a small measure of the concentrate tea would be poured out, to then be diluted by the hot water from the larger vessel. The tea was then served black in small glasses shaped like women's waists and drunk with a sugarcube held between the teeth*.

But when I began to feel woozy after my first few sips, I immediately deduced that I'd been drugged! That conclusion made me pretty light-headed anyway and I only saved myself from lashing out in hysterical defence, by remembering that tea always made me feel high and that I'd hardly slept on the train the night before. I was just paranoid from fatigue.

I cleared my head and calmed myself with a couple of deep breaths. I then refocused on the old man who made the tea and saw that he was delighted to have an Englishman as a guest in his humble home. His two sons sat groggily on their bunks, around which were pasted various pin-up girls. It was plainly ridiculous to imagine any skulduggery in this quaint scene!

We returned to the road and some time towards noon we crested the last hill to meet Istanbul in its impressive glory, with towering minarets cornering the city that sprawled over the landscape before meeting the sea in the South.

* *The people of hot countries always seem to have a fetish for sugar for it's cooling effect and the relief of a sweet taste in a harsh environment; anyone who declines the sugar is looked upon strangely, perhaps because an ascetic tends to spoil a party atmosphere!*

I was dropped off at the outskirts and I floundered around for an hour trying to find my way into the city. Eventually I realised that walking was no effective means of transport in a metropolis and a car fortuitously turned up to ferry me into the city. There was still no escaping the concrete tower blocks and I wondered how much further East I'd have to go before I'd be rid of them.

Things seemed much more hi-tech here. My senses were at once overloaded with an assault of sounds, sights and smells that seemed unashamedly modern in comparison to the gateway city of my imaginings. The traffic was intense, with roaring highways playing backdrop to the hooting horns of the street congestion and it took more skill in crossing the road than I was used to.

The first few signs of street life were here and that at least struck a familiar chord with the feel of the East: manned stalls sold cuts of Doner kebab and chickpeas with rice, whilst sandal salesmen sat on rugs beside piles of their leather footwear. The street fronts were lined with bureau de change outlets and handicraft shops. I struck out into the backlanes resolving to find the real Istanbul.

An hour later, I was completely lost in the suburbs and my clothes stuck unpleasantly to my skin as I dragged my bags up and down hills, desperately searching for some reference point. I seemed to be stuck in a never-ending labyrinth of deathly housing estates with large and empty spaces in between, which would give way without warning to sudden motorway passes that roared obnoxiously as I came across them.

I wandered as a small and frail figure beneath a sadistic sun. Then as I stopped to clean the sweat from my eyes, a gang of Turkish workmen on a building site beckoned me over. Maybe this will be the magical contact that my seemingly aimless trek has brought me to, I thought, always expecting the wondrous to manifest itself amidst the commonplace and dull, just like the lotus flower that flourishes in the heart of swampland. I walked up to their cabin where the mustachioed men sat in their white vests and shorts. The smallest and fattest of them contrived to say in English:

"Ho, Ho! Madam–Good fucking, yes? Madam!" Accompanied by the appropriate grunting gestures in a brave and magnanimous endeavour to cross the cultural boundaries that separated us, by means of a bridge of good-hearted common spirit constructed with all the poetic finesse at his disposal. So underwhelmed was I by this gracious extension of camaraderie, that I could not find suitable words for a fit response and walked away without reply.

Weary and worn, I chanced again upon my starting point, none the better for my labours and sat down morosely on my packed-up sleeping stuff to re-evaluate my position. I had about $20, most of which I wanted to save for the Irani border in case the officials demanded proof that I could support myself in their country. There seemed no point in blowing the cash on a hotel room if I was going to be in the same homeless position the next day. If I was going to have to adjust to getting by with no money again, it was clear that I should start now.

Besides, Istanbul had hardly met up to my expectations of a city of mystery and adventure. Apart from the beautiful mosques that were mercifully plentiful, this could have been any other European city, as far as I could see, ugly and uninteresting. Not so surprising when you consider that it has grown in size by about ten times in the past thirty years. And with none of the tens of thousands who once stopped here on the road to Kathmandu, there were no longer any freaks in the city to speak of. I was lonely.

I was just thinking about moving on while there was still light, when it began to rain tumultuously and I fled to the shelter of a nearby shopping complex. I shivered as I despondently watched the water fall, a few tears running down my cheeks in unison. Where was I? And where was I going? I didn't know where I'd sleep that night and a bed outdoors was now impossible with the ground all soaked and muddy.

There were no Indian ashrams to give me food and shelter here and all I could foresee was a long and lonely road for another four thousand miles across barren lands, where no one was going to open up to me and offer help, save perhaps for the occasional bread roll if I begged hard enough. Self-pity is a pretty seductive emotion and it tends to taint all past, present and future experience with its miserable brush–but at least when you reach rock bottom, the only way is then up and thus it can act as a kind of purification. By indulging in all of your fears about the worst eventualities, they are thrown out in the open and you can rebuild within.

With typical timing, the coin of fortune then flipped and gave me my first insight into the notion of hospitality within the Muslim community, which I would taste many, many times again on my journey. Naturally, when you're standing on the streets of a city feeling ill, hungry or sad, no one can know about it unless you give them the opportunity to find out through some kind of point of contact–this being the great advantage of hitchhiking and street-performing, that you inevitably meet and get to know a variety of people who will often help you out once they are acquainted with your position.

On this occasion, I asked the help of a couple of young newsstand guys to find a place selling roadmaps of Turkey. Passers-by became involved with the communication process and I ended up attracting the attention of a whole crowd, all of whom wanted to help.

I was just establishing the possibility of sleeping in a vacant office belonging to the uncle of a young guy that had turned up, speaking pretty good English–when a corpulent policeman appeared at my side intent on taking me off to the British embassy for assistance. No go. I was not a tourist in trouble but a pilgrim in search of a bit of shelter and though the officer just wanted to be of assistance, the inattentive manner with which he waved his rifle around was making me feel pretty nervous. It was also drawing a mob of onlookers who imagined that I was being busted.

In the end, someone had to lead the officer away by the arm whilst he complained in hurt tones that he was only trying to help. Meanwhile, I slipped away with my new friend, Ahmed, for some mutton and rice as we allowed the commotion to die down.

Ahmed then took me to the 'office', where I was due to spend the night. Upon arrival, I received an immediate interrogation from two young policemen as to what I was doing and why. Did my family know where I was? How much did I know about Islam? And did I want to become a Muslim? It took me a while to realise that these were the guys that were in charge of giving me a place to rest. It took even longer to convince them that I was in full command of my senses and knew what I was doing. More or less.

The 'office' turned out to be a small cabin at the end of a wide alley, beside a political building that the police were guarding for the night. The floor was dusty but it was warm and dry and I was pretty happy with my lot, though the policemen shook their heads disapprovingly that I should choose to subject myself to such conditions.

"It's perfect!" I cried.

"No, it's very bad for you!" They pronounced,

A few minutes later, a knock at the door produced Ahmed, bearing bread rolls, tins of tuna and bars of chocolate, apologising all the while that it wasn't much. All of this put my earlier self-pity to shame and my confidence grew in direct proportion to the generosity I was receiving, refilling that most essential of hoboing fuels.

I dreamt of shuffling shadows of bored policemen, come to peek through the windows at the weird English bum who begged for his beef and slept on floors. Otherwise, I slept fine.

Chapter 7

Losing Fear
(Turkey)

In the morning, I was informed that I had barely entered Istanbul and was only on the periphery. That was why it had all seemed so dull. Meekly, I allowed my benefactors to place me in a minibus to head for the centre. Soon I was back on the motorway as this crazy city is intersected by screeching tongues of roadway that any vehicle must traverse to get to any other area. 'The motor car will drive modern man to distraction' said Gurdjieff and he was right.

I arrived at the celebrated tourist centre of Istanbul, the Sultanahmed, where the famous giant blue mosques stood, untouched by the modern age. Within seconds, local guides were hustling me to buy postcards, maps and whole piles of other assorted crap. To them I was just another backpacker on tour with a bundle of traveller's cheques and a camera in my knapsack. They decided to leave me alone when they saw the condition of my boots, which didn't look like they'd last the course to India.

I strolled around the grand mosques and palaces, was dutifully impressed and then prepared to get back on the road. I got myself a Turkish-English dictionary and mailed a couple of postcards to my folks back home to let them know that I was still alive.

Now, hitchhiking out of Istanbul is no simple matter and it was almost impossible to find any kind of access point to the thundering monster of highway that could be seen tantalisingly below from the bridges where I stood. I spent three futile hours trying to track down a slip-road, before I realised that the best way around this kind of obstacle was to catch a bus to the next small town and try again from there.

This I did and by the time I was on the outskirts of the next village, the heat of the day had already passed before I found a reasonable place to stand near a small petrol station. I spent half my energies trying to flag down likely looking vehicles and the remainder dodging the cars that swerved in to fill up.

I got a ride with a toothless old man who spoke no English and I hopped in. With the aid of my dictionary, we established at length that he was from South-West Turkey where the English tourists really 'go to town' and that it was certain that if I tried to hitch through East Turkey, then I was a 'lunatic' as I was sure to be 'hijacked' and 'murdered'. He made the accompanying pistol-to-temple sign with his fingers.

He became pretty fond of me in no time and occasionally pinched my cheek with paternal care. Nevertheless, he became pissed-off when I declined his offer to go South with him as I insisted I had to go East. He shrugged angrily as if I was little more than a corpse-soon-to-be sitting in his passenger seat, for all my chances were against the heavily-armed Kurds on my route.

The early evening traffic was 'madness', my driver told me and we became stuck in an unmoving queue of vehicles. He pulled over into a gravel patch and began to lower the seats, suggesting that we sleep for a while. There didn't seem like anything else to do so I lay down lengthways with him over the front seats and he placed his hand across my belly–not an explicitly sexual act but more intimate than I'm used to with people of the same gender.

Occasionally, he would try to roll a bit closer and I would have to move him gently away; the whole situation was so comic that I couldn't really feel threatened by this tiny old cozen of skin and bones who I could probably have lifted up with one hand. There was no one else around and so what did it matter if I indulged his need for a little companionship and warmth? Just as long as it was not any more than that!

When the traffic had eased, we got under way again and I became concerned that nightfall was only about an hour off. We were only 40km away from Istanbul. My day's progress could only be counted as miserable. The sky outside was scattered with dubious-looking clouds and the prospect of rain deterred me from jumping out into the passing woodland to make a fire for the night. No way did I want to get caught in the open if yesterday's kind of shower came again. I was equally less sanguine about arriving in a town in the evening time and attempting to find a local to give me a bed.

At this point in the trip, my fears about my immediate well-being reached a head. For the first time I found myself poor and alone in a *very* foreign culture–Somehow having no money in Europe wasn't that big a deal, it all being so close to home ground. But now that I was in deep beyond the point of return, I was assailed by doubts and worries. What would I do if I became sick? And would I really have to lug my waterproofs all the way to India if the weather was going to be like this?

I began looking out of the window, in an anxious search for somewhere good to kip down in safety and warmth. At last, I saw a field that looked reasonably discreet and I bid my confused old man goodbye as I stalked off into the night. I laid my stuff down by a bush, some hundred yards from the road and trusted that the dim orange illumination cast by the streetlights didn't depict me too brightly. Occasionally, drifting conversation would come my way from local residents on an evening stroll and I just hoped that they wouldn't be expecting to see anyone. I closed my eyes to a curiously relaxed sleep. I'd often read of exhausted bluesmen who sometimes used to fall down asleep across the railroad tracks they were following and it seems that we are at our most trusting precisely when we are most defenceless.

But there is no rest for the wretched and sometime in the middle of the night, I heard a soft pattering sound that I knew meant something bad. I'm always reluctant to wake up to the unpleasant, half-hoping that things might just go away again if I keep my eyes shut but after a drowsy struggle I fathomed that it was the beginnings of rain.

"Fuck!" I said aloud and realised that to sit still any longer could be absolutely disastrous, as a full-fledged Turkish torrent could reduce me to a shivering pneumonic wreck in about five minutes. I dragged myself out of dreamland and gathered my stuff into my arms with all the haste that I could muster, before staggering like a lame donkey with a poor sense of balance to the nearest concrete road bridge. I sat under that thing for the next three hours playing the sleepless blues on my clarinet and munching miserably through bits of bread and olives that I had left, more for something to do than because of hunger.

The morning call to prayer eventually came and I wondered if Muhammed had ever spent half a rainy night under a motorway bridge. It's written that he had been in the habit of going to sit in a cave in the wilderness to fast and meditate many years before he received his first revelation from the angel Gabriel. He knew all about the loneliness of doubt too. After the absolute thunderbolt of the first transmission of the Qur'an that caused him to shake and quiver with its power, he had to wait another two full years before the Angel appeared to him again. During this time he had a difficult time maintaining his faith, like a candle trying to stay alight in the storms of scorn he faced from his community.

But I seriously doubted if any strident monotheistic religion would flower as the result of *my* night-long vigil and when no angel appeared before morning, I caught a bus into town. I realised that if I had difficulty here explaining my situation to people who spoke English, then it was going to be near-impossible in East Turkey where people were poorer and the levels of education correspondingly lower. I hit upon the idea of getting a small postcard with an explanation written on the back in Turkish to say that I was a spiritual seeker, travelling by means of God for my food and shelter.

I left the bus at a random point in town and wandered around aimlessly, until some shopkeepers hailed me and despatched someone to look for a speaker of a European language. A solid young guy named Mehmet was brought who spoke some German. Pretty soon I was being fed soup and rice, drowned in tea and being introduced to every man in town. Somehow, by breaking bread with them a bond of trust was established and I became surrogate, long-lost family. I was taken around to the cafes where, on Sundays, the working men played cards, dominoes and chess all day–much like the old guys in Northern England, though here hot tannin substituted for beer.

I was a novelty and everyone was happy to give bits of food and endless glasses of chai as long as I didn't mind answering the same questions over and over again: How old was I? What was my job? Was I married? Why did I have no money? Did I want to become a Muslim? And so on ad infinitum. The big joke which they went to great trouble to make me understand (by means of exaggerated snipping gestures around their groins) was that if I were to convert to Islam I'd have to be circumcised! All good fun amongst men!

Mehmet suggested that I come with him and his friends to the football match that afternoon. It seemed like a good way to escape the endless discussions-cum-lectures about life–my life in particular. This was the crunch with Muslim hospitality to one in my position; wherever I went, help would usually be given but almost always accompanied by a lecture on the faults and short-comings of my way of life. None knew of the age not so long ago when this mode of hand-to-mouth travel was commonplace, before the advent of charter flights, visas, insurance policies for everything and sticky red tape that ties up as much freedom as it can wrap itself around. But as much as I can rant here on the page (again!) There was no way I could go into explanations like that to every person who wound me up in this way. Thus I just leant back on the classic tactic of quoting from their own texts:

"Allah will provide!" I told them wearily. They nodded in approval, though secretly they believed me to be off my hinges. Some even doubted that I had come this far by hitching without money but I had nothing to prove to them. Did it really matter if they didn't possess the finer strands of their tradition in their heads if they carried the best of it in their hearts, receiving a visitor in the warmest of outward manners:

"We love you, Thomas! We do! We love you, Thomas! We do!" A coach of a hundred young football thugs sang in English, in between their songs of adoration for their football club, Karseilly. I was a Star! And the grinning, fresh faces of the young fans were excited to have something new to yell about. It's a strange thing but whenever they sang some football chant or slogan, their Turkish accent was inexplicably replaced by an oafish slur, that can be heard at any football ground in Europe–Had I discovered some kind of cross-cultural genes here or what?

But I was wrong–being a football fan in Karseilly had nothing to do with watching the game but rather about the pre and post match posturing in which they could revel away from the vigilance of their elders. Mehmet had suddenly been transformed from an awkward bachelor in front of the old men in the cafes, to a militant leader of idle youth, fully in his element amongst thousands of mindless supporters who all just wanted to be on the right side. The winning side. It wasn't clear what the stakes were as Mehmet strutted around, always in some urgent hurry to attend to some imagined contingency of great importance. He was trailed by a bunch of younger sidekicks, eager to demonstrate their worth.

Finally, he was given some justification for his clownish activities as the opposing fans suddenly scaled the partition behind which they were enclosed. The air filled with a volley of stones and rocks, falling just short of our main body. I was ushered protectively to the side while the boisterous young men of our side seized the chance for glory, by following Mehmet's example of charging forward and returning the missile fire with whatever debris they could gather from the ground.

My escorts turned to me with grinning faces, as if to say, 'fun, eh?' I didn't bother to conceal my anger and disgust. The police soon came in and Mehmet and his colleagues at once assumed the look of schoolboy innocence, before returning with a triumphant cheer. They were all very impressed with themselves.

"You fight and try to kill your fellow Muslims, for fuck's sake?" I cried. They all looked a little confused as if they couldn't see where the problem was. Why was I, a bloke of the same age as them acting like their fathers.

"No, no." They told me patiently. "This is not dangerous!" I gave up and became even more despondent when I found out that the match did not begin for another hour and a half. This pre-match mini warfare constituted more than half of their total expedition–the release of their frustrated testosterone in a socially-accepted way. What was I doing here? I asked myself yet again. I might as well have been in England. It was the kind of thing I was fleeing.

Fortunately there were no more incidents and to my relief, there was not enough room for all of us in the ground. A more genteel lad took me off for some *chai* in the sanctum of a cafe. There we attempted philosophical discussion about the duties of one's life with the sole aid of my dictionary. One word at a time.

Back at home, no one seemed to have given any thought as to where I was going to sleep that night. I eventually had to force the issue. For some reason, though everyone kept pressing food into my hands, no one was inclined to take me in so they had a whip round and got me a bed in the local hotel. I woke early and got on the road right away, pausing only to get one of the young lads to write me out a card in Turkish. He wrote that I was a 'friend of Allah' and needed people to house and feed me on my spiritual quest.

A sullen lift from a Romanian took me out a way and as usual I wasted a lot of time in finding the right road. After some time, I got on a very slow-moving truck heading North to the Black Sea. I fancied a swim and the prospect of drowning my troubles in a kind of baptism in the ocean. I sat tight as we moved inch by inch up the beautiful hills that separated us and the great salty waters on the other side. I tried to impress my driver with my Turkish:

"Beautiful, yes? Very beautiful! Good! Fantastic! Thankyou! Very good! Yes!" And so on with the enthusiastic and idiotic vocabulary every learner of a new language picks up. He smiled patiently.

Towards sunset, we came across the expanse of the Black Sea and the waters lapped against the shore with all the reassuring caress of a lover's hand; Nature's comfort for the weary wayfarer, who "ever seeks the sweet golden clime, where the traveller's journey is done." To quote Blake.

I was hoping the old man driving would concern himself with

where I was going to sleep that night but instead he let me out by a small town with some kind of industrial plant by the harbour, glowing with undeserved gold as the sun hung low in the sky. I began to walk to the main market area in the hope of flashing my postcard at someone and invoking some of the famous Turkish hospitality. But within seconds, a young guy in a car pulled to a quick halt and shouted "Come On!" So of course, I clambered in and he took me off to see his friend: a mechanic who could speak excellent English.

This turned out to be one of the least favourable of encounters I had in Turkey. I was ushered into a concrete garage and abruptly presented to a guy in overalls, who spoke to my young driver for a minute in Turkish, casting me sidelong glances all the while. Then he turned and spoke to me in a passionless tone of interrogation, to determine if I was a runaway from home. As I answered his questions, he turned to work a little at the underside of the elevated car by the wall. Finally, he faced me with folded arms and asked:

"So, are you hungry now?"

"Er, yes, a little."

"Well, we can drop you at the bus station and that's all we can do for you."

So I found myself standing by rows of buses on their concrete beds. Alone in a sleepless night that was too dark to find a safe place on the beach to rest and wearied by my fruitless last encounter, I felt low again. Up and down, up and down–this was often the story but fortunately with the Muslims, there were always enough ups just waiting to happen.

Nothing was going to happen unless I made the effort, so I summoned the energy from somewhere to approach a few people with my pilgrim's postcard to see if that humbling tactic would meet with any success. The first youth I spoke to didn't seem to comprehend and I wondered if he could read. My dejection was unexpectedly dispelled a minute later when he doubled back and put his hand on my shoulder, asking:

"*Ekmek* (food)?" Poverty is a great teacher of language and I recognized that crucial phrase straight off. He took me to a cafe and after placing money down on the counter for my mutton soup and rice, he bid me goodnight and left.

The guys working in the cafe also wanted to read my postcard and once they understood the score, they plied me with stuffed pepper casserole and *chai* until I could take no more. Afterwards, I was taken down the road and introduced to some young, long-haired guys with gentle smiles and shining hearts–it was immediately decided that I was to be a guest in their home.

My host was a guy named Selchuk, whose locks flowed blonde and free and he seemed a little embarrassed that his mother wore a head covering. He brought out maps of Turkey and we examined my route. He warned me that hitchhiking was 'absent' in Eastern Turkey and assured me that 'terrorist activity' would hinder me on the roads there. I'd have to take a bus.

I heard this story so many times in the West of the country that I began to wonder if I was crazy, heading naively towards violent militants with rifles and grenades. I didn't really have a clue as I hadn't done my homework on the area. I was just vaguely aware that the Turkish were in the habit of sending airplanes over to drop bombs on small Kurdish villages–serve them right! Goddamn suspicious, carpet-weaving, ethnic minorities with their own language, hanging about for thousands of years just plain old cluttering up the place!

Breakfast was big and hearty, with local breads, cheeses and olives. I only stopped eating when it occurred to me that it wasn't polite to be sitting by the meal mat on the floor, munching away when everyone else had finished 45 minutes before. Well, a guy's got to fuel up–never do know when you're going to get any more!

I was put on the phone to every English speaker in town and my friends were a little at a loss as how to satisfy their strong urge to help me. They were not at all simple-minded though, for all their untainted cheeriness; when the football came on the television Selchuk switched it off at once, pointing out the word in my dictionary: 'exploitation'.

Selchuk and I went walking on the promenade that would have

been beautiful if not for the leering industrial plant that crowded the view. We then turned to wander up a hill, climbing dozy streets whose concrete slabs were drugged with sunshine and the town wore a cheerful suggestion of aspiring to modern times without being in too much of a hurry.

With some consternation Selchuk explained to me that he was a 'bad Muslim', because of the way he looked and acted. I tried to console him in my poor but growing Turkish that there were 'different paths–different people but all same!' I'm not sure how that Indian logic translated but it seemed to cheer him up a bit. The bounding free heart of his nature struggled with the claustrophobic confines of his nurture–I wish he could have known that in some alternative setting he could find people of similar bearing and that there was nothing wrong with his bohemian way of life.

I wouldn't have minded staying for a while but I was not invited to do so. Selchuk and his friends put me on the afternoon bus back down to the main trans-Turkey highway, insisting that hitching would be easier down there. As I got ready to board the bus they hoisted a big bag of food on me and despite my protests, stuffed my shirt pocket with a million and a half lire (about $20), that would sort me out for a couple of days. I sat on the back of the bus and actually wept, stunned by their kindness and generosity.

It was this sort of thing that restored my faith in the goodness of the human heart and cured my bitter cynicism about the poverty of the human condition. From my perspective of material destitution, I was able to glimpse some of the hidden sides of people and found that the majority really *will* extend their help and means to you–at least, when there's no hiding from the fact that you're genuinely in need.

I came out on the Istanbul-Ankara highway and a group of kids that I'd been talking to managed to get me my next ride, by chatting up a truck driver on my behalf. Hitchhikers need to be on good terms with all folks great and small!

The road wound up through some pretty mountains and we seemed to be scaling more noble heights, leaving the Westernised influence on Turkey behind. Greater things surely lay ahead.

Towards the end of the day, the driver announced he was stopping to rest for the night and I scrambled out to stroll around the roadside village. I eyed up potential places to sleep. There were a number of derelict buildings with large gaps in the bricks where the windows once were. But my plans were foiled by a cruising police wagon that hauled me in and then drove me two kilometres up the highway hill to a side of the road restaurant where they said I could find a hotel.

Cops in Turkey were generally very kind to me and though it was never my first instinct to expect any good intentions from them, they were always more than friendly. I was, of course, more accustomed to the usual uncultured thugs who use their positions of power to obstruct any act of freedom—schoolyard bullies grown up, getting a rush of the power endowed upon them by virtue of a shiny black uniform and gun.

That's a pretty large and unfair generalisation of course and is certainly not true of the many who really do try to act as guardians of the peace, sorting out disputes with the minimum of fuss and stepping into nasty situations most of us would rather have nothing to do with.

However, not many of them have an interest in organic farming or in the magic of auric healing; being conservative by both nature and definition, they're not generally of a bearing that can absorb the weird and the wonderful. Thus they often respond to expressions of a culture beyond their expression with an aggressive and intolerant manner. If only they could all be like the cops in Holland, where they're required to pass psychological personality tests as part of their training (An easy-going and understanding manner is essential in dealing with the space cadets found in the European capital of decadence, Amsterdam.)

Of course, I say all of this as one who instinctively feels himself to be on the wrong side of the law. Whilst I've never done much that is illegal, I always have to give a second thought as to whether I might have a piece of hash in my pocket when I see a policeman coming my way in the street. The non-smoking, working population generally has little bad feeling towards the constabulary, simply because they are fairly unlikely to end up on the wrong end of the law which is where the *real* character of the police is seen.

I've been arrested twice in my life: once as a 16 year-old attempting to hitchhike home from a road protest–I was stupid and inexperienced enough to try and flag cars down on the motorway. A police car screamed to a halt and then reversed back to where I was standing. They were not happy men. It emerged that they had been stationed on the protest that had held up the entire motorway, as we all made a big party on the offending bypass that had cleaved a beautiful valley in two.

"I find it quite ironic that you're trying to hitchhike home, having been on a road protest!" A six-foot-three bloated pig with a helmet told me. After taking my details, he instructed me to return up the grass verge and not let him see me again.

"But I haven't got any money or food or anything warm to wear!" I protested.

"Well, quite frankly, I don't care!" He replied and I ended up walking 12 miles back to the protest site in the dark.

These kinds of experiences, together with the brutal horse charges, aggressive searches and general intimidation common to police world-wide, that I've seen on the street and at peaceful demonstrations–all leave me to conclude the average cop to be something other than my guardian and my friend.

Here in Turkey, though, the police had put me in rather a nice place at a restaurant that had an outstanding view of the plains below and the nearby habitat looked pretty friendly for one sleeping out. Somehow, the further I progressed East, the more acceptable it seemed to make a bed in the open as I came to lands that have no taboos about 'vagrancy'.

A smartly-dressed young Turk came out, who was assistant manger of the place and after he understood that I was a traveller of little means, he refused to allow me to pay for dinner. He set me up at a little table and the waiters brought me soup, beef and rice, all of it excellent.

I lay down to sleep in the garden that lay to the side of the restaurant that night and felt a large psychic load lift off me. I finally ceased worrying about my day-to-day welfare. Time and time again, circumstances were providing enough to meet the needs of the situation and fretting about it all just detracted from the thrills of the Journey.

After some time, you can become accustomed to any fear, even begin to feel indifference for what once turned your stomach with dread. It was all delightfully out of my hands and consequently, I felt more safe and secure than any time in the past. I had discovered the cosmic game of catch, falling without fail into the waiting arms of the universe.

Having finally overcome immediate fear for my physical wellbeing, it followed that all other aspects of my world would be catered for too, provided I conducted myself with the patience and respect to let Things Work Out In Their Own Time.

It was like stepping out over a terrible abyss and finding that a bridge appears beneath my feet with each step. Once I actually took that first fearful stride everything fell into place as and when needed. But there was no way any of it could be seen beforehand and I never could say with all surety how I'd find shelter and food two weeks hence–But who can?

Everything always came but it may be that I had to face a few things first as part of the lesson. In the May of that year, I was returning from my European tour back to England. A whole day's hitching brought me only around 60km along the French coast and I was still a little way from Calais, where I could catch a boat back to my tiny island. I had walked six miles out of Dunkirk to try and find a decent spot to catch a lift. I was aching, weary and miserable, the sun was going down and a vicious wind with an icy whip flayed my poorly-clothed body. I couldn't see any viable place to kip down from the harsh elements for the night and I seriously doubted if I had the strength to walk back to civilisation.

The sky began to grow darker and darker and the sunset splendour faded along with the warmth of the day, my spirits dissipating along with it. In a few minutes, no car would be able to see my out-stretched thumb and I seriously began to contemplate that Death by exposure might be my fate that evening. Ironic, true, to die so close to home, having been 3000km around the roads of the Continent but a sense of fair play and justice rarely seems to concern Fatality. I began to consider the demise of Tom–my carefully-constructed and crafted personality to die of cold in minutes after all these 20 years of struggle and effort. Was this to be it? Didn't I get to go down in glory?

I was rescued from this oblique perspective by a Renault bound for Calais. Within minutes of arrival at the port, a British car driver I chatted to pulled out a wad of notes and gave me £5 to get me across the water. Then on the ferry, I met another young guy who bought me pints of beer in exchange for my stories. All the comfort of the world was mine again but only after a close encounter with the Grim Side of Things.

Chapter 8

The Real Journey to the East

"Herman Hesse never did this!"
(old freak of Anjuna)
(Turkey)

I woke from my bed beneath some trees in the early morning and discovered with delight that Selchuk had packed some *halwah* for me. With the first bite of this honeyed sesame nectar, I drifted off to the dreamscape lands of 1001 Arabian Nights. I clutched onto the swaying hump of my camel, the finest silks of Baghdad draped around my head to fend off the noontime brilliance and yea, I did perspire with great perspiration and did find myself coming by chance upon the declining banks of a great river, that did flow with unhasty majesty.

Young Caliph Tom of the Aching Thumb did there bid his kinsmen depart forthwith and grant him the solitude for which his soul did yearn for with great yearning.

"Now," said he, "Shall I forsake all nourishment except such as may be granted me by the All-Merciful One! Bismillah!" And there he did sit in contemplative solitude for the duration of the day and night, steadfastly ignoring the clamours of his gluttony.

But the next morning, as he stared forlornly into the myriad deceptions of the current, a sealed package did wend its way through the high reeds and come to rest within the reach of his arm. Upon opening the vessel, the young Caliph did discover it to contain the sweetest of *halwah* and he did marvel with exceeding marvel.

"By Allah!"He cried, "Surely this is a boon from the Heavens, as such divine delicacy as this could only have come from the banquet tables of the angels!" Thus he did break his fast upon the *halwah* and was sated. But then he did once again sit with pious and steadfast austerity, immersed in prayer and devout worship of the Almighty.

But the next morning, another package of the same sweet stuff did arrive at his place of repose upon the bank and he did consume it with as much fervour as the day before, indebted to the generosity of the Lord. This pattern continued for three days, before Caliph Tom's curiousity could be contained no more and the songbirds heard him to exclaim:

"By Allah! I shall discover the source of my subsistence, or perish in the attempt!" And then he did follow a trail that led up-river, until he suddenly came upon a great stone castle, with a single tower that overlooked the course of the river. Gazing up, the young Caliph almost lost his balance as he beheld the turret window where a young maiden whose beauty put the sun to shame; her eyes gleamed as pools of cool lapiz and her smile was stolen from the third night of the moon. Espying Caliph Tom, the maiden did call down to him with sweet and slender voice:

"Oh, my Lord! May the mercy of thy heart bid to rescue me from my imprisonment in this dreadful high place—My captor is an evil hunchback lord who has locked me here until I succumb to his evil designs!"

"Most surely will I come to thy assistance, O Pearl of Pearls—but first mayhap thou willt be able to solve my perplexity of whence cometh the salvation of *halwah* that has saved me from starvation these last three days?" And he did hold aloft the cloth that had bound the dessert. The princess (for such she surely was) did then emit a laugh like sparkling water as she cried:

"Oh my noble hero! That which you call *halwah* is merely the leftovers of my daily cosmetic applications, which I then let fall into the currents below!" Caliph Tom knew a good thing when he saw it and scaled the tower vineage, rescued the princess and her vast stores of sesame sweet and settled down to a joyful future of nuptial bliss and early tooth loss.

The roar of the first truck of the day shook me out of these strange dreams as the overdose of sugar had put me to sleep again. I got on the road and caught a lift into the dawn in no time. A young family man at the wheel, he took me a long way through a landscape that would suddenly rip open into ferocious mountain passes, smouldering with the heat beneath a bleak coat of dust that made the prospects of life seem very harsh indeed. I dreamt of the odd cougar, purring in the shade of a rocky shelf, its merciless eyes lazily scanning the sparse and hazy land for its next meal. But then we'd turn a corner and be smacked in the face by the brilliant blue visage of a lake that would put the land to shame with a sweet splash of colour and relief amid the court of cliff faces, barren and stark.

We drove for six hours to Ankara, coming to the heart of Turkey and I hoped to see some really original culture. I didn't feel like entering another metropolis and I decided to skirt Turkey's second largest city and hit some lesser-known ways.

Practically every lift that stopped for me, warned me of the perils of the Kurdish 'terrorists' that lay a few hundred kilometres ahead. But when I failed to be duly impressed by their cautions, they wrote me off as another Englishman who'd seen too much of the sun and just helped me along my way as they could.

The terrain began to open out and become more bare and picturesque, with lumpy hills like frowning foreheads. They carried an imposing silence that only the bustle of the modern age could ignore. After a short ride from the outskirts of the city, I jumped out at a crossroads and my first sight was of a dead wolf lying in the dust, with flies fighting over a small wound in its temple and blood-stained mouth. So this is where the big animals live! I presume it was a wolf because I've never seen a dog with such a large and wild appearance and as the wind rustled its submissive fur it bore a tragic majesty, cutting its own raw poetry on an unseen page.

A quarry driver took me out to a gravel pit where I played jazz for him and his friends, all queuing up to fill their trucks with the loose rubble. Then I moved along a short way and had some afternoon *chai* with some guys in a small village. Everyone that I met made some effort to communicate with me. The people seemed slower and calmer and the atmosphere of content tradition was a relief in tempo after the frenzy of the other Turkish cities, which all aspired to be as Western as possible.

I was a little nervous that I seemed to be crossing Turkey at too fast a rate and thought that I might be missing out somehow on the kind of cultural experience that is the motivation for hard-core travellers. I hadn't stopped anywhere for more than a night in 11 days and I was hoping to find some niche along the way where I might rest and consolidate. In any event, I resolved from now on to stick to the small roads and thus deliberately sabotage my progress!

The next driver almost completely sabotaged the progress of both of our lives completely, as whilst searching through the pages of my English-Turkish dictionary, he failed to notice the approaching bend in the road.

"Bak! (Look!)" I shouted, my instinctive language cortex kicking in and he hit the brakes of the twenty-ton truck just in time as damage was limited to uprooting a small barrier post. I was a little shaken and I wished that the use of seat belts didn't have such effeminate connotations in this country. But if you're not dead, you're alive and what could I do except shrug it off with a laugh and resolve never to lend reading material to my drivers.

He let me off by a lovely small village with attractive shamanic looking hills. I decided straight away to make my camp in a cave somewhere. Before I could go anywhere though, I was hailed by a plump man in shorts working in a near-by melon field. He handed me three juicy Galia melons and then stuck his knife in the largest of them as he went off to rejoin his labours. This spontaneous generosity was typical of all that I met in this country and the memory of these encounters remains warm and vibrant.

I clambered up the rocky hillside and found a promising-looking cave. I tried not to be too put off by the large animal dropping that lay there. They seemed pretty fresh and I imagined the three wolves returning home to discover that I'd eaten all their porridge–but as I recall, Goldilocks got off scot free and so I decided my chances were good.

The sun sank softly behind a long curved ridge, that cast its glorious brooch-like image upon the delightfully turquoise lake lounging wide and flat beneath it. I sighed in peace and lay back to count the blossoming stars in the moonless night. This was my trip and, despite occasional twinges of the heart, I was making it just as I had hoped: happy and free with each day's agenda mine to set.

I awoke the next day to find that I hadn't been eaten alive by angry carnivores and I hung around until the sun had climbed high enough to warm the lake a little. I stumbled down to a quiet spot by the water, to wash myself and my clothes. Dirty-faced pilgrims are more usually identified as good-for-nothing bums. The lake was still freezing. I shivered in the sun, waiting to dry off and saw a couple of tortoises snuffling through the grass. As I stared and wondered at this meeting with these timeless creatures, I heard a distant tinkling of bells come drifting through the air, growing in volume by the moment.

Within a few minutes, a whole herd of goats came down to the water's edge for a drink, each wearing a bell around its neck of varying lilts of tone and pitch. The effect was that they approached like one huge, moving orchestra of tings and tongs, dings and gongs. I looked over my shoulder for the BBC audio team that ought to have been there to record this miracle. The goats wandered and flocked as an aural manifestation of the perfection of Chaos—woven of the most random of melodies, that told the age-old tale of wandering the hills and lakes; enduring the relentless hot days of summer and the icy winds of winter that cut to the scrawny bone, treading the land for all their days under the steady guidance of a shepherd whose life followed a pattern scarcely different than that of his predecessors thousands of years before him. He himself came at the rear of the herd and added his own gravelly cries to the music as he shouted:

"Brrrrrrrr! Brrrrrrrrrr! Hai! Hai! Ishca! Brrrrrrrr! Yoae! Ishaca Hai!" On and on, which all I assumed made perfect sense to the goats and added to my romantic fascination with the life of a shepherd. I imagined the peace and magic of a solitary working life, learning from the animals that I would herd. Eating pieces of goat's cheese and lulling the hearts of my beasts with mystical clarinet melodies from remote tors and valleys. But *this* is just the kind of dreamy perspective that prevents me from actually working, as the actual sweat of the labour never quite matches up to the sweetness of my imagination!

While I waited for my clothes to dry another shepherd invited me for lunch and before long, we were munching locally-grown grapes in yoghourt, scooped up in salty pieces of a pancakey bread which, for the second course, we filled with pieces of tomato and onion. We didn't share many words and I had the feeling that his shepherd's mind belonged to a vale of its own, where none save the walkers of many years could follow.

It was not the easiest of days on the road and I had to reaccustom myself to long waits–something that was pretty uncommon in Turkey, one of the best countries I've found for thumbing one's way around.

But on this day I was obliged to resort to my Zen-hitching practice. I try to make the mind wait in perfect contentment and equanimity to its fate and in appreciation of the beauty of every car that drives by without stopping for me. Everything becomes of equal significance and time itself loses its reinhold on events. The mind spaces out into the grand meditative, hitchhiker's waiting room, free to go places that the body currently cannot.

I evolved this practice in Perpignan, in France, near the Spanish border. I waited unsuccessfully for a day and a half for a lift going South and during this time various French police* may or may not have taken my passport details and read them out over their radios into a central computer–or it may have just been an interesting illusion for all that I was really conscious of it. If it did happen, then they certainly kept better track and record of my orientation and progress than I did.

The trouble with waiting in Turkey, in August, is that it's hot. Very hot. And standing around in flimsy shade is the kind of thing that makes you become ill. I started to feel quite ill. My forehead acquired a strange heat and it became hard to focus on my surroundings as I was assailed by a strange giddiness.

This was one of the more feared eventualities: that I might find

* *When hitching in France, don't stand in the area after the peage toll check, unless you want excess hassle.*

myself poor and sick in a foreign land and it was a contingency that my friends liked to present as a reason for not embarking on the trip. I was pleased they were not here to say 'I told you so!'

I eventually reached the next small town, with a couple of hours of daylight left and I set about finding some rest and shelter. My stomach churned in discomfort and my forehead burned in such a way that suggested another night of sleeping outside would not be a good idea. After some attempts at speaking Turkish I showed my little card around and an old German-speaking guy turned up, taking me to sit outside his kebab shop. He was one of the little helpers of the Devil who just wait on the blind corners of your path and prey mercilessly upon your helpless position for no other end than to make your time as infuriating and unbearable as possible. Thus they nourish their own perverted sense of mischievous delight.

He was a grey-haired guy with a stupid mustache that twirled each time he spoke. His eyes flashed like a madman and he made great theatre in translating our conversation to the crowd that had begun to gather. I had little choice except to suffer through his stage performance until he got bored with it all.

He offered me a night's hospitality for free which I accepted graciously—and then he asked for some payment. I maintained my position of poverty; knowing from past experiences that with this kind of person, once the purse is opened—it is soon emptied.

I had no choice except to endure while he dillied and dallied, all the time making jokes at my expense to the audience and I had no means of communication to appeal to their good hearts to save me from this mental torture.

.At one point, he began to rummage around in my bags and when I asked him what the fuck he was doing, he explained that he was looking for my wife that he was sure I had hidden away somewhere. That was the breaking-point and I started cussing him out in I don't know what language, with tears in my voice from the strain of illness. Only then did he surmise that he'd gone so far that he'd have to help me, if I was to be bullied again on another occasion. He arranged for me to go to his son's house; on condition that I return the next day to discuss my future–he wanted me to work in his kebab shop and marry me off to a local girl. He promised me she would be very beautiful. A cold day in hell, I thought but smiled and gave thanks for his charity in the present.

I was given a bunk to lie on in a house where six or seven young men lived, students of the Qur'an. After much extended hand-shaking rituals, I was left alone in a room where also sat a bucket of acid with wires from it going straight to the mains. I became absorbed with the dread of a horrific explosion, with a acidic face-spray ruining my good looks. My chances of sleep were further hindered by the door flinging wide-open every five minutes, as each new arrival wanted to witness their unusual guest with their own eyes before believing it.

They enjoined me to share their chicken and bread and were very good sports, if a little boisterous in the way of virginal males in their early twenties. Later they woke me whilst it was still dark outside and I figured it must be time for the pre-dawn prayers. It was Friday, the holy day of congregational worship for Muslims. I dutifully rose and followed them into the next room, where a small pornographic magazine was thrust under my nose depicting a couple caught in cunnilingus.

The guy holding the picture giggled hysterically as I shoved it away and turned to my right, where another student held the king of clubs in true card-sharper style between his thumb and first finger.

"Cards?" He asked, with a Las Vegas smile. The clock behind him told me it was only 1am. Cards? But of course! What poorly fool would rather sleep through the night-time hours when there are mean sessions of gin rummy to be played, with devilish 3-of-a-kinds and sneaky all-out straights. Giggling at the absurdity of adventure, I staggered back to bed.

In the morning, I was sorted out with a thick sandwich and I got on the road again, without going to see the greasy kebab man. By noon, I was down at a crossroads where the competition of hitching was quite intense, with whole families looking to clamber into the cabins of trucks that stopped. I never worked out if these people paid for their rides and if I was made an exception of, being a poor foreigner. Or maybe it was just a custom of general goodwill, part of helping each other along.

Getting by in a foreign language when you need to ask something other than directions to the beach, is something that relies more upon a willingness to communicate, rather than on technical expertise in linguistics, plus the confidence to not care too much when you make mistakes. It put a different flavour on hitching too as I was inevitably required to work that much harder to win the friendship of your drivers who often try harder than I might have liked to bridge the communications gap. In France that year, people who picked me up often chose to pursue me relentlessly through my minimal French vocabulary, to elicit my opinions on the threat of fascism or my existential belief in a collective unconscious! It would always start off simple enough but once the usual exchange of pleasantries was done, my command of the language would be stretched like cellophane. I'd be obliged to smile stupidly and admit that I had the verbal skill of a three year-old in their tongue.

Generally, the smallest attempt to speak the local language will bring favour but my next ride illustrated the pits to which the language barrier can descend. I was picked up by a truck driven by a man with a hard-set jaw and who left finger-indentations in the steering wheel. It took him around ten minutes to understand that I couldn't follow fluent Turkish, no matter how slowly he talked or how often he repeated the same word with growing irritation. He scowled and cussed and berated me for not comprehending. I retorted in abusive English, just to return the volleys of aggressive energy he flung at me. Unless you can really let that kind of antagonism fall off you like water of a leaf, it's necessary to give as good as you get to defend yourself.

I wondered what he lived for, this angry, tense man in tight jeans and high blood pressure–did he have any appreciation of beauty or love? Did he have small children that came running towards him as he returned home each day, crying 'daddy'? Was there *anyone* who could prise open his soft centre? A few moments later though, I was hoping that his house would burn down and that all his kids be of a mood to dose his coffee with arsenic, when he began another barrage of inexplicably offensive questions.

But I was in his vehicle and so I had to refrain from actually spitting on him, contenting myself to count the decreasing kilometre signs that indicated the distance to the next town. He confirmed the issue of having home territory by demanding:

"Passport! Passport!"

"Fuck you!" I told him and looked out of my window. He pulled the truck to a sudden halt and threatened to throw me out. I had to take off my left shoe where the document was hidden and wait until his primeval consciousness realised that the details were unlikely to be in Turkish, before we could move on again.

The sun was still at killer heights outside but it was only mildly more favourable to stay in his truck and hang tight till the next oasis, rather than jump out into the outdoor oven. Meanwhile, as we climbed a winding road, he sensed that time was running out and tried to find other ways to get at me. He mimed the same enquiry that all Turkish truck guys made by making the motion of cupping his hands on his chest to indicate the weight of breasts and asking:

"Madame?"

"Yeah, yeah, pal, I have–don't worry about that." I wasn't going to give him any satisfaction on that score.

We pulled into the town of Kaman, a few minutes before the actual onset of bloodshed and I jumped out without bothering to close the door behind me. I disappeared into the backstreets without a word.

I sat down on a bench outside a mosque and started to make a few notes while things were still fresh in my mind. It was the time for the Friday afternoon prayers and there was such an overflow in the small village, that men spilled out of the mosque and laid their mats down upon the pavement in lines facing towards the mosque. They prayed side-by-side, shoulder-to-shoulder, as Muhammed had advised, to 'prevent the devil from slipping in between the ranks'. On a Friday, the community is pulled out of their individual cubby-holes and all islands of personal introspection (except the women, of course) are thrown together in a grounding meet—communal prayer is said to be ten times more worthy in Islam than solitary prayer and the Friday is when all believers are reminded that they exist as part of a Brotherhood. All are then equal before God, regardless of whatever issues may have cropped up in the intervening six days.

But I'm an infidel and so when the mats started to line up facing me, I shunted out of the way. A Muslim will always pray in the direction of the holy city of Mecca in Saudi Arabia, regardless of what else lies in the path but I thought it polite to move.

My motion was detected by a young guy from Istanbul, who invited me to a cafe and placed doner kebab, rice and a yoghourt drink before me. That dispelled the unpleasantness of the last hour and he had certainly gained my esteem and trust. He nearly lost it when he proposed that we visit the police. As I believe I mentioned before, my instinctive reaction to that 'p' word, is to slink back to the shadows in horror. But he insisted, explaining that the policemen were good friends of his. I didn't really see how any good could come from this but felt that after the good lunch, I owed it to him to go along with any strong plan of action he might have.

The resulting scene at the police station was confusing. My passport was taken from me and various conferences were held whilst I watched from my wooden bench seat. After some time, the police chief came down from his upstairs office, to discover what all the fuss was about and he invited me up for some chai.

He was an outsider in the area and was in temporary charge of the village policing, in a break from his usual big city job in Yozgat, to the North. He was totally bored in this small place, where he did little other than sign his name a hundred times a day to the reports and where the only trouble was the firing of guns in the air at weddings on the weekend. As such, he was delighted to have the chance to make educated conversation for a couple of hours, in what was a welcome break from the usual small-world religious minds of the area. Then, totally out of the blue, he asked me:

"So, you say that you want to go to Iran?" I had mentioned that I was a bit nervous about the much-hyped dangers of Eastern Turkey and so now he arranged there-and-then to send me out to the highway with a couple of his officers–they stopped a coach and put me on board. They instructed the driver that I was travelling as a guest of the police and was to ride as far as I liked, free of charge.

So suddenly, I was hurtling through the night across the whole of Eastern Turkey that before had seemed like a daunting and dangerous prospect for a hand-to-mouth hitchhiker. Mother Fate had stepped in with a large sandal flop in the middle of the world and scooped me up and over the trouble zone and safely down 30km away from the Irani border.

The Irani border. Most people will never cross this border and most would never want to. Mention Iran and most will think of the stern and foreboding countenance of Ayatollah Khomeni, staring with the burning eyes of Islamic fundamentalism, ordering you to accept the True Faith or face the Fire!

"Salman Rushdie must die!" We hear and imagine the mindless fanaticism of the Persian proletariat, prepared to run onto landmines to secure their place in paradise in a holy yeehahing jihad. The ruthless dictatorship of oil-funded cult leaders prepared to let fly nuclear weapons at the touch of a button if someone should but cast the slightest aspersion about the cut of Muhammed's beard.

I knew better than this, having always been friends with the local Irani delicatessen in England. I went every week for the strange and rich *filo* pastry sweets and for the rowdy conversation.

"So what will you do with no money?" The more surly of the Irani brothers had demanded.

"Oh, you know; everything comes; and I'll have my clarinet to play."

"Ha! You think you can play your clarinet in the streets of Teheran?" He sneered in nothing more than a habitually rough tone. But then his brother interrupted impatiently with a sweep of the arm:

"In Iran, they will throw food at him!" And told me in a confidential tone, "You'll have no problem for eating in Iran- but in Turkey, you should save a hundred pounds for yourself!"

Every country in the world seems to have a centuries-hardened distrust of the character of its neighbouring states. Often when I was helped on my journey, I was warned that I was unlikely to find similar help in other parts!

But they were all Muslims and the lavish hospitality of these people is famous. The Qur'an actually commands its followers to feed a hungry person–it being well-known that 'a hungry stomach has no faith'. This custom undoubtedly saved me from starvation a number of times. I was pretty sure that the folk of Iran would feed me also.

But I wasn't so sure about the friendly character of the border cops and police–not a small part due to the stories I'd heard from my mate, Nik, who had hitched this same route four years before. He'd had some money with him but then the route was much more hazardous and untrod.

Having overcome his trauma of having turned around during a spectacular sunrise, to witness Turkish planes dropping bombs on a defenceless Kurdish village, Nik had approached the Irani border and was taken into a private interrogation room so that he could explain just why exactly, he wanted to travel through Iran.

After taking his luggage to pieces, he was finally let in to the country and he caught a lift on the back of a truck up into the mountains by mistake. It snowed* and he ended up being stuck in the remote valley for ten anxious days, worrying his head off about his transit visa that had expired whilst he was trapped behind the blocked roads.

* *The nutter had begun his journey from England in February, and whilst pitching his tent in blizzard conditions had often wondered if he would survive the cold of the night. He gave prayers of thanks when he would dig his way out of his submerged tent in the morning to find himself still alive!*

When he finally managed to come down to Teheran, he was thrown in jail for two days on suspicion of espionage. They finally let him out with a new transit visa but for those 48 hours behind bars he didn't know *what* was going on.

I reckoned that if I could get past this point, then I was pretty well home clear to India. The focus of my personal future lay on this particular checkpoint. If I failed to get through, I'd have to turn back to Greece and make massage on the beach or maybe become a roaming shepherd. I much preferred the idea of sitting on my reputation as a hitchhiking celebrity on a beach in Goa.

The trouble was that I feared one look at the state of me, my finances and luggage would bring nothing but harsh laughter and a refusal for entry on the grounds that no one could possibly travel like that.

Customs and border stations often take an immediate dislike and distrust to me if the last time I flew back to England was anything to go by. I was returning from three months in Goa and was pulled instantly as I shuffled through the green channel. The officer found my bag to be full of packets of beedies (Indian tobacco wrapped up in tree leaves that sell for seven times the price in London's head shops) and informed me that I'd either have to give them up or pay £1000 duty tax.

"Take them!" I said. Then they found a spoon in my bag and came to the clear-cut and unshakeable conclusion that I must be a junky–why else would someone be carrying a spoon in their bags, for crying out loud?

"What's the spoon used for?"

"Eating." I replied, trying not to sound mocking or ironic–for customs are God. They have more legal power than any policeman and can lock you up for 48 hours without so much as a phone call.

"Have you been heating anything up in this?" They enquired–that's the way! Hit me with the sneaky direct question! Oh nothing but the finest opium, officer! Here, try a piece!

"In addition to attempting to smuggle illegal quantities of tobacco items into the country, I strongly suspect that you've been in contact with illegal substances whilst abroad. I must therefore ask you to come into the back room." Possibly he'd seen the poetry and odes to LSD in my notebook. Either way, I had nothing else to hide–although you do put things in the strangest of places when stoned!

"I must ask you to take off your trousers, sir–Oh! I presumed you'd be wearing some kind of underwear!" He exclaimed as I stood nude and proud. He handed me back my trousers after the most peremptory of searches. They checked my ribcage from behind, maybe to see if I had swallowed bulging amounts of hashish to shit out at huge profit in some London pad

"Are you an addict of any kind?" He asked, checking my arms for syringe marks. No officer! I just throw heroin into my eyeballs from time to time like any normal person!

"So how much money do you have? How are you going to get home?" The customs guys asked me after the search, as though they wanted to arrest me for vagrancy.

"Oh, I've got some money and-"

"What! About 30p, from what I could see!" I had, in fact, returned to the country flat broke, having invested the last of my cash in the beedies. But I pretended that I had a friend who was going to buy me a train ticket home. They let me go.

It was very simple to beg my train fare in about five minutes, as people at airports always have lots of loose cash and are usually sympathetic to stranded cases. My mate Cal, had put me on to this, as he had done the same thing a few years before and had asked the conductor at the ticket office if he could travel free, given his exceptional situation.

"Certainly not!" He was rather primly told. He panhandled his fare and returned about ten minutes later. An astonished ticket-man asked him how he'd got the money.

"Well, I asked a few people."

"You mean to say, you begged?" What was expected exactly? That he should find gainful employment at the airport and work his way home?

So customs, police and officials will always be against our

anarchistic breed of people, whether we do anything wrong or not. We're clearly undesirables in a world-wide structure of power that gives 2000 television channels of dross to the connected public, whilst Shell liquidates the natives of Nigeria by the thousands. In a world where most of the major countries sell weapons of pain and mass destruction to anyone with the lolly in the world's most lucrative trade.

I'd be concerned if the free and happy in spirit weren't persecuted, for we're a living embarrassment to the evil and corruption that runs through the entire Establishment. But fuck it. We have to live within what's there and deal with it as we have to. Change and adapt.

"You'd better smarten yourself up for the Irani border, Tom." Nik had warned me, referring to my habitually sloppy appearance. Wherever I am in the world, I can usually be counted upon to be looking like a tramp without any conscious effort, regardless of my prosperity at the time. So it was with real focus that I got myself together to invest nearly all of my remaining money in a pair of new trousers, bought from a young guy selling clothes from a cart that he wheeled up and down the street of this tiny town on the edge of Turkey.

I got myself washed and shaved and wore my trusty grey shirt, hoping that the holes under the armpits wouldn't show. I ditched the postcard explaining my spiritual poverty and hid my small rucksack at the bottom of my big black bag; as it was adorned with esoteric symbols that Cal had scrawled on before giving it to me. I doubted the Irani authorities would find imagery of the Temple of Psychic Youth to be all that appealing.

I cleared my bags of all the bits of bread crumbs and burst packets of herbal remedies that had scattered themselves and in the end, I looked pretty good in shirt and trousers, clean shaven, carrying one black bag and a small clarinet case by the handle.

From the small town where I'd landed, I left behind all of the old men at the cafe tables who'd bought me *chai* that morning and caught a bus to the very last outpost of Turkishness before the border. The army patrols stopped the vehicle five times on the twenty-minute journey as the various checkpoints examined all of our documents. Tanks and other armoured cars could be seen here and there, ready to deal with the Kurdish militants.

The mountains began to dominate the forward area and the physical obstruction appeared as daunting as the bureaucratic. Mount Ararat lurched sharply up and I said a small prayer requesting the blessing of Noah; this was the first point of land he saw after the floods subsided.

There was no choice but to take a taxi to the frontier itself and that cost half of what I had left but I was now 100% focused on the crossing and cared not. To my surprise and relief, I met two Czech guys who had just come through from the other direction and they informed me that it was a sinch to get in. They said that visas could even be extended without any trouble inside Iran. I gave them my Turkish dictionary and went on to the awaiting formalities, which took about an hour and then walked through a corridor to face a huge board proclaiming:

"WELCOME TO IRAN!" With enormous pictures of Ayatollah Khomeni and his successor, Khomini, to either side. I was there. In Iran. Wow. Mount Arafat looked far more kindly now and I strolled past long rows of trucks waiting to be allowed through. I stopped to have *chai* with a few drivers, then I changed my money with one of the changer hanging around. I bought a bus ticket to take me through the night to Teheran, getting me away from the edge of the country and into the heart of things. With three dollars in my pocket and not a care in the world, the bus started moving and I slept the whole way.

Chapter 9

Sympathy for the Hitchhiker
(Iran)

What is it to be alone? To be really alone. One way was to stand out in the middle of nowhere and try to hitch a lift. When no one knew me, my identity became just an arbitrary story that I happened to know quite well but which didn't seem to mean all that much. My name is Tom. I'm twenty years old. I play ludo–blah, blah, blah–what does any of that have to do with who I am today and what I'm experiencing? Nothing. When hitchhiking, I had to continually maintain the foundations of my world and hold up the sky with my own hands. There was no one to haul me up from the ditch when I fell over and the only person who made sure that I ate, drank and stayed warm was myself. Naturally, when hitching I met people who extended their love and care to me but when I moved on I was a stranger in a new town, once again alone.

Maybe this doesn't sound so cheerful but it was a far-out state of mind to achieve for, by handling the lone travelling trip I could sometimes access a kind of self-contained strength that was the springboard for true independence. By the roadside, I entered into a kind of a dialogue with the silence around where for my every thought, word and action, there was a kind of complementing answer in the world about me; a response that could only be heard when there was sufficient quiet.

When alone, that existential silence was plentiful. Without any fixed schedule or responsibilities, there were often times when I had nothing to do except look within and talk to myself–the first sign of madness; the second was when I began to feel more comfortable on the road than when staying put–unless of course, I chose to make my home in India, in which case I'd be a complete write-off as far as the rest of the world was concerned.

But that's always been the way. The anthropologists tell us that there have always been people who have been possessed of the unshakeable urge to go walkabout and the roots of this go back to the nomadic way of life, common to almost all humans before Christ and still practiced by hundreds of thousands of people today. They lived off their livestock and moved on to find fresh grazing pastures, new markets to trade their wares or to stay with the friendly drift of the seasons and avoid the harsh extremes of climate.

Apparently, this was once common practice from the aborigines of America to the Bushmen of Africa, from the Bedouin of the Sinai to the Rajasthanis of India; all lived within temporary tent structures of varying design and sophistication, roaming as a tribe with no one owning more than they could carry. Because of the necessity of travelling light individual wealth was not an issue. Possessions and equipment were mostly of the communal domain, efficiency being the soulmate of Survival.

Hand-in-hand with this way of life was the ancient paradigm of a close and personal relationship with the world; the fortune of a tribe would depend much upon the favour of the seasons. Every culture had shamans, priests or sages who could place themselves in contact with the various spirits and deities of the Earth and Sky, to determine how best to align their activities with the elemental forces at play.

These practices don't require our belief or faith in the supernatural because the power that they thrived upon was largely based upon certain poetic symbols (for the various aspects of ourselves), as manifested in the external creation of a god or a demon–it's often a great deal easier to focus on say, an image of the lust for wealth, represented by the Hindu goddess, Lakshmi, than it is to identify the craving within our own muddled minds.

On the move, the distinctions of the outside world became a blur as their surroundings changed by the day. Most of their waking hours were filled with the sounds and smells of their way of life, moving with the jangle of kitchenware and breathing the musty scents of the pack animals. Their steps in time with the beat of their hearts.This lifestyle gave rise to a free state of consciousness of non-attachment to transient things. They were endlessly taught the lesson that they could hold on to no more than they could carry and that even these would not long survive the rigours of the road.

This nature began to die when people first started to cultivate their own land on a wide scale and erected settlements to last longer than a season. Then, with the seductive attraction of security and stability in a fixed community, in crept the evils of personal power and wealth. Families began to vie for influence and prestige in what was the birth of feudal politics.

This focus on the accumulation of fortune and prestige meant that their greedy eyes no longer dwelt on the poetic beauty of the world, save for a few pious mouthings in religious ceremonies that were but another tool in the spawning games of questing for power.

And look at things today—most people are utterly tied up in debt and fears about their financial security, as they endure lives of drudgery and misery in a gargantuan effort to 'stay afloat', for fear that the ground will suddenly open up and swallow them! No one buys anything or goes anywhere without extensive insurance policies to cover them in case the worst happens and hardly one person in every ten thousand can hold all he owns in both arms.

But the nomadic urge is inherent in just about everyone and is hard to completely eliminate. No matter how neurotic and paranoid the culture there always surface individuals who are ready to leave town for the next horizon. 'Drifters', 'hoboes' and 'tramps' they're called by those who stay put, these people are regarded with suspicion and wariness wherever they arrive. However, that's often overcome by the relief from monotony these drop-outs bring. People of the road are often also story-tellers and musicians, singing of the blues that comes with a freedom of movement that the common people both envy and fear. These free-rollers traditionally come into town to make a few nickels with their talents, departing the next day with a hangover and a few scars, leaving behind broken hearts and the odd pregnancy.

Such a man was the blues maestro of the 1930's, Robert

Johnson and he epitomised the image of the smooth itinerant musician. A comrade of his is quoted as saying:

"Me and Robert would be on the road for days at a time; sleeping in ditches and barns and playing on street corners and low-down bars for nickels and dimes; I'd just as soon as catch myself in the mirror and see myself looking like a *dog*–and then I'd turn around to see Robert, looking like he just stepped out of *church* !"

But it wasn't long before the black folk of the Mississippi, jealous of his freedom, began to make rumours and gossip that Johnson had sold his soul to the devil at the crossroads to gain his amazing musical skills. A legend that grew in strength after his first wife died in premature childbirth while Robert was off hoboing somewhere. The only way he could deal with these blues was to sing them:

"I've got to keep moving, blues falling down like hail,
And the day keeps on my need,
Like a hellhound on my trail."

The tradition continued with types like Woody Guthrie in the 30's and 40's Depression America. Tens of thousands of men, women and children got on the road to head for the sweet waters of California, to find health, wealth and prosperity in the promised lands to the West. Of course, they found only miserable refugee camps and hostility and these migrants from Oklahoma and Arkansas, whose lands had been desolated by dust storms, discovered the truth that travelling men like Guthrie had always known–the dreams of modern society were a con and that there never would be any absolute security from the perils of the world–not if you owned the largest farm in Texas! Everything could at any time depart just as easily as it came. You either gripped your handful of dollars until you developed heart cancer or you shrugged and moved on your way with Poverty and Insecurity as a friend that you knew, rather than a dreaded enemy who haunted your dreams at night.

This spirit was maintained by the Beat generation, as Kerouac, Cassady and co, screamed across America in stolen or borrowed convertibles. They introduced a healthy intake of drugs to the picture, generating an intoxication of the present that recreated a mystic appreciation of the relationship with the road, not so different from the ways of the nomads thousands of years before. These trends ultimately coalesced into the reunion of Eastern and Western thought, as the psychedelic explosion in the West instinctively sought its partner in the strong esoteric traditions of the Orient. Long-haired freaks began to establish a physical bridge between the two by means of the overland trail, that many thousands successfully made in the 60's and 70's and that many hundreds didn't:

"And I lay traps for troubadours,

Who get killed before they reached Bombay!" So sang the Rolling Stones, in a well-deserved tribute to those who went down along the way. Victims of illness, murder and overdoses, the casualties were high (Naturally, the Stones never hitched anywhere as they couldn't be sure of maintaining a steady supply of pharmaceuticals).

The movement reestablished a culture of being on the road. Modern counter-culture needed to get away and out there in the real Journey to the East, where they hoped to find some match in the philosophies of India and South-East Asia for the discoveries they were making in their own heads.

So what was I doing hitchhiking the overland trail 20 years too late? I'm supposed to be a Thatcher's child! Where was my portable phone, credit card and filofax? I guess I've always spent too much time hanging around with a crowd 20 or 30 years older than me, soaking up their stories and ripping off their anecdotes. Sigh, a mis-spent youth.

In some warped corner of my mind, I conceived of it all as a pilgrimage in tribute to the various influences that had turned me on to this whole new way of life. I had to earn my freak stripes, in order to really understand the origins of the whole Asian freak scene. I was due to finish my trip in Goa where I'd first really been turned on to the spiritual dimension and saw the Light! (where were my sunglasses when I needed them?) I hoped it would be there that I would find a clue of what to do next. Look out gang, I'm coming home!

Chapter 10

The Magic of Esfahan

(Iran)

I came into Teheran in the early morning, only 30 days after leaving England but it seemed that many months of experience had passed in the meantime. I booked a bus ticket to Esfahan straight away. Public transport is amazingly cheap in oil-rich Iran and I had no inclination to hang around in this notoriously-polluted city.

I made friends with a fat, smiling man who ran the find-out-your-weight machine and he gave me some of his lunch: a nutty paste sandwich, complete with the ubiquitious soft drink in Iran, called Zam-Zam–an irreverent reference to the Zim-Zim holy spring waters at Mecca. He told me of his joyful visit to England, where he had fully utilised the cultural experience by playing the fruit machines in the arcades. Gambling is, of course, forbidden in Iran, as the Qur'an clearly condemns the practice of trying to get something for nothing (though you normally get nothing for something). Because my friend had had a map of the symbols on each reel, I suppose it was technically more fraud than gambling, as he stood there all day using the nudges to win jackpot after jackpot.

Nobody had heard of hitching in Iran and there appeared to be no word for it in their language, Farsi. The entire 3000km length of the country could be crossed for about 15 dollars and so I don't suppose many people bothered standing around in deserts to get a free lift. I was feeling too lazy to find the motorway just then and I was busy assimilating the new vibes that Iran presented. Every woman in sight had her head covered with some kind of wrapped scarf, many of them wearing the full-length black chador that kept them nice and warm during the 40c. summer months.

The average skin pigment was only slightly dark and so I passed easily enough as an Irani. The men cut around in shirts and trousers, looking decidedly more busy than me. As I came closer to Asia, mats on the street sold food items or newspapers but the high-rise buildings lurked even here. I boarded the bus with a loaf of bread and about 300 Toman in my pocket–about half a dollar. I was quite pleased to be in shallow financial waters again. I couldn't feel much like a renunciate with a bulging wallet! I also hoped that my poverty might bring me closer to the Iranis, throwing myself upon their mercy as it were.

I sat up front with the driver and played some blues harp for him, while he plied me with cups of *chai* and with handfuls of one of the many kinds of pistachio nut, that take about thirteen years of practice to get the dexterity needed to open the shell. He insisted that I was completely crazy and after the 6 hour journey, he dropped me off in Esfahan with a parting present of another 300 toman so that I could afford the next bus.

Everywhere there seemed to be huge pictures of the previous two Ayatollahs and less frequently, of the new president. Big Brother is watching you? The sun was setting and all was magic as I strolled through the streets of Esfahan: still today the bejewelled prize of Persia, famous through the ages for its spectacular architectural tributes to heaven. It was too dark to really see anything much but I felt moved anyhow.

I passed a carpet shop and a young guy with clear English invited me to come in. Pretty soon, I was spinning stories about travelling with all the strength and glory of Allah behind me, whilst they plied me with eggs and bread.

"Many people *talk* about 'Allah providing'," They told me, "but you actually *mean* it!"

Then they led me down the lane that brought us to the Ayatollah Khomeni Square that they claimed to be the largest public square in the world. Closed shops bordered the stone-paved terraces that perimetered the area and in the middle were large lawns, with ponds and fountains in the centre and hundreds of families making picnics on the grass. Horse-driven wagons galloped up and down the terraces, where youths played five-a-side football with a tiny ball and hockey-size goalnets.

One of the enthusiastic carpet-lads took me to find a family who could give me dinner and watch over me as I slept on the ground. As we walked around, we met an off-duty policeman who wanted to find me a job in a local factory. I declined for personal reasons and because of an addiction for habitual sloth.

After a while, we found a visiting family from Teheran and I was invited to sit on their laid-out picnic mats. They served up an impressive array of rice, meat dishes and soup, that I had to accept for fear of causing offence–a very common dilemma for visitors in Iran. I took out my sleeping bag to lay it out on the stone tiles and saw the son of the carpet shop owner running down to meet me. He insisted that he would sleep outside also, to ensure my safety on my first night in his city.

His name was Ijaz and he looked like a second-hand car salesman from Liverpool, who had undoubtedly spent long stretches of his life both behind bars and sitting on stools in front of them. Actually, he was the sweetest of people I met in Iran but his scarred and battered face with suspicious semi-crossed eyes and bushy eyebrows suggested something far more devious and scheming. It was quite comical to watch his short figure ambling around the Square; dressed up in a smart grey suit that expressed an elegance that lasted from the feet up to the neck, where his head took over and exaggerated the whole dodgy effect. He looked like a defendant in court wearing clothes for the first time.

He spent his days on the lookout for the trickle of tourists that dared to brave the reputation of his country. He accosted them with a friendly style in English or German and they'd immediately shrink back in horror. If he was lucky, his charm would overcome their initial repugnance and doubts and they'd allow him to drag them off to see Persia's finest carpets. Even then, Ijaz told me, suspicions could still arise. He had taken a man from Taiwan back to the shop but the tourist had grown nervous and paranoid as they walked around to the side entrance–the front being closed in observance of the holy day of Friday.

"This is no shop! Who are you?" The Taiwani had suddenly cried with flaring eyes.

"Oh yes, this is my father's shop and-"

"No! No! Get away from me! I know Tai Kwon-do!" His customer had shouted in terror, exhibiting the kind of mental control intense training in martial arts can bring.

We settled down to sleep and I couldn't help grinning as I heard Ijaz's teeth chattering. I had to lend him my coat to keep him warm.

Amid dreams, I heard the call of the morning prayer before dawn, accompanied by a fanfare of horns and trumpets–at least, I think I heard that and then a while later:

"And behold! Morning's stone dropped into the bowl of night,
Has put the session of stars to flight,
And the sun has looped sultan's turret
In a single golden noose of light"

So wrote Omar Khayyam and thus happened here. The first rays of day struck the dizzy minaret towers of the huge blue mosque that commanded the Square and which draws tens of thousands of touristic faithful each year to pray within this amazing structure.

Bleary-eyed and dazed, Ijaz and I faced each other like a pair of old tramps and exchanged impressions of the cold and discomfort. I was vastly amused that my friend had chosen to endure it! We took off for some breakfast of bean stew and *nan* bread, courtesy of Ijaz and then I washed up at the local Hamam–here just a functional unit where a person can shower and wash in privacy; not the luxury variety of the Middle Eastern kind, which are equipped with steam rooms, dry rooms, icy baths, herbal fragrance and all of the rest. Staying clean has always been close to the hearts of Islamic people and it has always been a source of pride against the Christian infidels, who have only really taken to bathing regularly in the last fifty years (who needed water, when you had beer? Pour every tenth pint down the back of the neck and you stay clean enough, surely.)

Ritual Islam requires all believers to wash their extremities before worship and there has never been any separation of rank in the washroom or in the prayer hall. This puts to shame our own history, as according to George Orwell, working class estates of

England in the 1930's averaged only one bathroom and toilet for every fifty houses!

There was never really any consciousness of cleanliness in the West, until the governments eventually forced the rather obvious findings of science on a reluctant public who would have preferred to keep their cess pits adjacent to their water supply. Islam, however, has always had quite explicit guidelines in these areas from the commandments in the Qur'an and by the recorded practices of the prophet, Muhammed, in what amounts to a very large game of Muhammed says!

Muhammed says don't eat with your left hand–very good.

Muhammed says suck your fingertips after a meal–well done.

Write a book speculating about the depravity of the Prophet's family...

Wrong, Salman Rushdie! You're out!

So, looking a lot more Islamic, I returned to the main square and sat on the cool blue tiles by the grand blue mosque that gave beneficent shade at the South end. I had to sit outside as they charged foreigners fifteen times more to enter than for Iranis–it still wasn't much but it was more than I had.

I was actually quite content to stare at the patterns covering the front side in what is the crystallisation of Islamic artistic excellence. As mentioned in the commandments that Moses brought down from Mount Sinai, true believers should not make any representation of any form from the heavens above, the Earth in the middle or in the waters below.*

Thus for thirteen centuries the creativity of Islamic artists has been forced to internalise in the innocence of perfect symmetry, finding new dimensions of expression in patterns denied of any identifiable imagery.

It all seemed very reminiscent of the visions of my psychedelic past and I was so startled to see the pictures behind my eyelids staring back at me from 100 foot tall minarets. I soon fell into a trance and lay down to join the mass drowsiness that falls upon Iran in the middle of the day.

* *Hell was not always considered to be a fiery place*

The Square became quiet at this time as all of the shopkeepers closed up for lunch. It was hard to imagine this place full of screaming Muslim men on the frenzied demonstrations of the '79 Revolution.

In the evening, I met a gawky but intelligent Belgian called Garick. We gratefully exchanged experiences of fitting in with Iran's social mesh–especially concerning conduct towards women. The black chadors succeeded in depersonalising the females, so that we couldn't tell much about their appearance and age. Instead it made them into a kind of street hazard that we dreaded colliding with lest our eyes be plucked from us in accord with Islamic justice.

Garick told me that he had recurrent nightmares of tripping on a paving stone and grabbing out with his hands as he fell–straight on to the bosom of a young Irani virgin! Surely a shotgun wedding scenario!

It seemed so incongruous that all of these measures were taken to prevent the leering at women in public but yet in conversation we were often asked if we liked Irani girls! In fact, we did our utmost to avoid any kind of contact with women at all. It seemed that even meeting the eyes of a woman for too long would be an implicit statement of intent or betrothal. For all of that, the elusive charm of the fairer sex could not be completely hidden and even the flash of a dark pair of eyes could leave the impression echoing around in my fantasies for days afterwards.

In the evening we joined the local guys playing football on the tiles, the national sporting obsession and we embarrassed ourselves dashing and slipping about in sweaty clothes and with red faces. Eventually I had to collapse by the side and save some face by giving a small blues concert.

I passed a few happy days in Esfahan, recovering after the 35 hours of bussing from the middle of Turkey. It was the first time I'd stayed put for more than a day in the three weeks since leaving Budapest. I'd wake in the mornings to the prayer calls and shortly after, I'd hear the sound of water gushing onto the tiles. I'd have to rouse myself to make way for the hosemen to clean the area.

They patiently waited with big grins while I gathered up all my belongings.

I hung about exchanging English lessons for meals with the many students who came down to the Square to meet tourists. I'd make friends in the various carpet shops to extend my network of hospitality and keep hunger at bay. When no kebab-bearing benefactor materialised I'd buy some slices of flat bread and a bag of fresh dates, the most choice of all foods. I could eat six such meals for a dollar.

I made yoga and performed inadvertent clarinet performances, as crowds of entertainment-starved people would gather whenever I took the time to practise. Many forms of music and all kinds of dancing were banned in Iran,. It was thought to be the clear preliminary to the meeting of the sexes and the 'inevitable' illicit copulation that would follow. For these crazy reasons, I was always a little shy to play but one and all would urge me on. Their spirit of fun was alive and kicking beneath the layers of religious monotony.

Intelligent conversation could easily be found and the Iranis carried themselves with a kind of grace and sophistication that distinguished them as a proud race apart. Begging was rarely seen and the only observable life focused around business enterprise, the families that walked around together, or the young men who milled around dreaming of a life of fulfillment in either marriage or:

"How is it possible for me to go to your country?" I was forever asked all across Turkey and Iran. It was depressing to meet so many people who were dissatisfied with where they were and they could not understand why I should want to leave the idyll of England. Across Asia, it's widely assumed that strawberry jam runs down the sides of the buildings and that honey runs freely in the gutters. These people crave an honest police force, a free hospital service and the kinds of modern technology like heated showers and washing machines that are hard to find in the poorer countries. Iran wasn't that poor but its people were very quick to believe that all their problems would dissolve if they only lived in one of the more-developed states of Europe.

I wasn't much of an ambassador for England. I confused all of their expectations and images by ranting on and on about the drudge of everyday life in the West. I told them how a million people are without homes, whilst the same number of buildings lie empty; how Europe is in complete spiritual poverty and devoid of any peace of mind. I'm not really that down on where I come from but I felt obliged to offer a counter to the hopeful *naivete* of their dreams. What a misery-guts. But weirdly, when arguing with an orthodox Muslim, I always seemed to be holding up England as a model of personal and social freedom–something I never expected to do.

Whilst chatting to a student of English, I was reminded that this area of the world was one of the traditional centres of Sufism and it occurred to me that it would be cool to meet these mystics in person, having been a reader of Sufi poetry and stories for years. A Professor I knew told me I'd have to go to Kurdistan to see the Sufis. He related how he'd been in that area and had personally witnessed a devotee's head being decapitated, placed on a table and then reattached without any injury or loss of life.This sounded quite funky and before I could even make any plans to leave, I met a young guy whose father drove buses to Sonedad, the capital of Kurdistan in West Iran.

In a whirlwind of events, I was whipped off to this young man's house for the night. In the morning I acquired a 4 week extension on my visa simply by the temerity of asking for so long. By the evening, I was on an evening bus going West with an address in my hand of some of the professor's old friends.

It was all quite exciting and I settled down for another 12 hours of motoring across the land, glowing outside in the sunset that lay a smoky veil on the lines of hills asleep on the horizon like Arabic script or large reclining beasts. If one ignored the plastic rubbish that blew around as copiously as the tufts of bush, then it was all quite beautiful.

Chapter 11

In search of Sufis

"Come, come, whoever you are!
Wanderers, worshippers, lovers of leaving,
It does not matter.
For ours is not a caravan of despair.
Even if you have broken your vows a thousand times,
Come, come, yet again, come."
(Jallal u' Din Rumi)
(Kurdistan in Iran)

The Sufis. As I had grown up I had picked up various pieces of information about them from different sources and had the general picture of them to be a collection of poets, mystics and madmen. I'd learnt that they would attempt to lose themselves in esoteric activities like spinning themselves in circles for hours at a time, to enter a kind of ecstatic state of union with God. They're usually seen as the nice side of Islam, that allows Westerners to relate to what is otherwise a pretty austere and foreboding religion.

The intro poem was written by Rumi, the 13the century Sufi master and poet supreme and his lines seem to sum up the basis of this tradition–that all of the rules and details of religion are irrelevant when you become consumed by translucent love for God. The individual melts like a drop of water into the ocean and the illusion of separation disappears as we return to our original nature.

The image of the whirling dervish is popularly known–the twirling dancers who dizzy themselves in trance and many folk stories and moral fables originate from the Sufi traditions dating back to pre-Islamic times. Small groups of disciples committed themselves to the guidance of an accomplished master, who would destroy the false notion that they were separate from the Creation of God all around. Such practices also used to include the extraction of all of the teeth of a young student, to take away his 'bite' for life and to humble him, that he might approach the path of self-dissolution with a more modest step.

The Sufis adapted to Islam pretty readily. The intense ritual activities of worship required and encouraged by the new religion in the seventh century, suited the fervent inclination of these mystics and gave them an umbrella of orthodox community support under which they could cultivate their studies.

Of course, it was a case of accept-or-die in the early days of Islam, when every true believer ran around with a sword looking for infidels to slice up into geometric pieces. Despite their tacit conversion to Islam, the Sufis have always been regarded with suspicion and mistrust in many circles and they've traditionally faced persecution in less tolerant communities.

But like all the people of the Middle East, they shared a reverence for the Word that is nowadays probably beyond our appreciation. Teachings and knowledge had always been passed down by a strict oral lineage that was definitely not a case of Chinese whispers–the length of the chain of transmission added to its prestige with the weight of each link increasing the validity of the teaching: As told by Muhammed to Ali, as told by Ali to Abu Bakr, as told by Abu Bakr to Bilal–if all those guys said it, then we'd better listen up!

As such, the Sufis embraced the miracle of the Qur'an with open heart and faith. It was clear to them that the sound and content was of a divine nature and they took their reverence a step further than most. They would chant some verses for days at a time. Especially the sacred verse of *'lailahahillalah'*–'There is no God–but God' ie. There is nothing–except this! Meaning that there is not a moment of sensation or a single facet of existence that is not perfect Godness. Through the most intense of pain, sorrow, joy or confusion, this verse acts like an ever-ready log of truth in the sea of transience. The believer floats above the fixation of events in the present to receive an eternal perspective where all is seen as Divine.

I was given the verse when I first came to Goa as an eighteen year old. I conducted an intense psychedelic regime over the next twelve weeks and I clung to the Qur'anic words for all I was worth. Whenever my visions turned malevolent with the sea and sky rotating wildly and demonic grinning skulls came flying through the darkness–the chanting of the Arabic phrase would put flowers in the eyes of my apparent assailants and a smile back on my lips. I discovered that fear could only operate when I imagined myself to be disconnected and outcast–with the chanting of these words the whole universe was behind me, in front and all around–Demons, do your worst!

Since the 60's, freaks from America and Europe have been searching for the secrets that Sufism hints to yield and the giver of the Quranic verse to me was an American who had spent six years in Morocco, under the tutelage of an acclaimed master of a prestigious Sufi order. For most of that season in Goa, I did my best to extract stories of this time from my friend and so I heard second-hand of some of the less-than-orthodox devices employed by his master in the process of instruction. His teacher was a small, glowing man named Ali. Whenever anyone came to visit him, they'd be given a spoonful of *majoom*: a sticky sweet concoction of countless moroccan herbs, not the least of which was mountain hashish–all just to prepare the student's mind for the mind-blowing rap session that would follow.

On one occasion, my friend told me, he was taken out by Ali in an open-top sports car to be taught the art of invisibility. After whizzing around the main streets a few times (a speeding convertible was more than a little conspicuous in Morocco) Ali put him down in the full view of two notorious, undercover narcotics police and roared off. My friend was left alone with two large suitcases full of hash, which he then had to carry back to the house.

"Ali, why are you making me do this?" My friend had implored on what was a very long walk. These stories he told me to illustrate the many and various methods used to navigate the student on his path of bending to the will of God.

Islam. The word means 'peace' or 'submission'. For me it always conjures up the eternal image of a Muslim kneeling down on his mat, a finite form, prostrate before the infinite. In the West, the atheistic fashion has been to hold our heads up high in defiance, refusing to lower ourselves to anyone or anything–including God. Bow down? Are you kidding? What is not generally known,is that surrender is the greatest strength of all, as the Chinese Taoists never tire of saying:

"What is there more soft and yielding than water?
Yet what is there that water cannot move?"

(Lao Tzu sometime B.C)

By kneeling down to the will of the universe, the Believer then stands up with the might of the cosmos behind him. Once the mind is at peace with the will of Allah then it becomes a hell of a lot easier to deal with humans afterwards. It was with this kind of inner strength that the Muslims sliced seven shades out of the crusading Christian 'infidels'–literally 'one who will not believe'.

When a person becomes a Muslim, a Self is lost and a Brotherhood gained. All believers are equal before the eyes of Allah. The whining pride of our infantile spirituality is put away and we can take rest and nourishment on the breast of Islam, on the infinite resources of strength and wisdom that stream forth from the Source.

The further Eastern traditions of Buddhism and Zen also put extreme emphasis on the killing of the Self, in order to unite with the Oneness of existence–so Islam is not unique in this and many of the images used in the poetry of Sufism can also be found in Buddhist texts. Mystics of any religion are bound to get along.

It's just that like Christianity and Judaism, Islam is a mad desert religion started by camel pushers who thought that the world was flat–Honour the Lord your God! Vengeance shall be upon thee! Woe be to the sinful! etc. And that's simply the style that suited these harsh lands, where Survival and Death were two deities to be solicited at the campfire, when still alive at the end of another day.

Can you imagine Buddha preaching to the Pharisees or to the idolatrous Arabs about the perfection of the lotus flower and the myriad illusion of a world that ran on the cosmic wheels of reincarnation? He'd have had his fat belly slit open before he could so much as light an incense stick!

In the same way, all religions originating in these big sand pits have learnt to embody the Infinite in a set Father figure of a creator–God, Jehovah, Yahweh or Allah–whatever you want to call it. They're all just aids to give a focus on what's going on all around them and their role within it. It's as adequate a vehicle as any and the Sufis explain the seemingly arbitrary reference to a personal God, using terms like 'He' and 'Him'–in the same way that we speak about each other as you, me and the parson's daughter. If we're going to think of ourselves as separate from each other, then it follows that our relationship of existence will be of the same tongue. So maybe there is a God sitting up in the sky with kindly eyes and a long, white, Santa Claus beard!

So I'd read my books and knew my stuff–or thought I did–and I was kinda hoping to meet some crazed Sufi master who might give me special initiation into the secrets of his sect in the remote and lonely mountains. This business of lopping off the head and then whacking it back on sounded pretty cool, too and I wanted to give it a try myself. 'Off with their heads! ' said the Queen.

We arrived in Sonedad before dawn and so I had to wait around in the station until a more reasonable hour for visiting people arrived. As the sky began to lighten, I went outside to take in the local scenery and a young man came running out after me, yelling that I'd dropped all my money in the station–it only amounted to about two dollars but it was a typical example of the good character of the Muslims.

The town was surrounded by bulging, green hills with rocky tors that celebrated the first rays of the sunshine breaking upon the Western ridge for the trillionth time in its life. Around 8 o'clock, I went to look for a bus into town, failed and indulgently took a taxi that brought me to the spacious lawned grounds of the university a short time later.

Thankfully, the guy at the gate paid the fare for me and I tried to locate Mr And Mrs Sufta: old English-teaching friends of the professor in Esfahan. I only hoped to get some information on where I could find some Sufi contacts—but when I turned up at the door that morning (although she couldn't recall who the professor was), Mrs Sufta simply declared:

"Anyway, you are our guest! Come in!" Slightly bemused at this unreserved and spontaneous act of hospitality, I entered and sat down on the thick Persian carpets that covered the floors—as they do in the house of every family that can afford them. Within minutes, she had bought me a box of my favourite pistachio pastry sweets and two slices of cake, along with a glass of chai, obviously. This was the way to breakfast! I was then invited to sleep and I did so gratefully, straight down on the rich textured carpets that were infinitely superior to mattresses. Very happy, I fell asleep.

When I awoke, the rest of the family had been marshalled and I had to explain to the kindly but stern father of the house, just what I was doing asleep in the corner of the room, having demolished half of the reserved delicacies of the pantry. He couldn't recall who the professor was either but it didn't really seem to matter. I was simply taken to be a long-lost family member of some kind and was absorbed as a random element into their everyday pattern of living.

Their nephew, Fahrzad, was appointed to be my guide for my time in Kurdistan. He would take me to the Thursday Khan Garh, that night: the weekly Sufi meeting that I hoped would be the unfolding of the entire mystery.

We came into town by shared taxi though it took some time to hail one of these unmarked cars that drive the same fixed routes around town each day. In every town in this country, men and women can be seen trying to get the attention of these taxis, who act like they couldn't care less if you come or not. It was a curious reversal of roles where the customers were subservient to the whims of the drivers. Passengers hop in, out and shuffle about every couple of minutes. Things are especially complicated when a woman gets in, as then all is done to keep them apart from the other men in the car and thus allow her dignity to be uncompromised.

In the middle of the town was a glorious statue of a man with one leg bent behind him, both arms and head raised up in the air in the full immersion of ecstatic worship. Right on! I thought, becoming a little fervent in the atmosphere of things.

A little while later, Fahrzad led me through the old part of the town which looked very much like 19th century London of the movies. We wound our way through irregular contours of misty back streets and alleys in the dark evening that held the kind of character long dead in the all-pervading illumination of modern cities. We came to the house of his grandmother, who was apparently a dervish, herself. I didn't really know what that meant, other than it was a term for a follower of Sufism. She was small and wizened in the face and lived in a poor dwelling with a wooden ceiling that appealed to my heart more than any home I'd seen since leaving England.

I tried to imagine if I could live in a place like this and wondered how the locals would react to an Englishman studying Sufism in their neighbourhood. Could I find peace and contentment in this traditional area, with a loving wife and establish a family away from the havoc of the rest of the world. I was really beginning to lose the plot at this stage.

A few family and friends arrived and one happy man in his fifties, proudly showed me the scar on the left flank of his belly from where he'd had a sword driven through him in a Sufi ceremony. This was not the side of Sufism I'd heard about and sounded like a grandiose S&M club. It was the focus of the conversation though they doubted there would be any bloodletting on this night.

The ceremonies took place in an old, old building known as the Khan Garh and we men came through to the main carpeted room, while the women went off to provide *chai*. I bowed to the Sufi leader of the evening; a slender man in pure white cloth, with a green scarf wrapped loosely around his head and neck. He eyed me keenly as I sat back against the wall and took a look around.

All who entered kissed the unfurled flag that stood in the corner and some bowed to the pictures of Muhammed's followers that hung high on the walls, which were supposed to have been drawn from inspired dreams. About 20 men sat about and the ones who were official dervishes had long, flowing hair, which they bundled up under large floppy hats, Rastafari-style. Propped against the corner were three rings of wood, two and a half feet across and covered with leather, looking like Irish *borans*. By these sat a small and silent old man, looking much like a goat. Next to him was the preacher in white who delivered a passionate discourse about the miracle of pregnancy. His audience nodded and murmured in assent to his words.

Not long after our second chai, the scrawny old man picked up his leather-bound hoop, known as a *daf* and suddenly burst out in a voice born of a thousand mountain gales; his rocky voice rough and strong as the crags that surrounded the city. He howled beautiful renderings of *suras* from the Qur'an, accompanying his wail with light finger rhythms that without warning would erupt with a thunder clap of sound when he threw the *daf* into the air and caught it with his spare slapping hand. The walls seemed to shake under the impact.

The *daf* is traditionally used to alter the consciousness of the audience, to allow the miracle of the Qur'an to be fully understood—an aural intoxication that held as much power as the rasping voice of the singer. A conversational silence reigned under the majesty of the performance, only to be broken when the men would murmur the salutary ' praise be upon him', whenever the name of Muhammed was sung.

After about an hour of solo performance, the old man was joined by two other *daf* players and singers. I feared for the foundations when all three threw their *dafs* in the air to emit a boom to banish any unbeliever's doubt. When we left, Fahrzad asked me how I felt–I was amazed that he needed to ask! He told me that the sound made him feel like crying inside for joy.

We slept in his grandmother's house and rose a few hours later to climb the local mountains before dawn. Hyperventilating and nauseous in the 5am chill, I had no idea why we were punishing our lungs like this, until our path climbed suddenly and we met the full vista of velvet hills. A white light lay like a snow blanket on the Eastern range. We climbed up and up, toward the drifting sounds of drums and laughter from above. We came to a plateau where a fire now burnt shyly in the virgin daylight that seeped in all around.

Our throats were hot and dry and we moved towards the spring where icy water laughed up from deep in the mountain. It was so cold that we could only take small sips, not sure any more if we were hot or chilled. Further up the slope, small groups of young men and even women sat in little spaced out clusters, talking and tapping the odd drum–or less favourably, playing some junk on a portable tape recorder.

I pulled myself up on a rock and meditated on the view that reminded me why I came travelling in the first place. The sun was peeking shyly over the opposite ridge and the whole town of Sonedad could be seen nestling in the valley pocket, with rocky slopes chaperoning the outer districts. No way could this town grow no larger.

The hills ran as far as the eye's sight, with fuzzy brown undulations and play of shadows. According to Fahrzad, it was these ranges that were the source of pride for the Kurdish people. I imagined the battles that were fought in these areas when Kurdish nationalist guerillas hid out in the valley clefts and scanty tree cover, in their ill-fated battle for independence during the early '80's. I could picture the fearful image of Irani army helicopters scouring the region to pinpoint and destroy the brave separatists, who might have won their struggle in an age of less-advanced technology.

These are the moments that make all the long road journeys worthwhile. When you climb up high all of the psychic stress of civilisation is shed like a heavy coat. The breezes of a purer blend of peace and the harmony of Nature lift the spirit to lofty places.

Before I could verbalise an emerging hunger that growled inside, Fahrzad passed me up a sandwich from a shoulder bag of packed breakfast. He spoke to me in quiet English and I realised that in my smart clothes, no one twigged that I was a foreigner.

That accounted for the refreshing lack of attention I received. Most of the Iranis had a lighter shade of skin than many of the Turkish. With dark hair and unshaven chin I didn't stand out, despite my blue eyes.

It was Friday and so many had taken advantage of the holiday to lounge about on this elevated social spot. I guess more informal relations could take place, away from the watchful eyes of the Islamic elders below who didn't have the energy to mount so many steep steps this early in the morning. Other late-risers were coming up with panting red faces as we descended a little while later and all over town, the Kurds prepared for their day of congregational worship. It was also a day for families to spend some relaxed time together

Fahrzad shepherded me back down to the town, taking my arm every time we crossed a street. This was annoying but actually quite necessary, because the traffic was so chaotic that when alone, it took me ten minutes to reach the next kerb. For his part, it was his glad duty to extend his protection to a guest in his homeplace. It didn't seem to cut much ice with him that I had come four thousand miles from England without any problems. He was extremely reluctant to let me loose in the tiny town of Sonedad, lest I should become hopelessly lost or meet with some terrible calamity.

To this extent, Fahrzad embodied the nobility of the Irani spirit, carrying on his young shoulders a strong sense of honourable conduct. He once solemnly informed me:

"You know, Tom, I shall never drink alcohol in my whole life!" He strained to be as gentle as possible to all that he met–though perhaps his sense of humour suffered in the seriousness of his endeavour to act well.

Most of all, he displayed the remarkable talent so often found in Iran, for *listening* and waiting until the other has finished everything they have to say before making a considered reply. Perhaps this is the patience that is lost to the West under the barrage of modern media that seeks to assail our every sense through each waking moment. This drip-feed of data becomes so addictive that most people's first reaction upon arriving home is to switch on the box and numb their minds with the sedative of Australian soap operas.

The Iranis *did* watch television but only in rationed amounts and they still valued more the time to take a glass of *chai* and elicit another person's viewpoint–and *this* was the people that the American government chose to make their national enemy? A more absurd example could not have been picked to present as a race of evil, scheming terrorists than these sweet and generous folk. I could not help but laugh when I thought of what sinister images the notion of Iran struck in the minds of most people back in England.

Fahrzad spent much of his time making sure that I was sufficiently entertained and many of his friends wanted to meet me and practice their English. I was a novelty in Kurdistan, which doesn't receive much tourism and whenever people heard that there was a foreigner in town, they would rush to see what a non-Irani was like. They seemed slightly disappointed to find that I had the same facial features as them (one nose, two eyes etc...) and much the same living needs. Perhaps they expected me to hunt butterflies for food or something! In any case, I tried to entertain them with blues harp and clarinet performances whenever I could find the energy.

The Sufta family were pretty happy to have me as long as I paid the unspoken tariff of playing chess with their young sons (and let them win). When they had to leave town to attend a family function, I moved to Fahrzad's house where I experienced the uncomfortable side to Irani hospitality.

A couple of hours after a huge lunch, the mother would come into the room where we were sleeping off the last ingestion of food and force our fuzzy heads to eat slices of melon. Throughout the day she would continue to ply us with bowls of fruit and chocolates and when we returned from our usual aimless walk into town, feeling ready for bed, I'd be thinking how sensible it was to eat such digestible food in the evening–when it would be announced that dinner was ready! To my horror, we'd come through to the main room to see the mats all laid out with plates of rice, piles of *nan*, meat dishes, vegetable stews and soups, peppers and sliced onions.

The largest piece of meat would be placed before me, the guest of vegetarian inclination. Fahrzad's mother would wait for the moment that the mounds of food on my plate showed even the slightest sign of a dent, when she'd pounce upon me with a ladle, imploring that I should take more. My polite refusals would cause her the most grievous offence. All in all, the last mouthful would sometimes be finished at midnight, leaving me with no energy the next day to leave the house and escape death by enforced gluttony.

During this week, I began to hate the thought of food as I fell asleep twice a day with a bloated stomach–a habit extremely damaging to one's health, one explicitly condemned by Muhammed too. But there was no way out and a silent war began to fester between Fahrzad's mother and I. She would eat only after everyone else had finished, stuffing in spoonfuls of three of four dishes at once into her powerful jaws, chewing in pensive hurt at the slight done to her cooking by this thin Englishman.

The father was a big and bustling guy who seemed to be on the verge of a heart attack at any moment. When he heard I was interested in Sufism, he pulled up his shirt to proudly show me his sword scar, too. My arrogance was a little disturbed to see that just about everyone seemed to be an ex-dervish–I wanted to be of the precious few initiated into the magical secrets of the dervishes. But it's a fact that until about 60 or 70 years ago, just about everybody in places like Morocco belonged to some Sufi order or the other.

Fahrzad told me that the dervishes were only really active in the wintertime when there was less to do in daily life. Not much really went on in these September days. To make up for my disappointment, he managed to get hold of a video (that had been made on someone's camcorder) of a maiming session from the previous winter.

The whole point of these rituals, Fahrzad told me, was to reach a state of trance and immersion with God, facilitated by chanting and the playing of *dafs*. The physical laws of the world could be breached on a bridge of Grace afforded by the intense faith of the devotees held in the protection of Allah. Are you following this so far?

The film starts running. *Dafs* boom through the room, accompanied by some finger chimes and a continual fervent chant of 'Allah! Allah! Allah'. A very shaky home video recording shows circles of men with their hands linked: some with long, flowing hair, others cropped–maybe they were on their lunch break from driving buses. They all move slowly round, rocking their heads back and forth with the rhythmic chant.

Now don't try this at home kids but one of the grey haired leaders in white cloth took a volunteer and slowly pierced a sword through the spare flesh at the side of his waist until it came out the other side. Then he withdrew it with no loss of blood.

Other tricks included needles being stuck through the cheeks and jaws, spikes hammered into the head with mallets until they could stick there unsupported, shooting themselves in the side and eating sharp pieces of glass lamps and razor blades–*hors d'oeuvres* anyone? A little rough to digest but quite refreshing I think you'll find! Even little boys no older than seven got in on the act, slashing their tongues with razors–anaethetized by the high produced either by the divine ritual atmosphere or perhaps by the attention of the video camera.

This was all entirely credible as none of the people involved were professionals and none were looking to deceive anyone. This video was not being produced for an MTV contract and most of the participants were just ordinary folk who didn't want much more than what they already had in life. I couldn't believe that this kind of revelry was going on in Iran but there it was.

All interesting stuff but not really to my tastes. I was hoping for a bit more from the Sufis than ceremonial piercing sessions and so I continued to pester Fahrzad to the point of exasperation. He couldn't understand what more I wanted as I begged him to establish for me some contact with the Dervishes of the area. A day or so later, he arranged for me to meet the son of the local Sufi leader who would answer any questions I had.

It was then that I realised I'd been guilty of spiritual window-shopping. All of my enquiries about the possibility of study brought the answer that I'd have to spend some years living around the Khan Garh building if I was to be initiated. There were currently no two week vocational courses for itinerant English freaks with a liking for poetry.

I did learn the meaning of the term 'dervish' though and this gave me more than enough to chew on for the time being. It literally means 'one who has nothing' ie. nothing except God. Rumi wrote:

"The true believer of God lives in complete poverty." Not that a dervish should necessarily be scrounging for bits of bread but rather that he should acknowledge everything as secondary to his passionate search for the Divine. By exerting utter detachment to the things of this world his mind is freed to focus on the heights of heaven. It all sounded little bit austere to me. I wasn't yet quite ready to forgo the milkshakes, the pretty girls and the fast cars just yet. Better that I come back to the feet of the Sufis as a toothless old man, when my 'bite' for the delights of life had faded and my meditations and prayer would not be interrupted by the vision of creamy thighs of sun-tanned sweeethearts.

I then considered I might make the luscious legs and pert breasts *my* particular meditation on the illusion of life and pursue them with pious gusto! I even found backing in Rumi's poetry as I remembered his verses impying that if your driving force is the carnal energies of your lower half, then simply turn your rump around to face the light and it will surely lead you there by the back door!

Not too many female lovelies to be had around these parts though and I dreamt of the Israeli girls who would even at this moment be partying in the Indian Himalayas. The thought was unbearable and so I made plans to start heading back East as soon as possible–wait up girls! I'll be there soon!

Before I left, I spent a night in the home of a local Kurdish guy and learnt some things about these charming mountain people, who have been pissed upon in several countries for a long, long time. The 20 million or so Kurds are spread over the range of mountains owned separately by Iran, Iraq, Turkey, Syria and a couple of the former Soviet Union states. Yet they lack a homeland of their own.

The Kurds that I met generally had a lively and laughing disposition with a strong sense of cultural identity. They have their own language and are proud of their distinctive customs of dress, dancing and folklore that mark them apart.

The politics are mind-numbingly complex but it seems that the Kurds in Iran have the best deal of all the scattered people–for in places like Turkey they face public flogging if they are caught speaking Kurdish and the Turkish government refuses to acknowledge them as a people in their own right. One Kurd had told me that there they were regarded only as 'barbarian Turks'. There they face continual police intimidation, brutality and military assaults. This is also true for the Kurds in Northern Iraq, where entire towns have been wiped out by the use of Saddam Hussein's chemical weapons (each batch allegedly stamped on the reverse side with 'made in the U.S.A' or 'produce of Great Britain and Germany')

All complicated and muddy and it seemed inappropriately distant when spending the evening with this mustachioed teacher, his smiling wife and their playful children. There was a free and easy vibe that was missing in many of the other houses that I stayed at. We had a great dinner together of a yoghourt soup and fried tomatoes with eggs which we ate out of the pan, in a kind of communal simplicity that was light and refreshing after the usual conservatism of Iran.

"Now let us lay back and fart!" The teacher announced. Here my new friends acted with the unpretentious energy of a family, not straining to be 'good Muslims' but only to be good people–they took their religion in the *spirit* of believers.

Sonedad was definitely poorer than anything I'd seen before in Iran. On the main streets could be seen ten or twenty beggars in the course of a half-hour walk. Most pitiful of all were the women who slumped on the the sidewalk with their heads and bodies completely covered: motionless black shrouds with a small bowl before them containing the odd coin. I guess they were widows from the days of the wars in the early eighties.

Islam does require that every male who is capable of doing so, should pay two and a half per cent of their annual earnings in a special tax called *zakat* and once a year, he will go to a special *zakat* office. He and an official will determine exactly how much he should pay and then the office distributes the funds amongst the poor and needy as it sees fit. By the looks of things it wasn't enough.

Islam condemns beggary. This makes sense in a functioning society where everyone has a chance but though no one wanted to admit it publicly (And the people to whom I spoke often requested me not to repeat what I was told), there was clearly a lot more talk about an Islamic society than actual practice. Corruption existed here too.

When I asked about the beggars, my friends would sniff disdainfully and declare that most of them were millionaires who were just too lazy to work. This kind of shit made me really angry and I upset the atmosphere of more than one dinner party by saying so. Anyone who has tried asking for money knows just how tough it is and what sort of wear and tear it takes upon your self-esteem and morale. It is to abjectly lower yourself to the offhand charitable whim of the passer-by and reduce all of your thoughts to the dismal focus of the next few coins required to buy your food. I suggested to these decent folk that they try it themselves and then they'd quickly change the subject.

On my last morning, I spent three hours climbing to the very top of the local mountain peak and celebrated with a wild dance of release in the domain of fresh, sweeping winds–finally free of the orthodox minds of the general public, who regarded a stretch of the arms as a prelude to a form of arcane witchery. By the time I descended Fahrzad had gone out of his mind with worry but I was glad to prove to him that I could stand on my own two feet.

I gratefully declined the offer of the Sufta family to stay longer at their home and teach English at their institute, though they would have been quite happy to put me up for months. Living in Iran was like leaving half of my mind closed, suppressing the freakish flowerings of the imagination to which no one there was able to relate

Fahrzad's mother repaired my flagging desert boots (A constant embarrassment to my hosts when they took me anywhere) and packed me a lunch for the journey; together with lots of advice on how to keep myself and my luggage safe. I was given the bus ticket to Esfahan and the two families also gave me some money for my forthcoming journeys.

The source of the Kurdish pride, the velvet mountains, slumbered in the sunset yellow that blessed the valley. My bus rolled out and we wheeled on East.

Chapter 12

Robbed of my bed

(Iran)

I came in to Esfahan pretty early and predictably, the first person I saw in the Square was Ijaz; his crooked gait and shifty demeanour distinctive at 100 yards distance. In a typically good-hearted gesture of welcome he took me off to eat an Irani delicacy for breakfast–head of sheep. I'm willing to give most things a try and my earliest recorded ancestor was hung for thieving sheep in 1329–but a mouthful of mucousy mutton later, I declined any more, much to the mystified surprise of my friend.

I hung around in the shade for a few hours, then some off-duty soldiers took me to lunch and I learnt a little more of the mentality of a country living in the shadow of war. All young men must spend two years in the army, regardless of their education or vocation, unless they be a mullah–the bearded Islamic scholars to be seen stepping piously about the place. The soldiers had been physics students but now their expertise lay stagnant as they spent their days learning how to hoist a rifle around and march in strict step.

In the evening I met up with the professor who had sent me to Sonedad and he invited me into his home for the night, necessitating that we catch no less than *four* crowded taxis to his home in the outskirts of the city. We spent the kind of evening of straight intellectual conversation that results when there's neither any dope nor alcohol to be had–Not that this guy *needed* anything! One look in his eyes was enough to convince you of his brilliant insanity, containing a cool air of danger somewhere within. This was combined with a sharp foxish cunning and he bounced around all over the place with the maniacal oscillating expression of an actor in sped-up film.

He spoke the most educated of Oxbridge English and believed whole-heartedly in the flag of Irani Islam. He seemed to feel that the strength of his nation and religion were synonymous with his own strength and pride! In his company you could not help but feel the formidable potential of this man and I soon had the explanation:

When I asked him about the previous Iran-Iraq war (that had raged for eight long and terrible years), he disappeared into a far room and returned with an album full of photos of himself as a soldier. As he turned the pages, I saw the image of a brave and frightened young commando, armed with all he could carry.

"I had everything. Rifles, grenades, pistols, poison–you see, Tom, I was a commando–that means I always worked alone–killing Iraqis! Because they were trying to kill me, you see!" And so on, in an engaging and charming voice that never tired of its own tone and that held something close to genius–in that he spoke of all matters in the same relaxed manner making no more fuss about the bizarre than the commonplace. He told me quite casually that he had personally killed 57 Iraqi soldiers.

"How did it feel to kill someone?" I asked him.

"Well, of course, I had all manner of terrible hallucinations–I was seeing things, Tom, as truly as you are here at this moment!" For two years, he had been unable to sleep comfortably, tormented by dreams of his own seemingly-imminent death. He kept patrol in the Kurdish mountains, through which Iraq had launched a surprise land invasion. I had no doubt that the eyes of my friend had seen a lot of death, witnessing many ugly sights hidden from the everyday view of the rest of society. But as a talented mystic in his own right, he seemed to deal with it now on the same conceptual plate as the complexities of a game of chess.

He dropped me back in the square the next day with a book of Omar Khayyam poetry and an arrangement whereby I could enter the fabulous blue mosque for free. I didn't see him again but was thankful for the relief of his unorthodox company, in a country that is strong in uniformity of thought.

I was never short of conversation in Iran and people sometimes exhibited less surprise that I was travelling without money, than by the fact that I was on the road all alone at the tender age of 20. I was always asked if I had my parent's permission to travel and it was assumed more than once that I must be a runaway.

Irani family structures generally entail that sons and daughters often live with their parents well into their 20's. It's seen as heartless and incomprehensible that teenagers are often expected to leave home at 18 or 19 in the West–or that they should want to! The close and somewhat sticky family relationship works both ways, of course and most Muslims will feel a strong responsibility to look after their parents when they become old and feeble, to repay the debt of their upbringing. Old folks homes are spoken of with real horror in Iran and are seen as a vivid symbol of the callousness of Western society–where we'd surely turn pensioners into tinned sausages if they tasted good!

In these modern times the young men sensed that they were somehow missing out on the action. They were obliged to wait until marriage before having any relations with girls and many couldn't afford the expense that a wedding and setting up house would entail–carpets are not cheap! Consequently, there were a lot of youths jerking around in small boisterous groups with frustrated testosterone flowing through their tense veins.

After an evening of walking around the Square, with my hopes of an invite into someone's house frequently being raised and then falling flat as a *nan* bread, I was eventually given some food by a family on the lawns. I retired to sleep on the tiles but within minutes a crowd of socially-awkward onlookers came to stare and hover about. Finally I jumped out of my sleeping-bag in my undershorts and screamed in rage:

"*Pool nadaram*! *Pool nadaram!*" (='No money! No money!) At which terrible visage, they finally understood and withdrew in shame.

The next morning, I was woken by the guys with hoses as usual and went to wash in the public toilets, leaving my bag out for a moment. On this occasion my trust in the goodness of the common folk was betrayed because when I returned it was gone. In one bleary lapse, I'd lost all of my sleeping stuff, clothes and my harmonica. After a minute of cussing, I was overcome by waves of laughter and I figured that at least I'd have less to carry.

When Ijaz heard what had happened, he was more upset about my loss than I'd initially been. He held his head in his hands and exclaimed:

"How could this happen to you in my country? Please accept my apologies!" and he bought me my bus ticket to Yazd in consolation.

Much lightened in load and in spirit, I strolled into the Blue Mosque with my paper of special permission and saw a collage of artistic inspiration that I can't effectively describe in words. My mind was taken to an architectural astral plane where many miracles were done and I wandered through the inner areas in a dream. This was an oasis of the spirit for thirsty desert travellers. Not a single hot colour could be seen and instead all folds and soft yieldings of blue, purple and green fell in flower blossom of heaven, eternally drifting, spiralling and folding in upon themselves within the casing of the blue tiles that adorned all.

The minarets towered in undeniable turquoise and I left the sunshine to walk beneath the fat main dome. It's underside glittered in a song of the night sky and by standing on the centre tiles, my voice echoed back seven times as I shouted 'Allah hu Akbar!'

Such are the wonders of Islamic constructions and I was told about a building (no longer surviving) which contained a room whose walls were contoured with Divine cunning; musicians could come and play and when the Sultan and his subjects would come in two hours later, the music would echo back at them!

Now without anything to keep me warm at night, I hoped that the hospitality of the Iranis was consistent across the land and I took the bus to Yazd in a general effort to move East while I still had the energy.

In an hour or two, the desert began to silently swallow the horizons on either side. We thundered forward, powered by sheer resolve, fierce determination and a full tank of diesel, undaunted by the mocking expanse that made our motorised carriage seem very small indeed. This was not a desert of the swirling sand dune variety but rather a plane where nothing seemed to have the will to live or grow; flat, fey ground that stretched as an enormous potential grave to the North and South.

To the East some hills began to grow and we focused on these for all we were worth. I was filled with a euphoria at the prospect of new territory but also a strange reluctance to leave the simplicity of the desert. I was pleased not to be hitchhiking here. Standing by the side of the road I would have been an incongruous island of life in an earthy void that hosts the heat of day and the cold of night with equal passivity. I'd soon have joined this entropy for the sake of good manners, if nothing else.

When we arrived in Yazd I teamed up with a serious Slovenian, named Peter and a funny French guy, called Jaurice, who had been on the same bus as me. Peter stared around at everything with an intense gaze as though he was expecting it all to dematerialize and hide the moment he looked away. Jaurice made impressive attempts to offer pieces of fruit to the guys at the bus stand who were staring at us:

"Why is it," he asked with empassioned bewilderment, "that the Irani will never allow us to decline when *they* offer us something but will never except anything that *we* try to give them!" Shaking his head with regret.

We marched into town like three bold wanderers from the West, striding boldly with our travel-hardened thighs and looking desperately for somewhere discreet to piss. I left them at their hotel and began to stroll around town, employing my usual tactic of attempting to look as lost as possible, in the hope that someone might come to my aid. In the general bustle of a town or a city, no one stands out more than someone who looks like they don't quite know what they should be doing.

Within minutes, a large fat man approached me in loud and simple English and asked me where I was from, where I was going and the usual stuff about occupation, marital status and the preferred cut of tobacco of my father. Once done with the obligatory preliminaries, he began to expound on his knowledge of Western culture; music in particular:

"Ah yes! I know music of Europe very well! George Michael!

Michael Jackson! Yes! Ha! Ha! No, Please wait... Mariah Carey, yes? And Dire Straits–very good!" With the approach of night and lacking a bed of any description, I began to feel that this non-stop stream of verbal diarrhoea wasn't exactly furthering my chances of survival and I said as much. He *did* pay for me to get cleaned up at the local *hamam*, which was a good start but I soon realised that he was yet another mindfucker from some warped and weary hell, sent to prise open the cracks in my sanity. He took me to the fruit shop and continued:

"Kerrot! Yes? Ha! Ha! Potatoo! Please wait! Ah! Onyon–yes? Please wait–Melon! Yes! very good!" And so on, until my reason eventually overtook my apathetic fatigue and I realised that he was just a bit simple in the head. It transpired that he still lived with his parents, who probably gave him a little pocket money each day so that he could stroll about and enjoy himself naming agricultural products in English.

He didn't want to let me go and I eventually had to use an arm twist to remove his huge hand from mine. I hustled off to find some other help in the now dark streets. He stood there waving for minutes after I left him and I cursed that I didn't have the money to take a hotel room too.

The only grass areas that I could see were coated with an evening dew and I no longer had any bedding. The nights in Esfahan had been sharp with the approach of autumn. Yazd was in the middle of a desert and so was even cooler in the evening.

I remembered the new postcard in Farsi that I'd gotten the professor in Esfahan to write out for me, explaining my pilgrimage and I showed it to a group of students I met on the street. They at once adopted me and took me back to their flat, apologizing all the while that they couldn't offer me much comfort.

They lived in a one-room apartment and slept on a floor that lacked the usual carpets. As a special celebration, they rented out some movies and we watched some hilarious Jackie Chan acrobatic action whilst we munched from a meal of a a foot high pile of *nan* bread and some pieces of meat. Most welcome of all, though, were the surprise joints of hashish that their Arabian friend produced from his jacket pocket–evidence that there existed more than one set of moral standards in Iran.

The next day I was passed on to another Yazd student, who buzzed me around town on his motorbike and sorted me out with some new clothes to replace my shirt and trousers that had deteriorated to rags. On the way round the red stone walls of the city we ran into Peter and Jaurice who were delighted to see me still alive.

"*Merci*, for our friend!" They told my driver and we parted with the wish that we might meet again in the later stages of the overland trail.

A contact was set up for me in my destination of Shiraz to the South and I spent the rest of the day and evening with the students, who practiced their ineffective English on my poor temper until it was ready to split. Once my survival was assured, it was amazing how ungrateful and irritable I became when I felt the peace of my personal sphere was invaded.

This kind of reaction was like biting the hand that was pulling me up the cliff face and is an indication of the exasperation that can come with hand-to-mouth travelling. I sometimes went for days and days without any space to myself, so dependent was I upon the help of others. This made me go fucking crazy. I was almost always in the company of others and I had to adjust myself to the routine of the kind folk who fed me–even if that did mean dinner at one in the morning.

My bad spirits were utterly shamed by the generosity of the students when they put me on the bus to Shiraz. Not only did they buy me the ticket but they all gave me more money than they could have afforded and became offended when I tried to refuse. In addition, it was all I could do to prevent them from giving me any of the valuable items that were in the room. They tried to bestow upon me digital clocks and vacuum flasks that would have doubled the weight of my luggage.

They loaded me up with food, shaving equipment and promises to write or phone, embraced me with tearful farewells and kisses on each cheek and then stood around to wave as my bus pulled out. I said a silent prayer for the blessing of the sweet people in the world, resolved not to be such an asshole in future. Then I breathed a sigh of relief at finally being alone again.

Well, alone in a sense, for as soon as the other passengers on the bus heard that I was English, they poured handfuls of seed and nuts into my hands that were beyond my dexterity to open. As it was impossible to refuse on these occasions, my pockets were always crammed with bits of muesli throughout my time in this country.

We arrived in Shiraz at 4am. I was taken back to the house of a young guy I had met on the bus, to sleep until a more reasonable hour. Thereupon, the contact of my friends in Yazd came to collect me and soon I was stepping into a huge three-storied house, owned by my new friend, Mehrdad who, after 14 years of living in America, had returned to try and get his land back from 'those thieving bastards in the government'.

Mehrdad was well-off, with American tastes and high blood pressure; he laughed at his own jokes and swore without restraint–yet at the same time retained the considerate nobility of his Irani upbringing. He had a beautiful wife at whom I couldn't help staring; and a nauseating little boy to whom I never gave a glance. Mehrdad was perhaps a little suspicious of my aims and it was important for him to establish some kind of hierarchy between us. But when I yielded to his whims and didn't take offence at his vibes, he reciprocated with friendly generosity.

There was a large convertible in the yard but Mehrdad liked to leave it draped and unused as a tribute to his late father, who had owned the car. So he showed me the sights of Shiraz by motorbike, with his excitable little brat on the front doing his best to glue his lips to the handles with candyfloss. We visited the tombs of a couple of Sufi poets and saw a few other crumbling relics but it was all something of a let-down after the magnificence of Esfahan. It didn't really matter for it was simply pleasant to be in interesting company and a warmer climate again.

We ate a wonderful dinner of succulent beef, that I judged to be of the same texture as the breasts of Mehrdad's wife who served it. We spent the evening with a selection of Hollywood videos which let in some welcome air on the austerity of Irani culture.

At night, Mehrdad and I sneaked out to break the law and we slipped through the midnight streets, slicing the cold air on his bike. Half an hour later, we were puffing on a joint in an alleyway with a friend of his, glancing nervously up and down every few seconds in case of detection.

We then joined his other friends upstairs who, though rebels themselves (by virtue of playing cards and watching the prohibited satellite television), would have been outraged by our dope habits. Suddenly it seemed like I was a teenager again, doing my utmost to hold back my giggles of mental obliteration before a stony and sober audience who quizzed me on strange and surreal aspects of Western life. I hope that my answers made some kind of sense.

Mehrdad had the strange capacity for seeming as uncouth as only an LA salesman could be one moment and then pull me up the next minute for not following the proper protocol for entering a house—one should wait for the other person before entering and it's respectful to yell 'ya Allah' (=to god) as you go in, to warn the females inside; in case they want to don their headcloths or whatever. Likewise, in the middle of a blood-and-guts Hollywood excuse-for-a-movie, he would sigh wistfully:

" There's no love like that you have for your mama and papa!"

There was no doubt about how he felt about the Islamic regime in Iran:

"Those fascist sons of bitches!" He would snarl,"Man, you can't even go for a walk in those mountains without the fuckers trying to make out you're a spy or something—just to get *baksheesh!** You know what that means? Yeah, that's right—money!"And he seemed almost pleased about the

---

* *Baksheesh—a word meaning 'gift' in Arabic and which is used across Asia to cover any solicited payment of an informal kind, ranging from a bribe paid to an official for special favour to an offering of cash to a beggar!*

corruption–it gave him the chance to screw his pudgy, bald-headed features into one of the bad-ass expressions he'd picked up from his movies.

"And I tell you, man, if you walk down the street with a girl, one of the secret police–you can recognize them because their shirts are always hanging out–will come up to you and ask to see your ID–and man, if you're not her husband or brother or something, then you're in deep shit!" he cackled with satisfaction.

Once Mehrdad no longer felt threatened by my eccentric presence and realised that I didn't want his money, he assumed a gracious and patronizing air of a teacher to a mixed-up pupil and suggested I should stay and make some money instructing English in Shiraz.

"I'm worried about you, man!" He said, the day before he and his family got ready to leave town on holiday. "What you gonna do?"

"Well, I guess I'll just have to turn the next page of the story!"

"Oh yeah?" he cried with a cheery grin, "What happens next?"

"Dunno–I haven't got there yet!" It was nice that two such utterly different people could get along so well and I enjoyed firmly declining his offer of money when I left.

I did accept some blankets and a warm jumper from his mother. She was a lonely, handsome woman who, to my surprise, proudly declared herself to be a Christian. She showed me her silver crucifix worn on a chain about her neck. She told me in her pidgin English how on a number of occasions she had brought back to life babies that had been dead for seven or eight hours. She demonstrated her secret technique, which was to rub downwards with both hands on the stomachs of the babes, who would then suddenly gurgle with smiling life, before their parents' very eyes. I believed her–as since reading Peter Pan as a kid, I've always been afraid to say that 'I don't believe in fairies', in case one dies at my words.

Mehrdad put me in a shared taxi out to some famous ruins in the desert 50km away. I had my new sleeping stuff all wrapped up in a large sheet, peasant knapsack style.

The Persepolis. Legendary stone structures of a ruined great city of long-forgotten times. They looked more like crumbling pillars of clay from the outside but I figured they'd be more impressive on the inside. As with every cultural site in Iran, there was a ticket booth to fleece the growing number of tourists come to see the hidden wonders of Persia and I gave my postcard to the man at the booth, in the hopes of getting in for free. He bade me come in and play my clarinet. One Ray Charles "Hit The Road Jack" boogie later, he loaded me up with chai and let me share his lunch of rice and chickpeas, before giving me leave to go among the ruins as I pleased.

The inside wasn't all that impressive either and I can only guess that it *was* something special before Alexander the Great smashed it to pieces in a drunken frenzy. I met a couple of Czech girls (what were all these Eastern Europeans doing on the road?) who were travelling in the other direction, back to Europe. We made use of the sourcebook where real travellers get their information—word-of-mouth. They reckoned I'd get fed well enough in Pakistan which was a relief to hear and it was good to get a lot of the thoughts off our chest that we couldn't really express to the Iranis.

We decided to make the most of Nature and sleep out in the rocky hills that lay a few hundred metres away. The notion was all but incomprehensible to the kind man in the ticket booth and it took a great deal of persuasion and explanation to convince him that we wanted to be alone. On our walk up the trail, we were twice stopped by soldiers and as the male of the group I was obliged to be the humouring spokesman. Because of these delays it was almost dark by the time we found somewhere flat enough to put down our beds.

As soon as we put our bags down in our spot in the gorge of large rocks and boulders that probably once held a stream. We fell instinctively silent. Something was wrong. A minute later, we heard some approaching sounds come from down the trail. Then a few grunting and sniffling noises produced a short man stumbling through the bushes in the fading light, murmuring to himself as he found his step. I really hoped he might be a lost shepherd.

"Salaam Aleikum!" I shouted in the age-old Muslim greeting of 'peace be upon you', just to advertise our lack of hostility. He staggered forwards to clasp my hand and the stench of alcohol rose from his bleary features. He mumbled something and then lurched over to the girls on my left who flinched with instinctive foreboding. I interposed myself, still attempting to be of calming good cheer. He clutched my forearm and snarled with eyes aflame.

My heart began to race and I felt slightly weak and dizzy. I realised that the kind of violent situation I had always hoped to avoid was now on my hands and there was no way of avoiding it. I had trained in Kung Fu for three years in England under the guidance of a blind Irishman–but I'd never had to put it to use and I discovered that there's a distinct gap between practice and the real thing.

The drunk began to lean across me, forgetting my presence in his greedy focus on the girls and one of them screamed out:

"Don't touch me!" It was now or never and so for the first time since the age of 10 I got ready for a fight. I let fly at him with a couple of palm strikes and a kick at his sideways figure, that suddenly transformed into a scrambling pair of heels at the moment I made contact. A real warrior would have given immediate pursuit and reduced his head to *halwah* on the rocks, before he could say 'Allah hu Akbar'. But a real warrior, I was not, despite my martial arts training–I suppose I'd always focused on the 'Art' aspects more than the 'martial'.

Before the drunk had run more than twenty yards, he turned and picked up two large stones. He reapproached with his arms in a throwing position that threatened the integrity of my skull.

This I did not need. The nearest hospital was over an hour away and if I was taken out, the girls would have to fend for themselves in a very ugly scene. The violent tack having failed, I tried a more subtle method beginning with appeasement.

"I'm sorry!" I cried, with my hands open to either side, "I'm sorry! It was my mistake! I'm sorry!" He caught my meaning in the tone, if not in the words and lowered his arms cautiously, reaching out his hand in armistice. I began to shake a little less.

The Czech girls had gotten on the case in the meantime and had gathered up all of our bags. Already they had begun to move back on down the path. The crazed Irani became more desperate as he sensed the situation slipping away from him and he couldn't quite decide if he wanted to fuck the girls or me–he kept on making a smooching sound with his lips and pointing towards the bushes. Naturally, it would have been indecent to have forced sex in the open.

There followed an almost comic descent. He would remember the more desirable Czech girls and hurry down after them, jumping through bushes in his frantic chase. The sound of his approach would elicit shrieks from the girls and I would hasten down by a safer route to once again intercept his path.

The situation came to a standstill again. He became more and more forceful with his grappling and I wondered if I could summon the focus and the calm to floor this lecher with the vital injuries he deserved. I possessed both but neither seemed eager to make an appearance and so I made use of my reserves of guile instead.

"SALAAM! SALAAM!" I yelled with elephant lungs, causing him to hesitate as we all listened for a response. "TOURIST! DANGER! HELP! DANGER!" I was saved from feeling stupid by an almost immediate response of torchlights and an answering call from far below. Whatever wits the guy possessed shook themselves aware. He turned and fled up the rocks with an aptitude that stemmed from unmitigated fear at the consequences of being caught–had he been apprehended, I'm sure he wouldn't be walking today.

Pretty shaken, we drifted back to the ticket office and made our beds nearby under the watchful eye of the soldier on guard duty there. I felt shitty for having been so feeble against what was not a challenging opponent. I realised that all the combat training in the world wouldn't make much difference if I didn't possess the

100% intent and mental capacity to go through with the task. This is the superiority of the street thug over the peaceful passer-by–that he is prepared to land a punch because he's done it so many times that it causes him no more conceptual difficulty than buttering a slice of bread.

I seemed to be a lot more disturbed about the whole thing than the Czech girls, however and I was impressed with the calm perspective with which they handled the event. For the first time, I fully appreciated the ever-present fear that all women have to a greater or lesser degree–especially in the case of the travelling female who is so more vulnerable than the local women on account of the language barrier and because she is not within the protective folds of the community.

The nature of this kind of incident throws light upon Islamic customs regarding women which in its purest form is a paternal and protective dimension.The fundamental feeling is that no woman should ever have her intimate nature violated by the most coarse and despicable lust that has always existed in some men.

Any man who's had a daughter will know this feeling well; the nervousness of watching her grow and flower into a girl who will attract the attention of every guy on the block–and it only takes one screwed-up asshole to poison in a couple of minutes, an innocence that can be ruined for a lifetime.

As well as being a Prophet, Muhammed was a war-lord and many of the guys were being wiped out in the endless wars to defend/impose the Faith, thus there was a surplus of unmarried and widowed women. The rule allowing men to have four wives meant that he could offer security to the women unspoken-for.

One of the girls told me of a similar close call she'd had whilst travelling in Turkey the year before. She had been invited into the home of a Turkish guy, whom she presumed lived with his family. His wife and children were in fact away at the time and she spent much of the night running around the house and garden, trying to hide from her host, who had turned sultry and leering as the evening wore on.

"Why are you doing this to me?" She had cried, "Aren't you

supposed to be a Muslim? The Qur'an doesn't tell you to do this!"

"Oh, it's night-time–Allah is sleeping!" came the smug reply.

And yet she continued with this grassroots travelling and planned to hitch all the way back to Prague once they reached Turkey. I shuddered in admiration.

As we got ready to sleep, the kind guy from the office turned up with a huge cauldron of stew and some corn-on-the-cobs. It took him some time to realise that we weren't declining out of shyness but because it was way too late to think about eating. It was nice to have the girls there to share the humour of the Iranis practically forcing food in your mouth as you snored.

My new blankets were almost up to protecting me from the cold of the desert night but not quite and I was shivering long before the dawn came. The morning erased the vulgar feelings of the previous evening and we were still rubbing the dust from our eyes in dreamy appreciation of the new day, when a whole coachload of American tourists pulled up. They poured out with the accompanying baseball caps, sunglasses and video cameras. All of the women were decked out in full-length chadors which they assumed they had to wear beyond the confines of the bus at all times (The Czech girls just wore thin headscarves and never received any flak for it). I suspect they enjoyed the theatre of blending into their grand adventure of going on holiday in the enemy heartland.

"Hi! My name's Frank! Pleased to meet you!" What was this? We were polite but it was a relief when the ruins opened for the day and they disappeared inside.

We munched on a melon that Mehrdad had given me and the girls paid for a taxi for us back to Shiraz bus station, where they also invited me to share a kebab lunch in the cafeteria. All of their talk about India and Pakistan was getting me in the mood to return. I decided to get moving and bought a bus ticket to Bam. They left me with a parting gift of 7 and a half Indian rupees (enough for a few chais) that they had remaining and a shell from an Indian beach to act as my homing signal. I hope they got back to Prague safely.

As my bus crossed the middle of Iran the road wound about a climbing canyon ridge and every time we hit a bend, the view of the expansive, flat basin below was revealed in all of its vast glory; rolling on and on until the mauve sands merged with the soft blue shadow of what may have been a lake.

I got chatting to an Irani guy who had spent 10 years living in America and he filled in a lot of gaps in my knowledge of Iran's turbulent history, making it slightly easier to get a perspective on things. He told me about the time of the Shah who, in the 70's, had tried to Europeanise Iran in much the same way that Turkey had been partially dragged into the twentieth century.

The Shah had declared war upon the chador and had sent soldiers on horseback down the streets to rip off the black cloth from any women who dared maintain the custom. In the schools and on TV, the young were encouraged to be as Western as possible; whilst in their homes, they would face the contrary influence of their parents and grandparents who were generally against everything that the Shah stood for.

In addition to this cultural conflict, Iran was used as a playground by men from the neighbouring Arab states, come to flaunt their wealth in the pursuit of alcohol, prostitution and general thrills denied to them in their home countries.

When the economy began to fail, people speaking out against the Shah were 'disappeared' and support began to grow for the exiled Ayatollah Khomeni, who with the help of the Western media's hype, came to be a focal embodiment for a return to Islamic tradition–a yearning that had grown in response to the failing attempts at modernisation. As my friend related the story it all sounded very epic but history has shown that people in a shaky economy will put anyone in power who can give them a bit of hope–Heil Khomeni!

His pictures were still everywhere–in mosques, restaurants and street corners and the sight of his stern, rectangular face made me quite pleased that I'd never had to deal with him. However I was assured that Khomeni was quite a mystic in his own right and wrote beautiful poetry. By drawing upon inner reserves of faith he supposedly enabled to deal with the political world with all the might of heaven behind him.

Of course, Saddam Hussein probably thought the same thing and the immediate eight-year war really fucked up the finances of the new Republic. Iran was forced to pay exorbitant prices for supplies to Turkey–the only state willing to help them–and so Turkey became rich whilst Iran became poor. My friend insisted that consequent economy problems were the main reason that Iran hasn't fully evolved into a fluid and perfectly-functioning Islamic state–whatever that was supposed to be.

The bus let me off at a small garage outside the town of Bam and I made a wind-swept bed behind a wall that kept a little of the wind off my huddled frame. I clutched onto my clarinet with both arms as I slept.

I got up early because it's somehow less acceptable to be sleeping rough when daylight comes. I strolled down the road to the date Mecca of the world, this remarkable oasis being particularly famed for the succulence of its date-palms which clustered in thick orchards to either side of the road.

An old man in faded clothing was sitting on the pavement with a few rolls of *nan* and a bag of dates before him. He made a simple wide-armed gesture as if to say 'look how little I have!' and I immediately responded with out-turned pockets to say 'me too, mate!' At which, he beckoned me to share his breakfast with him. I demurred but at his insistence, put silence to my complaining stomach with the most luscious of fruit to bless the trees of this planet.

Few Western people are aware of the delicacy of fresh dates, used to the squidgy, semi-dried variety that are sold in most places. No teeth are needed for the fresh kind and when mine all fall out, I'll move to Bam rightaway to end my days squeezing this juicy black nectar off the stone with my tongue.

I held back after each mouthful but the old guy would pressure me to take more until I really was full. He smiled and pointed to the sky to indicate the source of our fare. If the lines on our palm contain the secerts of our Fate, then the wrinkles on the face surely tell of our history and I wished I could decipher the stories etched in wending grooves across this old man's face.

I gave him the Indian shell that the Czech girls had left me with, telling him it was from Hindustan. He examined it with eyes of sunshine and was still holding it to his ear as I departed, which was probably about as close as he'd ever come to the sea again. I parted with all the appropriate hand-on-heart 'salaams' and then realised that we'd communicated so much in five minutes with hardly a word in common. Short like a *haiku* it remained one of the richest encounters I had on the whole trip.

"Hey Mister!" came a hundred friendly shouts from grinning locals, happy to break the monotony of the day with a few words of English. One cry came from above and as I looked up, a young guy harvesting dates dropped me a handful to munch as I walked along. Produce of an agricultural area can always be obtained without much effort and Bam proved this to be especially true. A little further on, some men were loading trays of dates onto a pick-up truck and I hung around conspicuously for a minute or two, until one of them raised his eyes to the sky and came over with a sample to move me on my way.

Bam was dead and its only beauty lies in the wealth of palm trees and the ruined city that drew its tourism. My mate Nik, had told me that the locals completely ignored the area when he was there but now, as everywhere, the ticket booths were up. I played my usual postcard trick and was asked to play some clarinet. He bade me go in without delay after one recital whether out of appreciation or relief that my music had come to an end, I'm not sure.

Now this place was far out. A real, deserted old city with stout stone perimeter walls 30foot high around which the ghosts of sentries still walked A citadel stood regally at the far end and in the intervening distance was a labyrinth of crumbling walls, paths, domes and sidestreets, all of them carved of the same grey stone. This must once have been an amazing place to live, with all of the life of the place concentrated with the 500 metre long city walls on each side, robbing the dawn and the sunset from all save the sentry guards and the privileged royalty in the elevated citadel. Protected from the outside or imprisoned within, it would depend on your perspective and every man, woman and child must have known the finite dimensions of the settlement with their eyes closed.

Taking random turns, I came across the old mosque area and I joined some workmen for a second breakfast of *nan*, dates and melon. I played minstrel yet again but the dates were beginning to lose their appeal.

I spent a couple of hours hanging about in the heights of the citadel towers, from where the entire lay-out of Bam could be seen. The forests of palms surprisingly fertile, adjacent to the dusty terrain of the desert that crawled up to the edge of the orchards.

I returned to the street and discovered the less open-minded temperament, characteristic of small towns and villages throughout the world. First of all, a fruit seller gave me a pomegranate and warned me that I was surely bound for hell as a non-believer. Then a surly grouch walking beside me ended up by saying that I had no business in Iran, as the playing of music was unIslamic. His bigotry didn't merit a reply, though I think I might have thrown a few expletives in his direction.

The bad impressions were made good by an invitation of a local guy to stay the night in his house. He took me back to his family home with an inner courtyard where five or six date palms grew. He scaled the thick ridges of his tree barefoot and brought me down a good bunch to eat before supper.

Maybe all of this *was* done out of duty rather than an enormous extension of friendship but it kept me fed and warm. Maybe we *all* do our good deeds to add a little holy glow to our egos but this attitude swallows itself somewhere in an abyss of Reductionism. A hungry man can't sneer at a hot meal.

Chapter 13

Uneasy dreams of the desert
(Iran, Pakistan)

Fed up with bus scenarios I resolved to try hitchhiking the remaining 400km to Zahedan, the last town before the Pakistan border. Travel is so cheap in Iran there's no real concept of flagging lifts and when a motorcyclist stopped at my wave, he imagined I must be in trouble. Fortunately, he was an English teacher and eventually understood what I was doing. He proposed to take me to the next police checkpoint.

When we arrived, it took about an hour for the guys in uniform to understand what they should do and only after I performed a whole series of clownish actions, did they get the idea that I wanted them to stop a truck and suggest that I travel with him. Once on the case, it took only a few minutes to find a lorry bound for Zahedan and I clambered into the cabin. The driver was a wheezing old man who fought a strange daily existence of moving this ten ton life-buoy through the vacuous wastes of the desert.

The motor engine transformed all such wayfaring in these barren lands. In the past it would have been nigh impossible for an individual to cross these lifeless lands alone. The necessary amounts of water, food and warm clothing for the night required the organisational support of a whole caravan. The desert once lay as a vast, subtle barrier to journeys in this area of the world, an obstacle that is now surmounted by the time it takes to buy a bus ticket, take a few valiums and doze through the drive (*I* never sedate myself for the journeys as I find the road to be enough of a drug in itself).

We were soon back in the monotone landscape, flat and yellow on all sides. I returned to the images on my inner eyelids and recalled the dreams of Goa that had come to me the night before. I could picture the rocking palm trees hanging loose with the soft blue sky, beneath which lapped the rippling waves around my feet; with coconut in hand and- hold on! It was unbearable to even think about it.

My reverie was interrupted by the grabbing hand of the truck driver, squeezing my pocket to see if I really didn't have any money. My indignant response led to a moody silence that prevailed until we reached the mountains that began as just a tiny blip on the horizon.

The engine spluttered and coughed as we crept uphill into the domain of these rocky creatures. Here were a thousand faces all screwed up and scrawnched from a million years of ferocious, distorting heat and the countering viciousness of the icy nights.

But these immobile beasts let us pass. An hour or two later we were back into non-distinct plains again and the driver pulled up into a lay-by in the middle of nowhere. This was it–he was going to either shoot me and leave my remains to the dust mites or else strand me as I walked off to take a piss. As I urinated I kept looking nervously back over my shoulder and saw the driver move around to a side compartment on the other side of the truck–that must be where he kept his guns! But he put my paranoia to shame by pulling out a lunch of chickpeas and *nan* which he shared with me.

We squatted in the shadow of his great vehicle in a surreal and serene meal scenario. Apart from the occasional roar of another passing lorry, all was silent save for the rustle of the breeze and our own sounds as we munched and swallowed. If I had spent my life braving these kind of obliterating perspectives on infinity. I'm certain that I'd be praying to some stern God in the sky too.

Zahedan is reputed to be a dark and dangerous place, where the smuggling of arms and drugs is rife. It certainly didn't seem to have much spark or life from the general vibe as I walked through the main road. There's nothing romantic about contraband trade, as other than the risk, increased heart-rates and higher profit, it's ultimately just about making money like any other business.

I filled my water-bottle and wasted a bunch of money on a taxi to the border–an occasional and unfortunate necessity for hassle-free border crossings.

The taxi left me at the border gates, which were locked and I joined 25 others with their heaps of piled-up luggage. We stood in the howling wind that threw sand into our eyes and forced us to wrap cloth around our heads. Some huddled together for warmth and others squatted low and alone, meditating on the emptiness all around–save for the meshed gates and border buildings on the other side. We resembled a rag-tailed tattle of refugees, anonymous before barbed wire and guns that held utter control over our future. It was not a good time to need the toilet.

The gates finally opened and we all shuffled in. We waited another half an hour for a temperamental bus to shuttle us to the next processing block. I took the opportunity to hassle my companions for a few words in Urdu, my language cortex kicking back into gear after a period of complete indolence in Iran.

Two Bosnian guys turned up shortly afterwards and we waited for the customs officers to let us through. He snapped for my passport and examined it studiously, whilst holding it upside-down.

"Japan?" He asked. I nodded vaguely and he waved me through. The Bosnian guys came next. I heard the voice behind me demand:

"Japan?"

"No. We are from Bosnia"

"Open your bags!"

I squinted my eyes and tried to look like a noodle and sushi eater as I waddled through to the Pakistan desk, leaving behind the other guys with their luggage splayed across the floor. I whispered a sincere 'salaam aleikum' in goodbye to Iran, which had been bloody good to me.

The Pakistan admission counter was in a dark back room. It held the feeling of a place where any transgression against the human spirit or body could occur–my body and spirit, to be precise. I smiled and told them how happy I was to come to their country. They let me through after a brief check.

Skipping out into Pakistan, my view was immediately obscured by a crowd of money-changers who scrambled to rip off the new arrival. I proudly presented all of my money and received

62 and a half rupees. Their pulses quickened as they waited for the big money.

"I have good rate for dollar–45.3!" They told me.

"I don't have any dollars."

"Pounds! Pounds!" They cried.

"I don't have any pounds."

"Marks? Francs? Lire?" They asked with increasing incredulity.

"Nothing." It took a while for this to sink in before they finally understood–I was clearly just holding out for a better rate in petty and unreasonable bargaining tactics.

Once the mob dispersed a little, I had a look around. I was supposed to come to the town of Taftan–the only settlement before the next desert. I had to blink twice before I realised I was already there. The last leg into the Third-World had been accomplished in a single step and the paved streets of Iran faded into memory. I gazed at the shambly rows of shacks that seemed like a village lost in time, derelict and adrift, with its inhabitants clinging on by their fingertips to life and existence itself. There must be people who were born here and had never left–what would their perspective be on the world?

No concrete was in sight and that made for a pleasant rarity. Wooden structures proudly accommodated all the needs for shelter of the community; here there was a *chai* shop with paraffin burners cooking up sweet, milky froth; and there would be a stall with shelves of miserable-looking vegetables, aging a day closer to the manure heap. Where did all the produce come from anyway–surely nothing could grow here?

Good as it was to be back in Asia with all of its grass-roots charm, I still had to find somewhere to sleep that night. The sun sank lower and I began to drift down the street, slowly out of town to find a friendly-looking wall to bed down behind. I was hoping a voice would call out and save me but no one took any notice. I was coming to the very edge of the bazaar when I was hailed and beckoned to the last shop-front. Two brothers who sold modern music tapes invited me to join them for some chai.

It was subsequently agreed that I could sleep inside.

A wobbling gurgle in my intestines sent me fleeing for the toilet, which turned out to be a small, stone hut with a hole in the ground. It was crawling with cockroaches that split at the intrusion of daylight as I entered and then crept slowly back as I squatted. I stamped my feet in feeble attempts to disperse them.

The sub-continent with all of its delights was upon me again and I spent a happy evening of watching satellite television with my new friends, staring at the pin-ups of female Indian pop stars that adorned the walls. Even the sight of bare necks and arms seemed pornographic after the complete censorship of Iran.

We picked communally at a meat dish and pile of *nan* and I was hit with the first rush of hot chilli since Budapest. India seemed to be just a hot fart away. They pulled the metal screen down over the front of the shop–locking me in and I just hoped that my bladder could hold out for the night.

In the morning, I tried to hitch for a while but traffic was thin. I went off in search of the truck drivers who would hopefully be crossing the distance to Quetta, the capital of South-West Pakistan. They were not hard to find for Pakistani lorries are really something else. The immediate impression is that that the vehicles must have driven through the middle of a supermarket with their exterior covered in glue to pick up each and every piece of shiny packaging. Not a speck of the original coat of paint could be seen on these trucks, as every colour of the rainbow found expression on its sides and front which were printed with hearts, Urdu lettering, spirals and slogans reading: ' God is Great' and 'I Love Pakistan!' Bells on chains hung from the rear to emit an incessant tinkling sound in transit and all kinds of hanging, bobbling paraphernalia could be seen in the cabins.

I approached a few of the drivers who squatted in small conferences in the shade of their wagons. I asked in my one-day-old Urdu if there was any chance of a ride to Quetta. I was taken around, introduced, sized up, given chai and talked about for an hour or so. Eventually some kind of conclusion was reached and an older driver with a fuzzy dark beard, gestured for me to follow him through a twisting path of half-built walls and led me up to a rickety-looking old bus. He paid the driver for my fare and stuffed another 50 rupees in my hand, all having been gathered in a whip-around of the truckies. I would have preferred to save them the expense by squeezing in with them but to dissent would have been to cause offence and so I submitted meekly, finding myself a broken seat in the near-empty bus. Only 7 or 8 others came for the ride.

As we prepared to set off, I heard a voice outside ask in English the price of the trip to Quetta. Jumping to the front, I reached out my arm to haul in my Slovenian friend Peter, whom I'd met on the way to Yazd in Iran. He'd had to wait around in Zahedan to get his Pakistan visa, which he'd got for just a dollar (compared to the £40 I'd paid in England), by virtue that Slovenia wasn't even listed in the directories of the consulate. The baffled bureaucrat set the arbitrary fee to banish this incongruity as fast as possible.

After a few hours of the drive, I began to realise how ridiculous I must have looked trying to hitch a lift by the side of the road. A flat, shadowless desert vanquished memories of things green and pleasant. Nice as it was to meet up again, Peter and I exchanged little more than an apple and some biscuits during the day, both absorbed in our own unreachable thoughts. A silence prevailed within the bus, as none of us dared risk the wrath of Infinity, hoping to cross the unseen and unknown–small insects crawling across the forehead of God.

As we came towards sunset the vanquishing flatness was broken by an approaching cluster of small buildings–our driver had his schedule smooth enough so that we had reached a lonely roadside mosque in time for men to dismount and make their evening prayers. How long before the first drive-thru place of worship? I now had more confidence in the capacities of our driver and reckoned we might all be safely delivered to our destination after all.

But there was no indication that we were any closer to Quetta and it was into the night before we stopped at a roadside eating place. However time didn't seem to matter any more once we looked up and saw the most amazing sky of our lives. With no artificial lights to pollute the twinkling black canopy, the heavens held full fiesta for us poor desert stragglers and I began to contemplate a solitary life in the middle of the Sahara or somewhere, just to have the visual bliss each night of the swirling Milky Way. The crystalline constellations weaved strange and undecipherable inscriptions across the nocturnal fabric that surely held the secrets to the yearnings of a traveller's heart. Fucking cold though and so I said goodnight to the stars, abandoning my desert dream to stumble back into the bus in search of my blankets.

The cold began to bite harder and harder with unrelenting teeth of ice, as the bus strove bravely on and through the dim haze of half-sleep, I became aware that we seemed to be climbing through some mountain roads. I abandoned the attempt to close the defective windows, standard to these kind of buses and instead pulled my blankets over my head, crouching low on the cushions that had long ago detached themselves from the seat.

Sometime later, the bus came to a halt in some town or other and the driver told us we had stopped for sleep. A few hours afterwards, I woke up to find that we'd actually arrived in Quetta and I bounced out into the street ready for new Asian adventures. Peter lagged behind to continue the argument about his bus fare (that had been going on for the past 24 hours!), convinced that he was being ripped off. It seemed that he must be one of the breed of travellers now found by the millions, who make it a point of pride to haggle over petty amounts that never have and never will be of any significance to them–but which do matter to the locals they argue with.

This is a kind of travelling where the object seems to be to place one of your eyeballs inside your wallet, to watch the dwindling supply of traveller's cheques in endless calculations as to whether you're within your self-ordained budget. The blame falls at the feet of the guidebooks which, for a price of $20, provide the tourist with all the most useless and pedantic little lists of prices and costs for a place and utterly fail to mention fucking anything about the people, the vibe, or what one might want to get out of it on a larger level. It's just pure consumerism as the idea is fostered that you can buy experience! All these *voyeur* backpackers firmly resolve to get off the beaten path with the steamroller scout of the guidebook before them, revealing how he and the ten million others who buy these textbooks each year can become real travellers! I wish they'd all fuck off. A thousand beautiful places have been ruined under the colonising wave of these types, arriving like VIP's wanting hotels, restaurants, Coca-Cola and all the rest.

Where was I? Oh yeah—Peter turned out not to be one of those production line tourists and just had one or two preconceived ideas about bargaining in Asia. No one wants to feel a fool by being cheated, either! We strolled in to Quetta together and as he still had no local currency I bought us each a paratha (the chappatti fried on the thin black pan of a street stall). We breakfasted on the starch and cheap fat in the same manner as hundreds of millions across the Indian sub-continent.

Peter was due to meet the French guy, Jaurice, at a hotel in town and I came along to see our witty chum, without any clear plan in my head as to what I was going to do next. Peter solved that by renting a double room for us both in a totally unexpected gesture of generosity, that proved to be typical of the stoic young guy. He was as economical with his words as he was talented with his observations and not a minute went by when he wasn't observing events with his full attention.

Jaurice wasn't in his room so we took a more leisured walk through the streets. Nik had told me that I'd be on home ground once I got to Pakistan and everything certainly seemed like India; from the looks of the people to the chaos of the infrastructure and though it isn't quite accurate to speak of the two countries in the same breath, I'll refer to them both as 'India' from time to time in its wider sense—this land once being part of the many and varied domains which, until just fifty years ago, was within the imperial borders of India itself.

Were it not for our exhilaration of the culture change, Peter and I would never have survived the dense clouds of dust that weeped our eyes, the maniacal driving of the auto-rickshaws, the unceasing din that mirrored the level of peace in men's hearts and the stench from the vegetable matter left to rot in various decaying heaps. It was like I'd never been away.

After about an hour of aimless drifting, Peter suddenly exclaimed:

"Where are the women?" It was a valid question. Looking around, not a single female form could be seen, veiled or otherwise. At last, we caught sight of one or two scurrying figures dressed to the eyeballs in drab gowns. It seemed that most of the fairer sex stayed indoors and did not venture out into the world of men.

The rites and practices of Islam are stuffed with esoteric symbolism and are practised with quite an enchanting fervour but there is always the sense that something is missing–the women. It's the men who attend the congregational prayers in the mosque; the men who study the Qur'an; it's the men who enforce and adjudicate upon the communal Muslim rules and it's even the men who thrust swords through their sides!

True, women have a clearly identified and supposedly respected role as wives, mothers and hearth-builders. But many Muslims seem to use the umbrella of Islamic statements to back up their own disdain of anyone with a gap between their legs. The men have excess licence to feel righteous about their own cultural prejudices with the full weight of the Word behind them!

Male stridency seemed to be strong in these parts and I only hope that the men actually do pay more than just lip service to Muhammed's praise of the qualities and virtues of women. However I suspect most young guys lick their lips at the thought of marriage, as the chance to acquire a weaker and acquiescent slave to satisfy their sexual whims and craving for power; a servant of the home to provide all the services and needs to create the husbands own little kingdom of despotic reign within his own four walls (Supposing that he can afford that–otherwise they live in his parent's home and his wife must face the tyranny of the mother-in-law!).

Jaurice was amazed to see me that evening, thinking I'd not be able to keep pace with the more wealthy voyagers and bought me dinner in affection for my novelty value. His small, round face was lit up even more than usual, now that he'd reunited with his girlfriend, who had flown over Iran in distaste for the enforced modesty of women's dress. In his slightly domineering showman style, Jaurice stole the conversation with the admittedly good story of his journey from Taftan that made our's seem like a luxury tour! He had spent two days coming from the border by train and he received an involuntary education in the workings of illicit trade in Asia.

They had left Taftan okay and were just settling down, when they came to a halt after only a kilometre. Smugglers (the most popular profession in that border town) came on board and started to load their produce onto the train with an endless succession of boxes, crates and sacks. They stuffed, squeezed and stashed it all into any and every conceivable hiding-place in the wagons, undercarriage and compartments especially designed for the purpose.

Three hours later when all was aboard, the train got under way again at a good speed, if a little heavier now, until they came to a police checkpoint further down. The customs men then proceeded to storm through every section of the train, searching each passenger and compartment, discovering much of the hidden booty–there was a delay of about 4 or 5 hours whilst all of the boxes found were removed by a less industrious policeforce, taking their cut of the illicit trade.

Then, after a couple of breakdowns, the train came within 50km of Quetta when it was stopped yet again. The receiving crew of smugglers began to offload the produce that had somehow gone undetected. Boxes and crates came out of nowhere to be despatched at high profit! Another three hours of this and they were finally permitted to roll in to the city.

Peter was off to Afghanistan of all places, having acquired an unlikely visa simply by writing to the embassy and asking for one before he left Europe. He gave me his green foam sleeping-mat, weighing just 300 grams with the insistence that I'd probably have more use for it than he. His beard wasn't all that fully grown and I feared for him a little in Taliban country–but we knew we'd both be okay as we'd convinced ourselves that we had Angels on our side. (He made it, too, according to an E-mail that he sent me and had an amazing time–proving that almost nowhere is out of bounds to the truly intrepid!)

We shared a last breakfast and manly hugs before I allowed myself to be dragged into a bus, jumping out once I saw a truck. I hopped in through the open space where the passenger door should have been and exchanged grins with the driver. I gibbered something in Urdu that I hoped said that I was going North and he yelled back in a tongue that I could barely hear let alone understand. We both laughed at the obvious joke–no one was going anywhere fast in the thick traffic curry that simmered outside. Donkey traps thrusted and hustled to each side in an ongoing clash of the eras with the tiny three-wheeled auto-rickshaws, that could scoot through gaps impassable to the multi-coloured trucks and buses.

To the sides, fruit stalls paraded bright and vivid fruits that bravely resisted the yellow dust and exhaust fumes which increased the number of collisions surely never to be heard above the din of horns of varying hellish pitches, general aimless shouting and drivers with their heads stuck out of the window, cussing for all they were worth.

The market stalls made bantering sales pitches and flies buzzed erratically close to the ear. My driver then slid in a tape of some obnoxious Indian film music and I leant back in the ludicrous intensity of it all. This was the intensity of life I dreamed about in the lifeless streets of Europe, where this kind of anarchic scene would throw most of the population into a nervous collapse, the overload of sensory stimulus streaming through the air as thick as soup.

If I could survive this then I could surely survive anything!

Relaxing in the commonplace Asian insanity, the world became mine! If I'd had longer hair then maybe I'd have stolen a donkey from somewhere to ride into my long-awaited kingdom; somewhere down the trail, they were surely growing my crown of thorns. Probably sharpening the nails too.

Chapter 14

The importance of a rear guard

"There is a boy across the river
With a bottom like a peach!
But alas! I cannot swim!"
('The wounded Heart' an old Peshtun song)
(Pakistan, the Patan Country)

I was taken just a short way out of the city, towards the first outcrops of the rocky ranges to the North where I hoped to chill out for some time. The grey crags loomed as sentinels of my route into Pathan country, digressing a little from my Eastern drift as I'd venture into unknown mountainous parts. The traditional overland trail of the 60's had run through Afghanistan and into Kabul, the real jewel of the journey, where travellers blew their minds on the best hashish in the world and gazed out in stupefied wonder at the absurd Tolkienesque landscapes on the roof of the world. They were made to feel welcome in every way by the generous and kindly Afghanis, who still proudly carried their World War One rifles.

Now Kabul is in rubble and though the warring factions possess the most up-to-date military hardware, many of the basic amenities are absent. Not a functioning electric lamp but rocket launchers a-plenty. Peter was going by the more accessible Southern route, for most of the North is strewn with landmines and tourists are not so welcome there.

So to compensate for this dissolved item of the journey's programme, I was going up along the Western fringe of Pakistan where the culture and people are pretty similar to their warring neighbours. I hoped to get a notion of what it was that I was missing.

After a three mile walk out of town, I grabbed a ride with a plump and jolly civil servant called Asmat. He invited me for lunch in his home village of Pishin where his offices were based.

I learnt to fold up pieces of flat bread, here called *roti*, into triangular cones that would allow me to scoop up *dal* and vegetable dishes without muddying my right hand. Then we sat around in the office, drinking green tea and chewing the fat.

I found myself in the thick of Asian conversational character once again as I spoke to a rather academic chap who was clearly enjoying the whole intellectual encounter. He proceeded to make a polite and thorough investigation of the nature of my life and my reasons for it. He jumped at the bit when I professed a liking for the Sufis.

"But sir, aren't the Sufis a very aloof people, conducting their practices away from the common herd?"

"I suppose so, yes."

"But sir," his eyes sparkling with delight as he pounced, "does not Aristotle say that Man is a social creature?" In his charming enthusiasm, he went on to express doubts as to whether poets were very practical people and also put it to me that the English language was 'unreasonable, unhistorical and unimaginable'–apparently he expected me to leap to the defence of the lettering of my mother tongue because he seemed disappointed when I just shrugged, not caring either way. But he outdid himself when he asked me casually:

"So, what is the current state of Existentialism in England?"

After an hour of this another bureaucrat entered; a short, odd-looking guy with half-Chinese features and a strange vibe about him. He invited me to stay the night at his home in Pishin, as it was already becoming a little late to make much more progress that day.

I was more or less accepting his offer when I saw that Asmat was making a discreet shaking motion with his head. I couldn't understand what the problem might be and when I asked him, he replied that nothing was wrong. But as the Chinese-looking guy went on to elucidate the dinner we would eat and so on, Asmat stood behind him and shook his head in an exaggerated 'no!' Eventually, I accepted his signal and apologized to the sallow-skinned man, explaining that I had to get back on the road.

More than a little confused, I went out to join Asmat in the jeep outside.

"Asmat, what was wrong?"

"I tell you, my friend, if you had gone home with that man–in the night, he would fuck you!"

"Oh... but he is not so strong, he could not-"

"He would come with three or four men. They hold you and then they all fuck you!"

Oh. That certainly explained the weird feeling I got from the guy's general manner that, in retrospect, certainly resembled a kind of salivation: 'Ah! God has sent me some naive, fresh, white flesh!

That wasn't the first time in my travels that men were interested in my appearance with my back towards them. Twice in my tour of Europe in the Spring, I'd been approached in less than a subtle manner: the first, whilst waiting outside the train station in Amsterdam–two different German guys had solicited me, one of them offering me as much as 150 guilders ($80) for my services. The other encounter was a little more protracted and was perhaps the natural result of attempting to hitch in the middle of the night in Belgium.

I was stranded in Antwerp and had just been thrown out of the tube station, for attempting to make my bed there. Although it was the middle of May, the night was bitterly cold and unrelenting winds cursed the sinister streets. I dragged myself along in utter fatigue, trying to find even a half-decent place to crumple up and await the morning. However, all I could find were grisly alleys and glossy corners with glitzy bars, full of rowdy drinkers who stared at me with meet-me-not eyes. They seemed ready to run out and add my head to the garbage that strewed the gutter.

Eventually, I reckoned I'd have nothing to lose by standing by the main exit road and sticking out my thumb–even a police cell might have been a relief. I'd barely even started my hitchhiking mantras   of 'OmpleasegiveTomaliftohOmpleasepleasegiveTomalift' and 'HareRamanoharmtomeoh" before a car actually stopped for me. I ran up to the red brake lights and clambered in to the back seat in the carefree manner of the cold and knackered traveller, offered a warm and comfy environment–if only a temporary one.

My benefactors were called Stanley and Peter. I immediately hastened to reassure them that although I was hitchhiking at 1am, I was not a dangerous lunatic and did so by chatting away in an eloquent and charming discourse about my life and travels. They visibly relaxed and after a while of driving through the dark, Stanley declared that he could give me a place to sleep if I liked. By the languid drawl of his voice, I didn't anticipate it would be much fun but at that point I'd have said yes to a cave in the seventh layer of hell.

We dropped Peter off and took a country road that wound through the flat, flat fields of the Belgian lowlands until we came to Stanley's remote cottage in the middle of nowhere. I smelt a strange rat.

We climbed some stairs up to the main room, where there was a television and a double bed. Whereupon, Stanley removed all of his clothes, save for a pair of bulging underpants and sprawled out on his stomach across the bed, propping himself up on his elbows in an expression of bored readiness.

"Could you give me a massage?" he asked in a slow and strangely suggestive voice. I told him, quite truthfully, that I wasn't really up to it and left the room to go to the toilet. Inside the lavatory, my worst fears were confirmed with a sinking feeling of yet another comic episode descending upon me. On the wall was a selection of postcards portraying an unnerving amount of young men–nothing so bad in itself, except that the gentlemen in question displayed a remarkable lack of clothing and held themselves in the strangest of bare-bottomed poses–the most vivid being that of 'Bruce'–I know his name because the image was of him standing on a beach with proud muscled buttocks, spelling his name in the sand with a jet of urine.

Right. I looked out the windows but I didn't reckon that I could survive the exposure of the night. I trudged wearily up the stairs to the main room, with a grim premonition of the scene that was to unfold.

Stanley was quite a heavy guy and I guessed that he could easily pin me down if he got the advantage. But I suspected that he'd crumple into a pathetic ball of flab after a couple of jabs though I hoped I wouldn't have to find out.

"Would you like to take a shower?" Stanley asked, as I re-entered.

"Ah, no, not really." I said in complete truth.

"Couldn't you give me just a little massage?" He begged with pleading eyes.

"I'm just too tired!" I explained, pulling out my sleeping bag onto the floor.

"Aren't you coming into the bed?"

"Er, no–I can't sleep in beds!" His eyes looked doubtful and so I continued, "Er, yeah, I never can–not since I was fourteen. Problem with my back, you see–I need the firmness of the floor, to avoid any problems!" Get it, Stanley? No, he didn't.

"Aren't you going to take your clothes off?" he asked, as I crawled fully dressed into my canvas.

"Oh no, really, I'm so dirty that it doesn't really make any difference, now."

"You can take a shower.

"Er, no, it's the kind of deep down dirt that only a sauna could get out, you know?"

He looked as though I'd painfully let him down in the most unreasonable way and that he was very, very disappointed in me. However, he displayed his magnanimity by holding no grudges and coming over to pat my stomach as he said:

"Sleep well!" Some chance! In the middle of the night, his arm flopped down as if by accident onto my knees and I jumped up with an unnecessary shout of alarm. He apologized and withdrew the offending limb. Honestly, talk about someone just not getting the message! Why couldn't he just have asked 'Can I fuck you?'- 'No, I won't!' And that could have been the end of it.

When the alarm went off in the morning, I jumped up and packed away my bed at record speed, crying:

"Right! I must be off then!" He made me stay for breakfast and took great delight at the fact that I ate heartily as if he were proud of me! I watched his cooking procedure carefully as he fried the eggs from his farm and made sure that he wasn't slipping in any sedatives. I almost switched the plates when his back was turned. Whilst we ate, he told me of the four stallions that he kept, who never fought, as they 'loved one another'–contrary to what others might say. I bet.

Back in Pakistan, Asmat gave me the address of a guesthouse that he owned in the hill-town of Ziarat. He told me that I could stay free for a couple of nights and eat with the steward there. He dropped me off on a road going into the hills and with the help of some locals, I got a ride in a dusty old truck going North. I had to slump my neck down to sit in the tiny truck cabin, seemingly designed to obscure as much of the view outside as possible and I squeezed in between two grinning bucktooth youths assisting the bearded old truckie who never made a sign that he was aware of my existence.

It was such a beautiful day, that I was thinking about jumping out of this crawling metal beast to enjoy the early evening sunshine. The driver was clearly telepathic because he shunted the truck to a stop and we all piled out to the side where a stream flowed in the roadside ditch. It was wash-the-truck time. The driver threw buckets of water at the wheels and undercarriage, not troubling overly to miss his assistant who darted and dodged with a piece of rag, wiping away the grease between each shower of stream water; the drips tickled the tingling chains hanging from the side as they ran down to the road.

As we got going again, I clambered up the ladder on the side to sit on top–a luxury of slow-moving transport in Asia–and I lay back to enjoy the crisp blue sky. I discovered with delight that we were carrying a load of melons. I pulled out my knife and within minutes I was quenching my thirst on this dry and dusty road with succulent slices of fruit. I managed to consume two and a half of them before I had to leap down for my turning to Ziarat.

The fork in the road was by a police checkpoint and they didn't understand what I was doing there. Our small exchange of words was friendly at first but became more exasperated as they prevented me from flagging down trucks, insisting that I couldn't get any further that day. Eventually, as the sun sank lower I submitted to the weight of circumstances and accepted their offer of hospitality.

They gave me a bed on the floor of the chief's room, inside the compound. They fed me *roti* and meat and I had to answer their questions about Princess Diana for the hundredth time in the month since she'd died. I could have made a fortune on the journey, if I'd been selling badges and T-shirts of the dead blonde and I began to wonder if I should have broken into outrageous sobbing despair at the mention of her name–such seemed to be the depth of their expectations.

Seeking sanity, I strolled out into the rocks to enjoy the sunset and met a mangy-looking dog, in need of company. I often feel sorry for dogs in Muslim countries, as they're generally scorned as unclean creatures. Maybe they were all reincarnated Hindus who'd accumulated bad karma in past lives. When I gave it a little affection it suddenly became wide-eyed and maniacal. I had to keep its gyrating head at a distance by employing the age-old trick of bending down as though I was going to pick up a stone. It backed off fast.

In the morning I hopped on a minibus in order to escape from the police, who were keen that I should stay for a few days. I thought it better that I should clear out quick lest they decided to force the issue. My hopes of a free ride were dashed by the 50 rupee fare, which left me with just 20 rupees in my pocket. 'Money comes, money goes, money stays–death comes' So runs the Asian proverb.

Tiny habitations could be seen on each side of the gently sloping valley through which we shuttled. Farmhands or shepherds lived in humble abodes of wood, straw, canvas and tin, that were hardly much larger than the space required to crouch about or lie down. It looked like a bare sort of life and I hoped they lived elsewhere when winter came.

Ziarat was a small town with quite a few guesthouses to

accommodate the moderate amount of tourism it received in season, attracted by the reputation of the area as a green and beautiful place of peace and quiet. Now there were no other travellers to be seen and though we were not all that high up, I immediately sensed the atmosphere of a mountain village. My nose went wild at the transporting scent of the wood-smoke that brushed the air and I felt like I was in the Himalayas already.

At the address I'd been given, I found a group of kids to play with and they taught me my 1 to 10 in Pashtun, the local tongue of the Pathan people who live across West Pakistan. When the steward turned up he took me over to the guesthouse. I lost my breath entirely as he opened the gates and led me down to a ridiculously beautiful garden with 100 colours of blooming flowers playing in the breeze and six or seven apple trees standing around, all proudly in fruit. I was given the key to a large, carpeted room and told to come over to his place for lunch at 1pm.

I sat in stunned bliss on the short-mown grass as fortunate sole occupier of a grand guesthouse. I munched huge, red apples, reflecting that sometimes the cards really do fall right. It made up for all the hassle with the police and I'd been graced with the perfect opportunity to rest, recuperate and contemplate the meaning of this 6000 mile trial of endurance that I'd set for myself. William Blake appeared beside me, singing:

"Oh Sunflower, weary of time!
You count the steps of the sun.
Ever seeking that sweet golden clime,
Where the traveller's journey is done!"

It was the first day of October and after just two months on the road, Pakistan seemed to have arrived right under my feet. The Journey to the East had been all too simple and easy. Modern transport has taken a lot of the romance out of travelling as once this distance would have taken years to traverse. But I suppose if I was *that* bothered by the ease of automation, I could have started to *walk* the distance!

I spent two days in this small town, making yoga on the lawn and melodising with my clarinet in the mornings until it was time to go to lunch at the steward's house. I'd be sat upon a chair in the corner, whilst the bearded custodian tinkered with the smelly kerosene stove, hand-pumping the fuel cylinder as the flame spluttered furiously. He'd cut up onions and tomatoes for the traditional salad and then serve me with the best of the meat, veg and *rotis,* waiting until I'd finished and made my grateful leave before they'd tuck in themselves.

Then I'd hike up the hill to find a good spot for meditation; gazing out on the grassy ridges or sometimes by the sheer drop of a gorge with its sweet echo. I'd usually be seen dashing back down a few hours later as evening often caught me unawares. More than once I had trouble finding my garden. Once safely home, I'd lay down on the lawn and star-gaze for an hour or so, with yet another apple between my teeth that were recovering their bite for the world.

Chapter 15

Fear and Loathing in the foothills
(Pakistan, the Patan Country)

Suddenly alone, in a scenic and beautiful place, safely in Asia, in good health and at least 48 hours away from the prospect of starvation, the world caught up with me. Now that it was pretty certain that I'd reach my destination, I began to consider who was going to rescue me from poverty in India? Once there, I wouldn't be able to afford more visas for further on-land travel. I had no flight coupons and I would only be given 6 months legal stay in India itself!

What am I doing? Who am I? Who's even asking the question? I threw up this interrogation like a dog chasing it own tail, or a man digging beneath his own feet, with a shovel of insatiable enquiry. If the ego is unimportant, then what matter if its depressed or jubilant, wise or insane? If this life is meaninglessly transient, then what matter if I sit still in the darkened room, uncomfortable and cold?

A pressure in my bladder awoke me to the fact that I needed to piss and dragged me out of my introspective chasm. I had enough residual awareness to realise that it would be tiresome clearing up if I didn't make the ten steps to the bathroom.

I could share the basic faith of the Muslims that 'there is no God but God—sure, all is one; but unlike them, I had no clear idea of how to live life according to that ideal. What to do? Who to be? Why to be? In the solitude of the night I struggled under the weight of my freedom and for want of any better ideas, I sank down to my knees and prostrated myself in prayer. Submission. Did that make me a Muslim? It occurred to me, as my forehead enjoyed the soft texture of the carpet, that this would make a particularly powerful scene in a high-budget film version of my journey! The thought evoked a devilish grin, quite inappropriate to my devout posture. I sat up to shrug at the comedy of life, rescued from the unresolvable by the ever-springing fountain of humour. I reached for my blankets and recharged in the protective shadow of sleep.

After two pleasant days and soul-searching nights, I decided not to abuse the hospitality any longer. It was time to move on towards the mountains in the North that were supposed to be awesome. I managed to get three kilometres up the road before being called over by the local bureaucrat of the area and invited for tea. We sat in another well-cultured garden, with hundreds of dragon-flies performing physics-defying gymnastics, upon a wind that rushed and roared up the valley, heralding the conquering intent of the approaching winter.

By assuming my very best manners and middle-class accent–useful to be able to pull these things out of the hat, at times–I received another free lunch and was invited to the home of the assistant, Noor-u-din, who lived in a village somewhere up the road.

The working day ended by about 4pm and I followed Noor-u-din over to the pick-up truck that waited for us. It was the communal taxi service, holding around 20 men in various standing, squatting and all-out clinging postures in the front, back and on the sides. If one rides, they all ride and there was no such thing as no more room.

I grinned sheepishly at the collection of beards about me who, characteristically of people in this area of the world, insisted on knowing how much I'd paid for my green foam sleeping mat. My baby-faced, scraggly look was a little out of place amongst these stout farmers and it would not have taken long to spot the odd one out.

Gradually, access to oxygen returned as the men got off one by one at the stops along the way; until it was just myself, Noor-u-din and the driver. We then stopped by the cornfields and we all gathered armfuls of the harvested corn plants to hoist into the back. They tried to dissuade me from joining in the manual work but seemed cheered when I mucked in. After the last load was stacked I turned and smiled to see the poetic figure of Noor-u-din kneeling down to pray in the middle of the field, with the steep mountain wall as a backdrop. I lay with my back on the corn as we got going again and stared at the stormy puffs of cloud, turning pink in the evening sky that shrank as the valley narrowed to either side.

We reached Noor-u-din's village. While he chatted to a friend a whole crowd came out to witness the foreigner who just gazed at the clouds for Allah's sake! I then discovered the nature of Pathan hospitality as I was taken to an empty barn, a short distance from my host's home. A wood-stove was lit for my warmth and a meal of *dal* and *chapattis* brought to me. I realised that I wasn't going to be allowed to see any local household culture. That had been one of the chief delights in Iran–hanging out with a family alleviated the strain of being alone. Here though, it seemed that their interpretation of the Qur'an was such that it was unacceptable to have a non-family male in the house where one's wives and daughters are kept.

This, I would learn later, was typical of the Pathan people. Their attitudes towards women being the most extreme and restrictive (or should I say 'protective'?) of any of the places I'd seen. Already, it had been difficult to ignore the fact that nearly every woman wore a dress in public that covered her from head to foot, with a thick, webbed veil over her face. It must have taken years of practice to learn not to walk into trees and over edges. I was sick of the repressive attitudes towards femininity and so much did I hunger for female company that I was half-way to becoming the kind of threat that Pathan customs were supposed to prevent. But I was able to control myself–no doubt aided by the sight of the rifles that the Pathans liked to carry around with them.

This was par for the course. Every overland traveller rejoices to hear the call to prayer upon entering Turkey, as they receive the first taste of the Orient's magic. Though gladdened by the traditional hospitality of Iran, patience begins to wear thin after all of the pathetic conversion attempts made upon you. Then the wayfarer runs into the thick end of Pakistan Islamic custom, deeper in the petty oppression than ever before and there's nothing he can do except wade through it.

At any event, I went four or five weeks in this period without even speaking to one female. That kind of deprivation does strange things to a young guy I can tell you. After the meal, I stood outside beneath a very dark and starry sky, watching the whip of distant lightning that cracked and flashed further down the valley. Noor-u-din however, could not understand why I was enjoying the display.

"Night-time–no view!" He informed me and once again I was blown away by the utter indifference local people in this part of the world seem to have to the beauty that they live in. The sea is generally seen as just a large and convenient toilet (many Indian beaches have a shit line, as well as tidal marks); the mountains are large rocks that make it harder to get around and 99% of the men would sooner look at a cheap piece of pornography, than a spell-binding sunset or dawn.

To be fair, this is probably more symptomatic of the last half of this century than any inherent insensitivity to Nature. All of Asia has swallowed the Material Dream of the West with great, greedy gulps–knocking down bamboo in favour of concrete, abandoning herbal knowledge for the instant magic of modern medicine and discarding the slow wagon of the spiritual search for the fast bike of the three-second orgasm.

I assured the nervous Noor-u-din that all was well and he left me alone–that rare luxury on this continent. He woke me six hours later and, after determining that I didn't want to stay for an extra five days to join him on the long trip to Lahore to deliver his apples, he put me on another pick-up truck. Again I squeezed in amongst twenty bearded men. My attention was only partially distracted from my bloated stomach nausea, by the fate of three chickens who squawked and flapped beneath the stout boots of the men aboard.

An hour later, we arrived in whatever town it was. I promptly started to walk down the one-road town, sticking out a futile thumb at the few passing vehicles. Given the distances involved on the route I needed to take, I was being hopelessly hopeful. The photocopy of a map that I had didn't convey the reality of the road

I'd be taking, nor the passage on it.

A petrol garage owner beckoned me over to partake in some chai. He gave me a pretty thorough interrogation, including an examination of my passport to verify my story. This is just the kind of thing to which you have to submit sometimes, without getting too caught up in reactions of personal pride and stuff. It was worth it too because he ended up giving me 100 rupees and arranged for me to travel with a friend of his who was taking a truck up and over the mountains, down into the Punjab and the plains.

We were due to leave in the evening time and as I couldn't see anyone smoking dope, it looked like it was going to be a very long day. It didn't help that I felt miserably ill and matters didn't improve when I succumbed to the temptation of some sweet goo on a stall that had probably been sitting there for days.

It wasn't easy to find some amusement in this town whose economy was presumably based on the traffic that passed through this major trade route and by the livestock trade that I guess was the older focus of commerce of the place. There was only so much food that I could eat and I tried to make lunch a more feasible option by getting a bit of exercise and walking around to the edge of town.

Here, I found the area where the shepherds brought their flocks of sheep and goats. I sat in the shade, digging the sight and no longer conscious of who was bringing me pots of excellent green tea. It was nice to watch the lean and bearded types in dull jerkins and scarves, as they tried to keep their animals distinct from the other groups and simultaneously conduct business with the other odd trader. The preliminary bargaining discussions that certainly wouldn't be completed today.

Time moved slowly. I had nothing to read and felt too ill to play my clarinet or make any notes. Wherever I stopped, twenty people would gather to see what for many, may have been their first foreigner. These were the kind of long and dull days that comprised the less romantic parts of the journey and they seemed like a complete waste of my time–who'd want to spend their precious hours here? I dreamed of California and girls with bronze flesh in mini-skirts and rollerboots.

The only guy of any real interest was the petrol pump manager–a mustachioed, energetic type who looked into the distance when he spoke. He'd travelled around within his own country and announced himself to be a dedicated communist. Accordingly, we had wildly irrelevant conversations about politics, that would never have any bearing on the place in which he lived but allowed us to lift ourselves into the large picture for a few pompous moments.

7 o'clock came and went. My driver didn't show. At the insistence of my communist friend I made the mistake of eating a little. My stomach worsened. With reassurances that my lift would materialise eventually, I crashed out in the office and woke a few hours later, feeling indescribably unwell. Straight after, my truck appeared and the clock on the wall read 1am. I seriously doubted if I could make the journey in my sick state–but I was darned if I was going to wait around in this town for another day. I crawled into the cabin where the two old drivers sat, together with the two sons of the first.

Crowded or cosy, depending on the mood, our first few hundred metres began with jolts and bumps over the pot-holed road and unpleasantly enough, continued that way–'On the Road, Again' de dum, de dum–but Canned Heat never had to deal with this!

We stopped for breakfast just before dawn and only just in time–I flung open the cabin door and dashed out into the bushes to fertilise the land with what first light revealed to be strange green liquid! I immediately began an emergency fast. I scooped together what I could of the fenugreek powder that had burst inside my bag and swallowed it, hoping that that its constipative powers were what they were supposed to be.

The trouble really began a few hours later, as we crawled through the winding mountain passes. The land had become colourless again and matched the blandness of the communication in the cabin. My new companions were determined to get the most out of their grumpy English freeloader.

Of course, they were blessed with the expressive gesture of enquiry, innate to everyone in Pakistan, consisting of a sharp, friendly poke with the fingers, which then sprawl in the motion of penetrating several anuses at once–the final position of the hand appearing ready to hold either the contents of your life or a large pair of testicles. So often was I approached with this gesture by strangers in the street, that I toyed with the idea of carrying around a small dagger, with which I could then sever the hands at the wrist and thrust it down their gaping and imbecilic necks, shouting 'There! Does that answer your fucking question?' Salaam, peace, my child!

I knew around 30 or 40 words in Urdu at this point and nothing in Pashtun. But mere facts weren't going to prevent the driver from delivering lectures to me in his tongue. Perhaps I'd miraculously learnt the language in the half hour that had passed since his last load of questions. I shouted back at him in English–in these situations you have to maintain the illusion that you're holding your own.

Favour was restored when I accepted his offer of charas: the resin hand-rolled from the marijuana plant. He leant over with a cackle to squeeze my cheek with his thumb and finger. My spirits were sufficiently restored by the excellent smoke to sing a few songs for them, including "I Heard It Through The Grapevine" I think. They were all pleased to have a jester on board, however cantankerous he might be.

Generally, one driver slept whilst the other took the wheel and they'd exchange places every eight hours or so. In the meantime, the two sons and I would fight for the comfortable seating. The mystique surrounding me as an honoured guest wore off towards the end of the first day and I was close enough to their age to be regarded at best as an equal.

The younger of the two sons was constantly bullied by his father, who would scold him with angry shouts and then cuff him sharply around the ears. He would bear in stoic silence, internalising the hurt. His dad would then relent shortly afterwards, trying

178

to cheer his son up with jokes and affectionate pinching of the cheeks. None of which would elicit any change in the features of the boy, who as a result of all of this was quite an unpleasant youth.

The elder of the two sons had an easier time and suffered only from having been weaned too early in infancy. He incessantly popped boiled sweets or cigarettes between his lips all day.

The second morning brought us down to the green plains of the Punjab and we'd been in constant motion for 30 hours. I was sick of the sub-continent already. Just as it had all seemed so far away when I was in Turkey, now it all seemed too close. I was fed up with the smells, the sickness, the stares and the ignorance and I wondered how I could ever imagine living here.

There was nothing glamourous about this whole trek. I now knew it was possible to get from A to B without any money–so what? This trip now seemed to be proving something to everyone but myself but it was me alone who was having to endure it. I felt like I'd been given a ticket for the wrong show.

Nevertheless, we had a few good moments in the truck: the best of which came when we broke down at the end of a 200 metre-long major bridge and we held up the entire flow of East-to-West inter-state traffic–good timing guys! The crew all jumped out to deal with the problem and I scooted off in search of a map to see if this would be a good place to escape from my tormenting benefactors.

Suddenly, there erupted a great wave of shouting and I could see my driver scrambling back to his seat; being chased by an angry policeman with a rifle. The cop wanted him to pull the truck over to the side but my Pathan friend recognized a baksheesh-trap when he saw one. He started to wheel his vehicle away with sharp twists of the wheel and a priceless look of schoolboy caught-in-the-act fear on his face. The policeman swung his rifle around to target the escapee with the more realistic threat of the butt but he was already pulling away. I began to sprint down the opposite side of the truck, shouting to the other old man to hold the door for me as he swung in.

His hand had barely hoisted me up before I had to do the same for the two sons who came bursting out of nowhere. We all united in the thrill of our defiant mischief and, thanks to the absence of radio technology, we got through the other checkpoint without any fuss. On other occasions, my driver would simply pretend not to see the officials who furiously waved at us from their little offices where he was supposed to fill in forms and pay a toll.

The incident brought us together for a while but by the time we reached the city of Faislabad, we hated each other's guts again and I came very close to actual fistfights with the two boys. Curiously though, it was the kind of antagonism that simply vanished once we left the tiny world of the cabin and melted into the larger context of the bustling market town. I guess it brought us back to some kind of normalcy, warped as we were after 40 straight hours of being on the road.

I went up with my driver to the office of some bureaucrats, above a large, square courtyard where arriving trucks reversed and manoeuvred their way into offloading their crates of farm produce. These guys seemed to be his bosses and they adminis-terated the fruit and veg *markeet* below.

At length, I gathered that we had reached our destination and that I was going to stay the night on the floor of this third-story room. The officials engaged me in small-talk about my life and I reeled off the appropriate answer with my mind in neutral gear, just humming at the bare minimum.

My driver didn't return at the hour promised and I began to imagine that the whole escapade had been a ruse to strand me here, whilst he made off with my bags which I'd left in the truck! Everything seemed to point to it and I rued my *naivete* with a fury. I'd never be pyschologically able to make the return journey in search of my clarinet, my only item of value.

Oh Woe is me! Just then my driver resurfaced with a kind smile and twinkling eyes, that denied the memory of the devil in the driving seat sending me insane with cross-examinations in Pashtun! I put my paranoia down to the excellent dope and warmed in heart to this nice old guy who soon had the bureaucrats laughing and merry; their favourite raconteur had showed up again. I began to suspect I had simply lost my sense of humour in the past couple of days.

Sleep came as never before and I awoke with a new-born eagerness and excitement about being in the sub-continent. Even as the pre-dawn call to prayer sounded, shouts and cries of activity floated up from the marketplace below. When daylight came, I slipped down to find some breakfast; my stomach now healthy and hungry. I was feeling rich with the 100 rupees in my pocket, given to me by the communist at the garage some eons ago.

I had to jump from each island of a paving slab to the next, across the foot-deep mud that held sway outside. When I came to the main courtyard, the air was thick with the smell of cheap cooking fat that deep-fried everything from samosas to sweet battered gunk, looking incredibly suspicious in bright green, red and yellow. Everyone rushed around at a frenetic and crazed pace, attempting to get as much done as possible before the sun rose and made work that much more oppressive.

Coolies ran by with flat circles of wicker lids on their heads, which supported impressively large sackloads. They used the force of momentum to bend the laws of gravity that would otherwise have crushed their necks. They commanded absolute right of way. Crates of fruit stood about in rectangular stacks with youths sitting on top. They guarded invisible distinctions between lots and munched apples procured from their charge.

Around some of the stacks, business had already begun and frenzied auctioneering took place by each pile. The supervisor stood on top to take the bids from the tooth and claw merchants below, whose shouts and arguments mingled with the hum of generators and the various banging and hammering noises that came from all sides.

A poor family searched through the piles of the discarded corn leaves, gathering the pieces that had been missed–typical of the efficiency of the Indian continent where nothing salvageable goes to waste. Near them, a fat *dal*-and-rice wallah sat on an elevated chair and held imperial sway over the people that he deigned to serve bowls of steaming food.

I watched one coolie take a break from work to have a glass of chai. He removed the head scarf used to soften the loads and sat down on a large mound of corn leaves. In between sips of hot chai, he stared thoughtfully off into the distance. A wistful reverie was expressed in the wrinkles on his face and the tired light of his eyes–features that in themselves told the whole story. When he finished his glass, he put his turban back on and moved off for his next shift.

There was a lull in the middle part of the day until the new deliveries arrived in the late afternoon and evening, prompting a new rush of speculation and striking of swift deals before the iron could even be heated. It was all fucking madness. It was sense. Chaos or order–use what words you like–it was Asia and I remembered why I had returned.

It turned out that my driver and his crew would not be going further North but would be returning to the hills where we started. I guessed that their whole lives followed this pattern of 40 hour drives, interspersed with break-downs, police confrontations and lots of *dal*, *chapattis* and chai at the roadside places with rope beds to sit on.

Then they'd get a couple of days off to go to the brothel and test the strengths of their livers with illegal brew. What a fucking life–no wonder their imaginations were so stunted. In fact, they did rather well under the circumstances, for these people had never been given a tenth of the attention, opportunities and stimulus that I'd received and I felt almost guilty about the annoyance and ill-feeling I'd borne towards them. Easy to be a Buddha, when you're well rested and fed.

My driver then further outdid himself, by buying me a bus ticket to Peshawar. A little later, I was flying through the night to the North, at what seemed lightning speed compared to the slow-worm pace of the truck. We arrived in the early morning and I jumped straight out of the bus, ran past all of the touts and into the first hotel that I saw. I flung my bags down to the side while I bolted into the toilet without a word of explanation.

Peshawar was supposed to be a fascinating mix of cultural and racial identities but the only real evidence of that were the poverty-stricken presence of Afghani refugees who had come to the city in great floods. To their credit, they didn't wear the sorrow that they must have felt at being estranged from their war-torn homelands, where Muslims shot one another in the Name of God. Their pride betrayed no sense of self-pity at being poor and I had fun sharing a joint with a couple of young Afghans in the park.

Then I played at being English *sahib,* sitting under a tree with a newspaper and a pot of tea. Within minutes, I had another crowd of twenty onlookers, all keen to talk to the foreigner. I say, old chap, can't a fellow get a spot of peace around here?

The general vibe was friendly and inquisitive and this was true of most Pathan people, whose sense of hospitality was very close to that of their national pride. People would frequently come up to me in the street and ask:

"Do you have any problem that I can help you with?" So by looking lost for a few minutes, I could generally get my food and shelter problems sorted out. I wouldn't want to get on the wrong side of them though and an American friend of mine would later put it this way:

"A Pathan would peel the skin of an enemy with a razor blade without a moment's thought or concern–but he is simultaneously quite capable of going into a complete tizz if his daughter grazes her knee!"

The only offensive side to life, were the guys who worked for the buses, both local and national. Whenever I passed the bus stand, I could count on at least twenty guys hooking my arm and asking:

"Lahore?" Before trying to pull me into a bus bound for that city. It never bloody occurred to them that a foreign guy walking around without luggage, might have some objectives in mind other than travelling on their bus for half the day. I was quite convinced that if I let them take me to Lahore, then upon arrival the same guys would pull me into another bus, shouting 'Peshawar?'

Sometimes I would grab one of these touts and give him the whole harangue that there was more to life than going to Lahore and did he really think I hadn't been asked ten times already? But then I'd see his smiling face, not understanding why I was so angry and I'd realise that it was stupid to get pissed at any one of them. Like attacking a single locust in a swarm.

The local bus crews weren't much better either. The vehicles had a system whereby the driver would spend all day trying to leave behind his conductor; who was forever hopping in and out of the bus or hanging halfway in between. He'd shout and implore pedestrians to join them, all the time urging the metal beasts along with slaps on the side and shouts of '*chalo!*' (='let's go!')

At any rate, it was easy to find small adventures which illustrated the charm of the people here. On the Sunday afternoon, I found myself strolling with some small Afghani kids to the park for a cricket match. They had one bat and two stumps and soon found some other boys who had the other pieces of equipment to make a match. They more than anyone took me at face value and had the tact to hide their disappointment when I lost my middle stump on the third ball delivered. Humiliated by players half my size, I withdrew to observe the general cricketing activity that took place throughout the park. The very small, were relegated to bowling practice in the corners, using the trees for stumps; whilst the older kids played small-level games; sharing bats and using balls ranging from professionally-bound leather to tightly-wrapped bundles of rags.

A street picture from a Pakistani city would be pretty much indistinguishable from that of an Indian town. The bazaars bulged out into the crowded streets with colourful anarchy and food stalls lined the sides of the roads, selling everything from fried rice to chopped papaya.

Unfortunately, I had to be careful when eating from these side stalls because much of the food had been sitting around for half the day, exposed to the mandibles of large and aggressive flies. I'd occasionally get paranoid when eating something that felt like it had been reheated too many times. Then I'd rush off to eat some hot chillis to kill any unfriendly bacteria.

The streets were congested with weird vehicles, piles of dust, dirt and rotting vegetable heaps which the endless crowds daintily stepped around. This certainly *looked* like India but the differences lay in the character of the people themselves. Here no one tried to cheat me for a rupee, whilst with the Indians you have to fight for every last coin. Muslims have a much clearer-cut code of action than many Hindus and it's in this sense that religion can be a very groovy thing–us intellectual *dilettantes* are used to sizing up and judging other cultures and religions; debating bits of metaphysics and philosophy until the pubs shut–But these guys work about ten hours a day on average, and when they.ve finished they don't *want* to engage in discussions about morality and good conduct. Far better for them and for society if they take to heart an all-encompassing guide to 'how to be good in today's world', as laid out in their holy books.

The locals were very giving with their pots of tea and spliffs and I tended to just drift about the streets, chatting and chilling with whomever I bumped into, whilst trying to avoid anyone from clinging on too much. There were some dark influences around of course, as just 100km West from here, were the unpoliced tribal territories where you could buy anything from grenades to tanks. Less orthodox Muslims produced heroin, in their contribution to the contraband trade that grosses around $100 billion a year. No one hears about these places because it's in no one's interest that such places are exposed–there being too much money involved for the many powerful players in these world-wide scams. It's well-known in some circles that most of the worldwide trade in class 'A' drugs is conducted by the CIA and their respective agencies. Just a little investigation into these things reveals that it all stinks and that you can't afford to take anything you hear all that seriously.

After a while on the road, you're pulled around by the winds of fate to the extent that you begin to develop an intuitive understanding of when you're in trouble and it would be a good time to leave. It can sometimes be a struggle to maintain the balance of being on your guard and being open to new meetings and adventures. After having been fed and housed by other people for most of the year, I'd formed a deep trust in the fundamental goodness, knowing that 99% would do right by me.

Sometimes I got paranoid in Peshawar, especially if the dope was too strong and then I'd look up through a smoke-filled room to realise that I was hanging out with some very dodgy people–but then I could always check my instincts by looking into their eyes. If I didn't like what I saw, I just picked up my things and left without a word of explanation- that was the freedom I had and it was my greatest defence.

A student I met gave me 100 rupees to catch a bus up to the mountainous Swat valley, the birthplace of Tantric Buddhism; though the orange cloth had long been kicked out by the sharper sword of Islam. I'd heard that the place was beautiful and I reckoned on a couple of weeks of meditation beside babbling streams and jagged rockfaces.

Not long before dark, I caught a minibus and smiled as we soon began to climb up, up, up. The journey was made murderous by my troublesome insides and we arrived just in time at the town of Kalam. I stumbled out with my cloth-style bag (now shredded in many parts) my blanket and small backpack containing my horn. From above came a shout and I saw a hotel manager on his balcony. I dashed up the steps to use the bathroom and prevent an embarrassing disaster. I apologized to the man, explaining that I couldn't afford a room and just needed to use the toilet–his reaction was brilliant:

"No money? No problem!" He said and handed me the key to a double room. That was the kind of thing I couldn't imagine happening in India and was one of the most endearing things about Pakistan. Here, people could step outside of their everyday money-making roles to deal with you on a human level, thus increasing the timeless riches of the soul, rather than the piles of rupees that disintegrate in the first rain-storm.

The morning came against all odds, so cold had the night been and revealed a small and quaint village with charming wooden houses and bridges, that forded a loud and gushing river of turquoise, bounding down from glacier sources. These icy giants *peaked* their heads over the valley and hinted at a land of snow that would soon be upon these people.

The delicious aroma of woodsmoke floated in the street. The men went about their business with blankets wrapped around their shoulders. Women were not to be seen. The few that dared step outside appeared as shuffling figures of cloth. Kalam was more conservative than the big cities and I couldn't imagine the women seeing unmeshed daylight here for a couple of centuries yet.

Tourist season was well and truly over. All of the many, many guesthouses and flash hotels stood empty. Development had not been slow off the mark here to entice the lucrative tourist industry and a few nights stay in the monstrous resorts on the edge of town would easily match the monthly salaries of most of the men living in Kalam. That was pretty horrible to see and I was pleased to be spared the obnoxious presence of Westerner tourists in jeans and sunglasses, wielding video cameras around with utter insensitivity and thrusting 500 rupee notes like daggers at the simple mountain folk. These I knew, would be the kind of travellers who fly everywhere, block up toilets with toilet paper and who continually whinge about the lack of hot water baths, satellite television and hot dogs with pepperoni–the fat-walleted fuckers should stay at home.

Even the money brought in by tourism often does more harm than good. The prospect of wealth seduces people who were previously content with a simple life in Nature into the pursuit of material riches. Along with this comes an impoverishment of spirit, as families begin to argue about rights to land that was previously considered worthless and jealousy grows towards those who are sharp enough to profit–They in turn become paranoid and possessive about their wealth. What price can be set on peace of mind?

I had enough rupees for a couple of days up here, if I ate meals of *nan*, apples and walnuts which were stuffed with the freshness of the valley. I made lunch by the turquoise brilliance of the river in a secluded meditation spot. The water played a collage of sounds as it skipped over the rocks and began its epic journey to the sea. I resorted to my usual game of trying to focus on each individual voice of the river, each gurgle, thump and gush singing its own tumbling water song of the narrow mountains.

But on this occasion the more I listened, the more agitated I became. Instead of the desired peaceful trance, I became more jumpity and anxious than before, as though I was being delivered a lecture that I didn't really want to hear. Minutes passed like hours and in the brilliance of the noon sunshine, everything seemed too stark and real.

I tried to break myself out of this mood by walking up river and into a forest of tall and thin trees. The leaves created a hypnotic filter effect of light on the shaded area, carpeted with soft, green turf. The trees were too tall for it to be possible to view the bottoms and the tops at the same time and I suspected that the two might not be connected at all. The turf undulated in smooth sloping dips and rises and I tried to enjoy the whole fairyland effect, hoping to hear the songs of merry elves in green jerkins. But here time hung still and ominous as the frozen shards of sunlight that filtered through the canopy. A sense of pensive foreboding prevailed and I began to flick nervous glances over my shoulder to see what might be stalking me.

All creatures and plants of the woods pricked up their ears in apprehension, as a lilting rustle of leaves warned of the swooping flight of huge air elementals that rode the wind on the hunt for free souls. I scanned the area for somewhere to hide but to no avail and so I just stood rigid and rooted, hoping to pass for a deformed sapling. The breeze parted for me as it rushed past, probing and stroking my body for any signs of life, wrathful and hungry. The ghosts of the air knew of no fixed abode and charged on to wreak havoc and terror in new glades and valleys. Severed from the nourishment of the Earth, they were thus shaped into bitter carnivores with the senseless fury of an army that's lost its banner.

Gradually a calm restored itself but nothing in Nature smiled or glowed. All sank under the veil of the condemned on death row, every living moment an expansive agony to be endured until the final mercy of the Executioner's swinging axe.

When I moved again my bones creaked and cracked and my blood began to sluggishly circulate once more. I was draped in a weary mantle now worn by the whole woods. The plants, the trees, the insects and I, all lurched in a passionless limbo, our inner fires quenched by the age-old songs of the winds that echoed yet, bemoaning with a piercing howl the bitter misery of the nightmare realm whose dearth spilled over from some perverse overlap of the worlds.

Some time later, some children saw a young wanderer drift among the fringes of the forest; his clothes ragged, his hair all blustered and his eyes wild and forlorn. In my low moments, I have every reason to believe that he walks there still.

Further down, I met a teacher who wanted me to come and see his school. I had no remaining will to refuse and was taken to see thirty young boys and girls recite in sweet chorus, the rote lesson the teacher recited. I sat unmoved and unable to communicate, depressed by this primitive attempt at education. The children all filed out to attend their next lesson with a retired army serviceman, who was going to teach them drill.

The teacher insisted that I should stay for dinner and wanted to employ me as an English instructor. He was a nervous and soft-hearted man, whose anxious eyes told the story of his broken loneliness. He told me of his great heart-ache, that came from his affection for a thirteen year-old girl whom he used to teach. She had been his pupil for two years; during which time they had developed a strong platonic bond before she'd been transferred to another school. He desperately wanted to see her again but knew that if any of her family ever found out, they would surely shoot him at once and with full community support.

He felt that the world was tragically unfair and he couldn't understand why other people didn't make the effort to be as good and conscientious as he tried to be. Sometimes, he felt like he should end it all and he looked to me to give him the words of wisdom to put his heart at rest.

The sight of someone deeper in despair than I dragged me out of my melancholy. I tried to give him every reason for living though as we faced each other at the opposite ends of the bed on which we sat, wrapped in every available blanket for warmth, it was hard to find many convincing arguments–what did I know? Maybe suicide *was* the best solution.

I headed back to my hotel that night in a weird state of mind but I resolved to give Kalam another chance in the morning, knowing the way that first impressions of a place are liable to be fickle and influenced by fatigue.

The morning was grey and dreary and even the desert would have been preferable to this place. It was still cold at noon as the clouds lay siege to the spirit. It all seemed so unreal that I wanted to take a sledgehammer to the whole thing and shatter this morbid illusion. I made a quick farewell to the teacher and caught the next mini-bus back to Peshawar.

I changed buses in Swat and ate a couple of bowls of beans cooked by a little old guy on the street in his massive wok-like cauldron. He made flexing muscles with his arms to indicate the nourishing value of his food and as I chewed, he thrust a bag of snuff under my nose. I thrust it away in exaggerated disgust that set the whole gathered crowd laughing and with the fresh chilli in my blood, I began to sweat and laugh, too. A deep cackle roared and raged inside and without, purifying and dispelling the dismal gloom of Kalam. Colour returned to my world.

Chapter 16

The rusty gates of India
(Pakisan, India)

As a result of a couple of punctures–a regular feature of mountain drives–it was dark by the time I arrived back in the city. It wasn't long before a conductor had pulled me into a bus and an hour of shunting through traffic later, we came to the university. It was my plan to try and find someone I knew there, or else just sleep out in the campus grounds. But I was befriended at once by a big and black medical student, called Farooq. His hulky body stretched even the most expansive of the traditional long *kameez* shirt and baggy *shalwur* trousers, though his plump-cheeked schoolboy manner suggested that he'd be at a complete loss at how to use his strength aggressively.

He fed me and let me stay in his room for the night, after an enjoyable few hours of getting stoned with some guys who had lived half their lives in England. They felt more dead than alive here and spent the majority of their mental energies in calculating the most effective schedule to kill the time that dragged upon them like lead. They couldn't understand why I was bothering to visit a country this dull. When they asked me how I'd liked the mountains, there didn't seem to be any words to describe what had passed.

I was tired. Tired of the world and the people in it; tired of guys trying to shove me into buses to Lahore; tired of maniacal truck drivers and 40 hour journeys; tired of side stall wallahs trying to sell me snacks; and really tired of shitting canal water, eight times a day.

So I hid away in the university for about a week, hanging out with people of education, who could express themselves in English (my Urdu only being at primate level) and who were more than willing to house and feed me in exchange for the enter-tainment value I merited. Travelling hand-to-mouth *didn't* mean that I was only taking from people. In all the situations I found myself in I was effectively an ambassador of another vision, an alternative perspective on life. I must have answered half a million questions during these months (most of them the same!) but each sprung from a genuine curiosity and so deserved an answer. I always had the responsibility on my shoulders to give hope and cheer to those that I met, regardless of my mood. In places where not much ever really happened, I'm sure that I'm still mentioned in conversation:

"Hey dad! Do you remember that dirty English guy who spat at us when we tried to sell him samosas?"

The campus grounds were unreasonably noisy with the hoots and horns of the college traffic but there were wide, grassy areas where the birds made melodious song at twilight and I treated the whole place like a kind of a holiday camp.

In these days, I would skulk in the library, reading Sufi poetry and Tales from the 1001 Nights like this one:

The king returned from the battlefield, where he'd been fighting for weeks in disputes about territory and shouted to his jester to bring him a glass of water. The fool brought it to him and watched his lord enjoy the drink before asking him:

"O my most majestic of Sires, what would you have given for that glass of water, if there had been none to bring it to you?

"About half my kingdom!" The king replied, leaning back on his throne.

"And supposing, O great and glorious King, that some mishap occurred in the functioning of your most blessed bladder–what would it be worth to you to be able to release the liquid then?"

"Again, I'd say half my kingdom!" The king laughed, wondering where this was taking him.

"So my most wise and esteemed Majesty, is a humble fool to suppose that this kingdom of yours, over which you fight such long and bloody wars, could be bought for a glass of water and a sloshful of piss?" The king wept at the truth of this!

Who'd be wise, when you could be a fool? One day the king decided to reward his jester and began to elaborate on the wonderful titles, gifts and lands he would bestow upon him. In the middle of this, however, the fool simply stretched out his legs towards the king in what was an unbelievably rude gesture of disrespect. The king was furious and shouted:

"Fool! You had better to be able to explain yourself, or else you'll lose your head within seconds!" And the fool replied:

"Well, I only meant to say, your Majesty, that if I were to reach out my hand to accept all these fine favours from you, then I should no longer be able to stretch out my legs!"

This last story rang some bells for me. Because I was almost always indebted to the people I met for their generosity and help, I often had to take a lot of shit in the process, swallowing my tongue every day. What did I expect? If people were going to give of their hard-earned resources to a lazy hippy like me, then they were going to want to exercise swaggering rank as a result.

The poor of the world usually seem to find some way to get by but most of them first have to endure humiliation at the hands of the more privileged; you can make a buck collecting rags on the street but only at the price of the well-to-do looking down upon you in the process. I was beginning to understand the value of financial independence.

The students were like all unmarried young men in Pakistan; bored, frustrated and tense. There *were* female students in the university but it was dangerous to talk to any of them, in case their families took exception and decided to bend some of your bones in the wrong direction to make their point. Still, it was naturally the main orientation of the thought and activity of my friends and they engaged in protracted and elaborate eye-contact rituals as a preliminary to actual conversation. They would also devote whole evenings to going out to public exhibitions where they might see some chaperoned females, to whom they might be able to slip their telephone numbers—and god help them if they were caught.

Not only did the students tread carefully around courtship behaviour, it was also highly imprudent to voice any unorthodox thought that might be regarded as un-Islamic—something that would probably merit an immediate expulsion from the university, at the least. Farid, a thin and awkward graduate, was one such intellectual who lived in constant fear that it would be discovered that he was not a Believer. In our conversations he emphasized the trouble that would befall him should I betray his confidence. He was probably the only feminist Pakistani that I met and it was a comfort to meet another dissenting island in the great ocean of Islam.

Not that all the students were ardent believers though, as every morning at 5am someone would do the rounds of knocking at each door of the hostels announcing that it was time for prayer, with the reminder that 'prayer is better than sleep' -the general response seemed to be 'Oh no, it's not!' as sleepy heads mumbled excuses until the attendant moved on.

The only drawback to being around people of able and eloquent minds was that there were the inevitable few who would make conversion attempts in pious efforts to correct my life. The Qur'an commands its followers to spread the True Word and puffed up with this spirit of righteous evangelicalism, arrogant adolescents would of times lecture me with ferocious sincerity as to the evils of my ways. I wasn't impressed. The whole *con*version-trip just stems from a doubting insecurity, gnawing away at the foundation of their own faith. To see someone who is a living denial of all that they believed in was just too much for them to bear! In a more barbaric age, they would have liked to kill me rather than allow my example to thrive in happy defiance.

It was bloody rude. When he had finally exhausted my patience, I told a Somalian student this and with waving arms and a reggae rhythm, he responded:

"What, man? I have to tell you! I mean if I *see* someone walking down a path and I *know* there's a lion there–I've got to tell him, right?" But the point was, that he'd never *been* down any other paths and had no idea of what a lion looked like. I didn't travel for three months on the mercy of Fate to be lectured to by these self-important prats. Some were indefatigable.

"There must be something wrong with your life, for you to be living like this!" I was told by a Russian guy, who seemed particularly offended at my hand-to-mouth existence. He was a recent *con*vert to Islam so I could forgive him his enthusiasm but not his condescension. I think I might even have threatened him in the end, to make him shut up–but I'm not sure as someone always got me absolutely bombed every evening.

The drag with living with medical students was that they kept leaving scary books lying around. One day, I made the mistake of picking up one on the nightmare world of parasitology. Ten minutes of morbid reading convinced me that I'd never touch food or water in Asia again. I'd been drinking local water and apart from mild inconveniences I'd been lucky so far. What to do? No way could I afford bottled water and you can't use purifying tablets forever.

Suddenly, my whole route lay ahead of me as a treacherous obstacle course of hepatitis, cholera and giardia bacteria; tapeworms, cysts and amoebas all waiting around the corner! I burned a five rupee note in offering to whatever god might be responsible for the health of poor travellers–Captain Cook, maybe.

The students were all very nice to me but it was tiresome to hear the way they'd continually run down all their countrymen who were not at university, calling them 'backward' and 'ignorant' as though they had to apologize for them. It was also these educated that had the strongest urge to emigrate to Europe, having heard some exaggerated stories from a relative living in Manchester or somewhere and they dreamed of the easy sex and big money that would surely be waiting for them.

Were it not for the immigration laws and passport restrictions, I have an idea that most of Asia would be on the long and dusty road to Europe. The whole issue is very mixed-up and at the thought, I was reminded of an old Palestinian I knew in Brighton. Whenever he saw a right-wing politician he'd approach him saying:

"I come from Palestine and I want to thank you very much for allowing me to stay in your country for the past seven years–during which I've not worked a single day! I've written home to all of my relatives and told them how the government here will give them a place to live, pay the rent and give you money each week for doing nothing! They'll all be coming soon!" He rarely got the chance to actually finish his monologue for the sight of his maniacal, wizened features and the insufferable spiel generally proved too much for the bigot in the suit.

I decided to get on with things and re-entered the city on a hot and smelly morning. I had to move on to Islamabad to get my visa for India and I whipped out the traveller's cheque I'd kept for the embassy fee. It had been stuffed into various pockets, shoe soles and crannies of my bag in an effort to keep it safe on my way. I'd succeeded but at a cost, as although it could still be recognized as authentic, it was covered in creases, holes and tears and the colours ran in washed out stains. It had very clearly not travelled in the normal fashion.

It was maybe for this reason or more likely due to the similar appearance of my person that I had trouble in cashing it. From the moment I walked into the only money-changing place I could find that took TC's, the owner looked me up and down with a contempt that he didn't try to conceal.

"Passport." He barked. He compared the two signatures and saw that on the cheque was just the initial of my first name, whilst on the passport it was written out in full. "This is not your cheque!" He said. I tried to explain, suppressing my surge of annoyance and he demanded that I prove my signature on a piece of blank paper—now who can make the same perfect signature twice?

"This is not same signature! this is not you cheque! I cannot take it!! He muttered in surly tones.

"Are you calling me a thief?" I cried, grabbing it back.

"No thief! This is not your cheque!"

"Then fuck you! You call me a thief! You're a pig and a dog, too!" I shouted in a fiery explosion of rage and I stormed out. Immediately, that I was outside in the street again, I started laughing. How could I be so ludicrously bad-tempered? I put it down to the amounts of chilli I'd been eating. It was no way to deal with that kind of problem as I completely blew the chances of either of us saving face. Yet again I proved myself to be a clueless klutz in Asia. It's always a far better approach to make the guy feel guilty by reminding him, 'Why do you talk to me like this? Aren't I a guest in your country?'

Furthermore, though things seemed civilized, this was still Pathan country and it's definitely not a good idea to stir them up as they're prepared to take things further than most. I was reminded of this as I bumped into a Danish guy in the street, called Martin, who had cycled all the way from Europe; baby-faced and blonde, with scarcely a bristle on his rosy cheeks, his toughness resided among his inner sinews and tendons and was reinforced by a self-reliant confidence that had won him the respect of the Peshawar locals. His story went like this:

"Man, you should have seen what happened yesterday! I was just getting out of one of those little minibuses and a French girl was coming out behind me–I heard her scream and I turned around to see that this Pakistani guy had put his hand around her breasts. Well, I was beating him up, when this shopkeeper comes running towards me, puts his hand down his trousers and pulls out a gun! Then, before I have time to think, he puts the pistol in my hands and shouts 'Shoot him!'" Martin raised his eyebrows in reflection, " now, that was going a bit too far for me, you know and so I said to him 'But I'll go to prison if I kill him!' This shopkeeper just smiles with a shake of his head and says proudly, 'No,no–this is *Pathan* country!'"

"So what did you do with the guy you were hitting?" I asked.

"Well," Martin chuckled, "there wasn't really much left of him by that point!"

I took a bus to Rawalpindi, the twin city of Islamabad and re-entered the Punjab. The bus got there in the evening and I spent the last of my money in getting a cheap hotel room; praying that someone would accept my cheque in the morning.

I awoke at 7am and walked the bitterly-cold streets. The thick grey clouds above seemed reluctant to release the day. I drifted largely unseen, due to my disguise of a grey *shalwur kameez*–wearing these, most people took me for an Afghani with my lighter skin colour and left me alone.

Men sat around huge Karom boards (the Asian version of pool), flicking the discs towards the pockets whilst only twenty metres away, a young guy off-handedly slit the throats of chickens. He tossed them into a dustbin, where they squawked and rumbled against the sides until their life ran out.

There was no trouble with the cheque at American Express and I dashed out before they could change their minds. The money was enough to buy my India visa and leave me with about 20 dollars to play with. The rest of the day was spent buying books and little dainties of food to cheer my spirits. I did my best to revive the feeling of being a prince in my particular kingdom, where I could have anything on display. I didn't need much, just a few luxury tastes to convince myself that I was amongst the favoured. From this elevated stance everything became far easier to handle.

I'd fucked up my timing for the embassy which was conveniently open to foreigner's applications for one and a half hours each day. So for the afternoon I took a minibus to Gorlarsharif, a Sufi shrine where I was told I could get free food. This place was on the outskirts of town and was a beautiful palace of marble white with a towering minaret that could be seen from miles away.

Ignoring the guys who asked for alms at the entrance, I left my decrepit boots outside and stepped into the main area of smooth and cool white tiles, with pillars making an avenue around the perimeter. A wide open courtyard in which was another structure, housed the tomb of an exalted Sufi saint. Around the shrine, there was a constant display of prayer and kissing of the cloth draped on it.

It was a relief to hang out in such a peaceful place and I got chatting to a visiting Pathan pilgrim. He disappeared for a minute and came back with a warm hat for me, before pointing out where I should go for the evening dinner that followed the sunset prayers. Around fifty men sat on the floor, facing one another (the women ate separately, of course) and we were each given two *nan*. These had to be broken up and folded into small triangular shapes to scoop up the *dal* from the shared bowl between each pair. Not easy and it made for anxious eating as only about half the *dal* I scooped up seemed to reach my mouth. I had to resort to using my spare *nan* as a safety net.

It turned out that one could stay for three nights in the place to make the most of the pilgrimage. I was just getting comfortable on the string bed in a dorm with ten other men when the manager came to personally greet me and insisted that I come with him. Much to my protest, he gave me a room of my own and brought in a tray of green tea. When he produced a cake, my solidarity for the guys in the dorm began to weaken and I decided to humbly accept my lot. It was a nice room, after all.

He left me with a book to read about the Sufi saint, to whom this place was dedicated and I read the story of a devout ascetic who had never missed a prayer in his life, spending all his time in study and contemplation in perfect observance of Qur'an and the Sayings of the Prophet. So where were the swords through the waists?

The next day, I was introduced to the current spiritual guide of the shrine and I was made to feel what an honour this would be. My brash English manner, however, shattered all appropriate etiquette as I strode forward and held out my hand to shake rather than bowing and prostrating or something. Before he knew what he was doing, the great *pir* responded by extending his hand. I grabbed it with a hearty squeeze and found myself holding a limp piece of fish.

We had about thirty words in common so we could be forgiven for the lack of dialogue and I stepped aside to allow two local women to approach. They came onto their knees straight away, trailing copious and cheerful dresses upon the ground. They paid homage with bowed heads and humble offerings of praise. One tried to make him a present of sweets, which met with a disdainful refusal and the other donated twenty rupees which he accepted without a word. He then bade them leave with a slight dismissive flick of the head.

This all made me feel utterly nauseous but I needed the hospitality and so I withdrew to my room. I'd lay money that this guy had never known what it was to need twenty rupees, having almost certainly been groomed for the position of a scholar and saint from birth–with a silver spoon in his mouth since day one and a golden shit pot from day two.

Apart from this oasis of calm, the city was typically loud and obnoxious and for me, Pakistan was fast running out of redeeming qualities. The embassy game didn't improve matters and was a picture of bizarre inhumanity in some warped sacrifice to the god of red tape. When I finally managed to arrive on the correct day and at the correct time, the heavens broke loose and rained upon all visa applicants waiting outside; not so bad for us small group of foreigners who gave our forms in at a separate window but for the Pakistanis hoping to visit India, it was a complete nightmare. They stood against a wall in a queue of about two or three hundred and all tried to shelter under a sheet of newspaper or an overhanging bush. I met one guy who had waited from 8am to 5pm the previous day without reaching the window and had to return again today, no better off than before.

I met a couple of Europeans who had cycled all the way and one or two others who had come by motorbike. I finally understood why locals were always asking me: 'Where is your bike?'

Inside the Consulate, we had to pay for a fax to England that would determine if we were wanted criminals, or political enemies of the Indian Government. In addition, it was sprung on us by a smarmy and uncompromising official that we would need a letter of recommendation from our home Embassies–what the fuck? A cold sweat broke on my forehead as I learnt that the cost of such a letter was £35 which I didn't have.

Contrary to popular belief, embassies are often not heavenly oases of sanity and sense in the midst of chaotic foreign lands. They have very little time for people who refuse to play life by the rules as they see it. Thus I decided against telling the British consulate that I was a wayfaring pilgrim, living in poverty to complement my search for a simple spiritual sanctity.

"I'm in the most terrible fix!" I began explaining in my most well-mannered English to the clerk on the other side of the reception window, "As I was travelling between Faislabad and Peshawar my bags were mislaid when someone opened the luggage hatch at the side of the bus during one of the stops–by accident or purpose, I really don't presume to know–but the real embarrassment of the whole affair is that my money belt was in the bags that were lost!" And I babbled on for a while like an aristocrat on amphetamines, standing close to the window, so that my torn and holed boots couldn't be seen by the patient clerk on the other side.

I was taken through to the interview room where I repeated my story to an older official. To my utter surprise, he responded in the warmest possible manner, assuring me of the recommendation letter for free and asked if there was anything else they could do for me, such as contacting friends and family in England. I was tempted to ask for a cheeky loan but reflected that I might someday be really in need of it and so reserved that option for the future.

I ran back to the Indian consulate and submitted the form just in time. I spent the next three days playing clarinet and making yoga in my room, wondering when the manager would finally throw me out–but then I was given the visa and boarded a bus for Lahore on the same day.

I arrived in Lahore around about getting-dark time and after a lot of hassle, found the YWCA (there were no rooms at the YMCA), that any foreigner could safely stay at for fifty rupees a night. A couple of grinning guards at the gate made me write down my name and time of arrival and I marched up the gravel path with gardens to either side. I met up with a whole load of other travellers who came here rather than risk the horror stories of robberies, rapes and police stitch-ups pervading about the hotels in Lahore.

I stood in the hostel gardens, enjoying the moonlight shadows and singing to myself a song by The Specials.

"Just because you've got nobody,
Doesn't mean that you're no good."

"It gives you a pretty good clue, though!" Piped up a voice behind me and I turned to find Jaurice, the French wit whom I'd not seen since Quetta.

Soon we were all laughing and joking in this large house that didn't seem to be run by anybody, catching up with each other's stories. As a result of keeping the more pyschedelic side of my mind closed for so many weeks, I now let fly with my imagination and humour and went into complete hyper-mode for the next couple of days, joking, piss-taking and fantasising about the future with excited abandon.

Jaurice had been up in the freezing Hunza valleys in a brave last romance with his girlfriend, who'd now gone on to China to take up a job in Peking as an English teacher. Whether because of this or just general *ennui*, Jaurice was weary of travel–happy though he was to be escaping the Muslims, whose conversion attempts he'd endured for seven months since starting off in Egypt. The thought of India daunted him a little, though, as he'd been there before and knew what to expect:

"How do *you* keep from going completely crazy there, Tom?" He asked me as if I was a priest in a confessional box. "I mean, the Indians really get on top of you after a while!" He sighed and shook his head with regret, "I don't know why we travel–I think maybe we're just running away from life in our own cultures, where we can't cope! I tell you, I'm just sick of the endless schedule of bus journeys, hotels and special places to see–okay, it's nice for a while but then I just begin to think, 'what are we doing here?' You know? I've got to do something different soon–I think I'll just fly to Bangkok and get a job in a bar or something." His voice had a weariness to it that he'd not revealed before and I wondered if the comedian has tears in his eyes when the curtains are drawn.

We dug Lahore a little the next day, visiting the museum where the famous fasting Buddha had its home. A truly austere-looking statue with all of its ribs painfully evident, I bought ten postcards of it to send back to friends as a wry indication of my fortune and fate.

I teamed up with a guy called Steve, who looked the archetypal English country gentleman, with an arable orange/brown mustache and scarecrow hair. He had, in fact, spent most of his youth hanging around on New Age Traveller sites, smoking cheap dope and absorbing non-conformist influences from the fringe. He'd done the East Asia tour by making money in Thailand where he was hired to take a Thai businessman with a false British passport to Japan–the Thai couldn't speak English and so Steve was employed to do the talking for him. It all went off smoothly as, to every question that the customs men fired at Steve's client, he replied:

"Oh ho! Yes sir!" The one expression he had mastered and which seemed to see him through okay.

We rode on the top of the mini-bus to the border and Steve hid all of his cash, for we'd heard that the officials were very corrupt. They weren't very friendly, either and when the Pakistanis learnt that Steve had some dollars, they offered to give him an exchange rate to Indian rupees. Steve refused and the policeman said:

"Okay. You not change–I not let you through. You can come back tomorrow." What to do? At least the rate was reasonable. They ripped apart all that we owned and much to their disappointment, found nothing untoward.

The Indian side was much more relaxed with a polite though thorough Sikh on the desk. On the form, we were required to state our means of support and I declared that I had £700 in traveller's cheques–fortunately, they didn't ask for proof.

We strolled triumphantly down the Atari road that linked the two countries, that have been at each other's throats since Independence. The distance was clearly a lot less effort for us than for the blue-hatted porters on the Pakistani side who carried huge loads to the border, where the burdens were transferred to a team of red-turbanned Indian coolies. The sight would have given a chiropractor a headache. These guys were creating wholly original spinal ailments, supporting loads on their heads that men were not meant to carry.

Before letting us through the final gate to the promised land of India, the Sikh on duty enquired if I wanted to sell my green foam sleeping mat. My laughter was not so much out of refusal but from a reassuring amazement that the very first thing that could occur in this land of merchants and frauds was to be approached for a cash-in-hand transaction!

Me and Steve took a cycle rickshaw to the Golden Temple; heartplace of Sikh faith. We rolled slowly along the road and felt like the arriving British Raj. The old man on the cycle puffed and sweated as he pulled our idle loads. His bony legs went up and down with a heaving effort that made us feel guilty for being so heavy. The clicks and whirrs of the chain and wheels were drowned out only by the whizz and hum of the mopeds that overtook us with automated ease. But we didn't care for we had arrived and we felt good. We were the bold new champions of the noble cause of hedonism; our banners painted in huge smiles across our faces. So what if we had to get out and help push when we came to the hill?

The Golden Temple. The Sikhs–a splendid people, with enormous hearts and courage that make them as fierce and daunting in battle as they are kind and beneficent in time of peace. And this was the place, the centre of their pilgrimage and man, what a place! We entered the massive complex and met with the unbelievable visage of the 30 ton Golden Temple, sat slam in the middle of the huge square lake, accessed only by a two-lane walkway that leads to the centre of the place. There we discovered that the song and tabla music heard through every waking and sleeping moment of the next few days, was being played *live*–and it was no problem to take a seat against the rails to just absorb the *shanti* contentment that abounded here, the peace beyond understanding.

I liked it. Even better was the handful of sweet semolina that they gave you as you returned from the centre–to reaffirm the potential sweetness of life on Earth, I guess. We'd chew on this and then just waltz around the tiled walkway that bordered the lake. The centre carpet warming our bare feet, our tranced steps were in time with the endless Punjabi song and our minds got lost in peaceful dreams.

When hunger overtook us it was only a short walk to the 24-hour free food hall and as we waited our turn, we'd squat down outside with businessmen, sadhus, families with uncontrollable children and Sikh warriors bearing pole-axes and swords (one guy even had a morning-star -the small spikey metal ball swung from a chain on a short metal pole!).

When the current session ended the hall would empty in a clattering exodus of satisfied pilgrims, carrying their plates and cups to the washing-up area. Then we'd all bustle inside and scramble to find places to sit on the long rows of thin carpet, that were arranged so that each line sat back-to-back. Down the long walkways came the guys with baskets of *chapattis* and buckets of *dal* which they dolloped out by hand. Before eating, we'd be led in a Punjabi Grace and the communal chant put an exquisite edge on our hunger, as aromas of hot food drifted in from the kitchen.

There was not a veil in sight anywhere in the complex and as Steve and I chased pieces of lentils around our plates with scooping shovels of *chapatti*, we often had the distinct feeling that we were being sized up as potential marriage material. We looked up and sure enough, quite dazzling young girls were returning our gaze with bold and saucy smiles. Their mothers were egging them on and to hear clusters of pretty maidens giggling and tittering was like feeling the first spray of rain upon our faces on a hot summer's day.

The Pakistanis now seemed like some cultural relic of the Dark Ages. One old Sikh chap with full grey beard, rocked with laughter when I told him of the taboos regarding women in the Pathan territories.

"Crazy, no?" He cried with gleaming eyes. It was hard not to agree. India is at least equally as prehistoric in its regard for women but in the Golden Temple an easy going vibe prevailed; with the intoxicating tranceful song of the Sikh holy books that sailed through the air and also with the constant excitement of the bustle and rustle of new arrivals, eager and enthusiastic and the departure of those who'd completed their three day stay, calmed and content.

Perhaps it was due to this relaxed vibe that on my way to wash in the bathroom, I received a full-blooded sexy wink from a Sikh girl who could not have been more than fifteen–she turned around excitedly, to see if I had caught her signal but I was so freaked after so many weeks of deprivation from female energies, that I collapsed on the spot in riotous hysterics! I hope that I didn't hurt her feelings too much as she was a sweet little thing–but this was not Thailand and there were way too many well-armed guys around to make that point with the ends of their daggers. Still, it was still nice to have these shining beauties around to fill our spare fanciful moments.

The Sikh were in some ways similar to the Pathans as can be confirmed by a quick glance at the history of this ferocious warrior race, that evolved to meet the threat of the invading Muslims. I'd rather face a hundred lap-top carrying English commuters than a single Sikh in blue battle-dress, carrying a sharpened toothpick.

But like the Pathans, they're determined that their guests should not lack for anything and they have a natural disposition to providing welfare to the less fortunate, in order to strengthen the communities they've founded.

The focus of the Sikh religion is on the happiness and fulfillment of people in *this* life, rather than the usual con-trick of other faiths where the believer's rewards are in some pie-in-the-sky Paradise or auspicious rebirth. In every city in the Punjab they provide a sleeping area in their temples and at least one free meal a day for those who wish to come.

Of course, there's a limit to how much help can be given and you're only allowed to stay for three days, which is deemed enough time to rest, recuperate and put you back on your feet–and is in fact the intuitively recognized length of time appropriate for hospitality in traditions all across the world; ranging from Arabia where lavish reception of guests has for ages been bestowed upon travellers for three days and three nights, to Germany, where the saying is that 'guests are like fish–after three days they both begin to smell!'

Naturally, within the Temple we had to pay respect to the values and traditions of our hosts–but it was easy to forget as when our Australian friend, Brendan, commenced to shave Steve's head in the middle of the courtyard. Only as the attendants came dashing up with outstretched arms of panicked protest, did my friends slap themselves on the forehead in a 'Oh, of course' realisation that the cutting of hair is forbidden among the Sikhs–that being perhaps the *most* obvious feature to be noticed about this folk where all the men wear long beards and stash their hair up under their turbans!

We kipped down at night-time in the area reserved for foreigners and it was good fun to meet up with other freakish travellers who got by without the use of guidebooks (and the accompanying demeanour of spoilt brats). The people I met here used their creativity to write their own movie plots, living whatever life they liked to live. We sat around exchanging Asia travel stories, each anecdote sending fresh sparks into the fire of experience, kindling our burning urge and seek out the jewels of one-off incidents that are booned upon the intrepidly curious.

The funniest story was that of an Australian girl, whom I called Baby Roo on account of her tiny figure, pretty mouse-like face and fuzzy, tumbleweed hair. She had come out travelling with the fierce determination to do things differently and had recently spent six weeks living almost entirely around the Indian railway system. She'd discovered that if she squashed into the lowest class of carriage and nestled somewhere in amongst the human jam, then she was rarely asked for a ticket and travel often became free. She further cut costs by sleeping in train stations, sometimes getting thrown out of the waiting rooms for being the freeloader that she was.

Her entire travelling luggage was even less than mine, coming down to one medium-sized, brown handbag with a couple of plastic bags hanging ragatat from the sides. The contents of all this consisted of a change of clothes, a bed sheet for a sleeping cover and, until recently, her travelling essentials in this miniature survival kit had included two cacti plants (sharp ones, mind) and a stand-up portrait of Barbara Streisland–she used to get these out and establish her personalised mini-environment any time, any place.

She'd reluctantly abandoned this practice, because two German guys had laughed at her and she suddenly became conscious that people might think that she was weird! In her spare time, this angel would buy chai at a small stand on the street and charm the shopkeeper until he'd ply her with the coconut sweets that she'd coveted all along! I was amazed to see someone who had adapted to and absorbed the weirdness of this country with such speed and ease. She was clearly an India-freak natural of outstanding talent.

Nevertheless, we were now in Tourist-Land. India has become a hugely popular destination for straight-laced young travellers on a limited budget. Such *voyeurs* tend to make the disastrous mistake of bringing with them the haughty expectations of their own cloistered cultures, with the result that they embarrass themselves time and time again with their inappropriate indignation.

On this occasion, it was the turn of the Swiss to be ambassadorial buffoons for the West. Around about midnight, two frigid-looking girls rose from their beds and marched to the other side of the plaster partition to ask the Sikh attendants if they wouldn't mind 'talking more quietly please' as some people were 'trying to get some sleep, thankyou-very-much'! At the other end of the room, we had to repress our guffaws of disbelief at their cheek; it was the accepted paradigm that we ought to be grateful for receiving a free bed in the first place! What was next? Room service? *Those* people would never have made it overland!

Now that I was in India, I had to get myself some decent-looking sadhu clothes, the orange and saffron colours that this brand of religious renunciates wear. I wasn't a sadhu, of course, as that would mean going through a whole process of being accepted by a guru, learning complicated mantras and a whole load of initiation rites, that might include attending my own funeral to renounce my previous identity.

These customs ensure the integrity of the tradition, as no one could pretend to be a sadhu by just wearing the appropriate colours, growing dredlocks and scrawling a few Shiva lines on their forehead with ash–unless they could answer the appropriate questions that another sadhu would ask them–they'd be found out immediately for being beggars on to a more respectable way of hand-to-mouth living. The sadhus usually have prestige in India because it's a facet of Hindu philosophy that every male should, after the periods of study and establishing a household, then renounce all of that, distribute his money to the poor and devote his life to the pursuit of self-realisation. But the word 'sadhu' just means 'practitioner' and so, in effect, any one who makes his or her meditation practice the focus of their lives, deserves the title as much as any grumpy old guy smoking chillums around a fire in a Himilayan temple.

My reasoning was that if I wore orange, then I'd have less questions asked of me and it would hopefully be apparent to others that I had no money. Offers of help might then be more forthcoming.

In my search for a good cloth shop, I rediscovered the joy of side-streets; an aspect of India I'd forgotten all about. Me and Steve delighted in becoming hopelessly lost in the alleyways that were thick with religion, commerce and general chaos. Retail operated in different zones; in one area the air would be thick with hanging scarves, lungis and sheets and then a few hundred yards away we'd clink into the hardware stalls, with pots, pans and cauldrons shining bright in all glistening directions.

Altars made their homes in ancient trees, that had merited enough respect to be built around, rather than through. Data streamed in a dense and invisible river from all sides. The street space that existed was still fought over by fierce traffic as the smaller vehicles wheeled through in skidding bursts, braking every half-minute as a cow would come strutting through, gnawing at anything resembling vegetable matter. That would be followed by a procession of chanting and singing Krishna devotees, playing instruments and burning incense in the Indian version of song-and-dance men.

It was our misfortune to be caught up in *Diwali*, the HIndu Festival of Light. It sounds nice but seems to be nothing more than an excuse for every child old enough to stand, to get hold of obnoxiously loud and dangerous fireworks which let off at the feet of anyone walking by (especially jumpy tourists, who fly into a delicious rage at the least prompting!). On the night itself, five of us sat on a lawn outside the Temple, eating masala spaghetti and feeling pretty nervous about being in the middle of a war-zone. The fireworks became more and more random, with a minimum of colour and a maximum of sound.

Then Brendan, with his remarkable talent for attracting tricky situations that belied his slouching, easy-going manner, suddenly outdid himself by producing a last joint he had remaining. We debated whether it was safe to smoke it, given the numbers of people around. You weren't supposed to smoke anything within a few hundred metres of the Temple–but in the midst of all this gunpowder and noise, who would know or care anyhow? We looked up and down with conspicuously hunched shoulders and paranoid tilts of the head, as full bearded Sikhs hung about in the distance carrying their ceremonial halberds.

"Wait, Wait–that guy over there is looking! No, it's okay, he's moved on."

"Okay, we'll just wait for that policeman to go round the corner"

"Right, do you think it's safe now? Yeah? Okay give me some cover, so that I can light up." And just as we were about to smoke, a great shadow loomed over us and we all turned around with stomach-wrenching fright. Standing two metres tall was a Sikh warrior in majestic blue battle dress, with one hand on an enormous sword in its scabbard. With his beard and turban he was utterly ferocious and for a long and dreadful moment, it flashed through all of our minds that he might chop off all of our heads with one mighty stroke.

It turned out that he was concerned about some rupees lying on the ground and thought that we might be gambling. He left and we all breathed again. Trying hard to be undismayed, we lit and finished the joint in record time, barely holding back our hysterics.

Chapter 17

Freaks in the mountains
(India, the Himalayas)

The next morning, on which we all had to leave, I woke early and struggled to put on my pink dhoti. I had to enlist the help of the Sikh attendants to work it out. I left behind an amused crowd, as I had entered as an apparently normal and mild-mannered tourist, found a phone box and emerged as Super-Sadhu! Wherever there's a free bowl of rice–I'll be there! Whenever there's a spare seat in a truck going East–you can count on me! And whenever there's a nation of 950 million people grappling with confused cultural identities, struggling with an economic and social infrastructure that's sick to the core–I'll...Well, there's only so much that one hero can do!

No one swallowed my bluff, however and I still got just as many solicitous shouts upon my wallet from rickshaws, stallholders and beggars. It was too cold to go barefoot and my clarinet made my rucksack seem bulky enough to belong to a tourist. Maybe I should just have completely covered myself in ash.

I was going into the mountains again. A quick glance at a map had shown to my surprise that I was very close to Dharamsala, the homeplace of the Dalai Lama. I'd had no idea that I was remotely within range but it was only a centimetre distance away on the map and from there it would be but a short hop to the Kulu valley, where I'd spent my first couple of formative weeks in India as a newly-arrived and green traveller two years before. I hoped to find some friends there.

The train station was decked out with Sikh warriors with axes and spears and also with sadhus of different colours, all making use of their privilege to travel free on the trains (no longer a *de facto* right but many conductors still turn a blind eye). With winter firmly in the air, perhaps they heading to warmer destinations.

I'd missed my train so I hit the road with ten rupees in my pocket. I stopped to ask directions of a young student, explaining that I didn't know the way and received the charmingly typical response:

"Indeed! Which one of us can truly say that he knows which direction to go in life–" I was in no mood to let him finish as discussions of this kind in India tend to wind, bend and circle inconceivably around to the starting point, whereupon the tracks found there serve as fuel for further happy speculation! If there's one thing at which the Indians have traditionally excelled, it's sitting about drinking chai and talking philosophy until the milk runs out. The results can be seen in the various Vedas, the Upanishads, the Gita and in the mountain of treatise on minute aspects of yoga, meditation and the transcendental–most of it an excellent cure for insomnia.

I strode off and managed to grab a lift in a truck after a few hundred metres of walking. I was taken North for a couple of hours and the guy at the wheel even bought me some excellent spinach and *chapattis* at a roadside bhaji place beside outrageously beautiful fields of purple flowers. Conversation didn't get too far.

"England! Good fucking, yes?"

The next truck was driven by a happy and laughing guy, with his two sons beside him in the cabin as assistants.

"Fucking girl, ha!"He cried joyously, though without the sultry sleaze of the previous guy. He was far more energetic in his appreciation for the women he saw walking down the road, honking his horn voraciously and making the in-out gesture with his finger and cupped hand. Hard to make a conversation like that last for two or three hours.

They weren't bad guys, just with very mixed-up perspectives on the whole thing. They'd seen Madonna straddling a cross on stage, gyrating passionately and, with the thousands of degrading movies produced within India, the general conclusion is that women can only be sex objects. For many Indians, Television is Truth and no two ways about it.

I began to sympathize with the Muslims again–I'd be nervous if I had daughters with gawping frustrates like these guys around.

On the other hand, perhaps the only way they're going to overcome these mountainous sexual repressions is by maximum *exposure* to breasts and bums–then maybe they'll be able to relax about it a little.

I got off in a small village at the foot of the mountains and as the day had somehow mostly passed, it made sense to kip down somewhere near rather than go any further up where it would be significantly colder.

Some jazz floated through the air and I pulled out my clarinet and went to join a sax player in a small shop. We played for an hour or two (a crowd of faces a*peer*ing, naturally) and my new friends paid for the rip in my trousers to be repaired. They also gave me twenty rupees so that I could eat at the train station where they reckoned I could also sleep.

The waiting room in the station was nice and I hung out there in the warmth. A father and mother ate *dal* and *chapattis* with their children from a shared bowl and the expressions of the kids moved with fluid ease, without trace of self-consciousness. Near the door was an elderly Tibetan nun and a teenage monk, sitting by their luggage as they returned from some mission or the other. The boy gently sobbed as his guide admonished him for something and I felt happy to witness all these expressions of human warmth, in one of those rare moments where everything seems just right.

The morning brought me a ride from another Sikh, who fetched me some breakfast from his home and I was soon curving upwards on mountain roads, waving a gentle goodbye to the plains of the Punjab now presented more simply from on high. Monkeys loped around and in between short rides from guys on scooters, I walked the sloping curves of the gently climbing road.

Turning a corner, loud and tinny music came blaring at me in the honour of a Hindu festival. Four guys stood by with a cauldron of sweet semolina, a handful of which they forced into the palms of everyone in the vehicles that came along the road. Indians are always keen to be in on the act, especially when there's plenty of potential for fun, mischief and a sense of self-importance

Beautiful walks and chilly but exhilarating rides on motorbikes and scooters brought me up to the first of the Dharamsala villages by mid-afternoon. I'd hoped that the Tibetan monks might give me shelter if only for three nights. But a polite secretary sitting at a computer, regretted that they were already full to overflowing point and that they couldn't help me.

I headed up to Mcleod ganj and ran into the usual marks of an Indian tourist town with Kashmiri jewellry, carpet and clothes shops, cheap hotels and bakeries and restaurants serving Western food. It was way too cold to think about sleeping outside but my problems were solved by some Kashmiris I met in the street, who let me stay in the house that they used only for cooking, eating and watching television.

Thank Allah for the Muslims! Saved the day once again and the odds on my blood turning to ice fell to the longshot chance that there might be no windows in this gaff. Gaping holes there were not but chronic damp there was, so bad that fresh layers of newspaper had to be laid down every two days and the layer of mats put out to dry on the rooves.

I was supposed to help with the cooking but fortunately the chef liked to do things his own way and relegated me to the task of smoothing through the rice on a plastic mat, to remove the tooth-crunching small stones that invariably find their way in. Contrary to many worldwide traditions where spicy foods are served in tropical climates to relieve the heat, my friend was of a mind to prepare hot chilli dishes in the icy evenings to ' put some fire' into our crew. We ate so late at night that our food didn't really digest but put us all to sleep okay. As a once-a-week treat they let me join them in getting snow-rat-arsed on Indian whiskey and Coke.

In the days I hiked up to Dharamkot, the highest village up a steep and gravelly path. I'd be passed on my ascent by Tibetan kids sliding on wooden planks in practice for the imminent arrival of snow. Monkeys lurched across the path with truculent aggression and the forest stood thick in this rain capital of India.

215

The lush vegetation dispelled any notion that all mountains were bare and rocky places.

Further up, the snow glaciers presented their god-like craggy heads and they were so close as to be surreal. But by the afternoon a floating dream of cloud would impose itself, just a stone's throw away and the white peaks would commence a game of peek-a-boo with the swirling gassed water.

Dharma-types hung about the chai-shops at this village and I quickly remembered this kind of holier-than-thou India heads. They engage in endless battles to determine who possesses the more superior of spirituality, hoping to flaunt their refined humility, modesty and understanding upon others. An older chap and I were chatting about snakes and scorpions in the area, numerous on account of the jungle terrain and an eavesdropping ashram kid from Vienna chipped in with:

"But you know, I just hold the scorpion in my hand and I feel no fear! I just feel love for it and there is no danger!" Gazing at us with earnest blue eyes that urged us to accept the wisdom of his words for our own good.

I realised this two years before, when I sat in a teepee in a Spanish commune on the verge of disrupting the Native American-style 'talking circle', as I came close to throwing the talking-stick into the fire. We were only allowed to speak when the stick came round to us. The person previous to me had announced that he knew beyond doubt that, in a past life he had been King Arthur of the Round Table–it seemed that it would be reasonable to incinerate the lump of wood as a metaphorical comment straight from my heart!

My scorn was alone, anyhow, as I realised when no one else laughed when an English girl told us that the flies buzzing in erratic orbits around us, *were* in fact stitching together the holes in our auras. Each to their own trip I suppose–it would just be nice if they could do it in silence... and elsewhere.

Dharamsala was full of stunning natural beauty and was full of easy walks that led high up winding jungly cliffs, painted in webbed shadow and host to an orchestra of insects, including the odd guard bee that would buzz in threatening proximity to let me know what I was up against if I went foraging for honey.

Towards the top, piles of stones could be seen in simple stone stacks monuments to the elements about. They were usually accompanied by colourful prayer flags that hung like the forgotten washing of an absent-minded god. It was a *shanti* place to be as long as I went early; the clouds began to encroach by about two o'clock and more than once I was sent scampering down the rocky paths, before I could get lost in the invading fog.

The Tibetans were pleasant people to be around and the religious thing is quite open and merry, compared to the austerity of Islam or other religions that take themselves more seriously. I've always had an affection for the Tibetan Buddhists since one of them winked at me in a visa office in Delhi, two years before. His well-timed bit of irreverence to the bureaucratic atmosphere had relieved my nervousness and reminded me that it was all just a game–I succeeded in getting the vital extension to my visa by ingratiating myself with the official as we talked enthusiastically about cricket!

The Tibetan trip is weird yet compassionate to the core. Their meditations can be of a highly shamanic order, relating to a whole cosmology of deities and demons but always the focus is on opening the Buddha-nature inside of all of us–however they recognize that it may sometimes take a pretty strange-looking key to open the doors of some psyches. As such, the Tibetan tradition is to dive into your fears head-first and one well-known saying that they used to sign off with is 'Into the mouth of the lion!' It's for this reason that they're well-known for their absorption with the most feared of all things: death. Conquer *that* particular hang-up and who can then touch you? Tibetan trainees used to spend entire nights sleeping with a corpse to overcome their heebie-jeebies about the dead!

I didn't have any special urge to take up the maroon robes of the Buddhist monks though, as it's much more fun being free. Anyway, was the Buddha a Buddhist? He was just a guy sitting in meditation in the jungle that finally understood his inner nature and supposedly received enlightenment.

Whatever else, the Tibetans have to be admired for the miracle they've worked in achieving such remarkable prosperity since they fled their homeland after the Chinese invasion, stumbling down as refugees into the mountains of India. The more famous of the rinpoches now buzz about between public lectures by private helicopter and the Dalai Lama receives financial support from the mega-wealthy bods of Hollywood.

An amazing lesson in how to turn utter disaster into a position of fantastic influence and prestige. And it's still possible to see the small guy himself. Around two thousand people queued to shake his hand when I was there–how many other people of such controversial fame is it possible to come close to with such ease?

After three nights stay, it seemed time to move on down the road and hopefully meet up with some old friends in the Kulu valley. I walked a long way and caught a series of short lifts on scooters before I finally got a ride in a truck going to Mandi, about halfway to my destination.

My drivers weren't shy as to their first thoughts concerning their new passenger.

"Currency? Foreign currency? Dollar?" They asked with hopeful grins after a few minutes of trundling along the pot-holed valley road. I responded by launching into an immediate lecture on the blessed nature of a life of renunciation, spared from the pollution of greed and avarice. I'm not sure that they understood a word but the gist was clear. Whenever they tried to mention payment again an exasperated snort was sufficient to bring silence, lest another full-force monologue should fall wrathfully upon them.

They were more offended though, when I denied them the satisfaction of their perverted desires–the only urge stronger than their lust for rupees–as I refused to join in a communal wash in a stream beside the road. From then on it became bitterly clear to them that I was neither going to rain golden dollars upon their dashboards, nor scrub their backs with a soapy rag and they lost complete interest in me, sulking in silence until I was dropped off in Mandi.

Somehow it was already mid-afternoon and it felt cold in the shadows. The river that roared through the middle of the valley basin had run down from the Kulu valley and beyond. It spoke of ice, cold and the insanity of attempting further travel to Northern heights without the surety of a warm bed at the end.

But there were no men in white coats around to stop me and so I caught a lift with a jolly local truck driver. He took me a kilometre and then insisted on buying me the ticket for the bus to Manali.

There was hardly room to breathe on the bus but none of the locals got uptight about it and they demonstrated their admirable capacity to be cheerful and relaxed in the most uncomfortable arrangements. Anyway, it was at least twice as fast as the groaning and decrepit engines of the lorries, that made only torturous progress on these rocky roads.

I was going home–back to the place where India really began for me, the place of watershed where a whole new life began to unfold and a beautiful new vision materialised. I met people and influences that surpassed all that I'd previously heard and seen; old heads who'd been on the road for thirty years as well as younger freaks just a little ahead of me in track-time. I learned how India gelled as the focus of their lives and its panoramic landscape the backdrop for temporary psychedelic communities, where it would be quite common to overhear conversations like:

"... and so advances the theory that the human race is slowly evolving into the next dimension" without an incredulous eyebrow being raised. Of course, there were still all the hang-ups and shortcomings found in any community but it represented a whole other way of living, a potential that no one in England had ever mentioned.

Lost in these vague reminisces the conductor shouted loudly in my ear, that we were coming into Manali bus station. I was out of my seat and into the darkness outside in seconds. Manali itself is now a horrible, bustling place with one long road and over a hundred autorickshaws. It's the villages nearby that are the choice places to hang out and I got hold of a candle and some matches and started to march up the hillside road.

Twenty steps later, I realised that I had as much chance of getting there on foot as... well, as an Englishman attempting to walk three kilometres in pitch darkness, along uneven roads with a pitfall of hundreds of feet to one side and with only a thin blanket wrapped around him in sub-zero temperatures.

Fortunately, all the cards were on my side that day and a mini-cab came by with some English travellers. A quick chat established that we had mutual friends up the hill and they gave me a lift up to the village. Ten minutes later, I was running into the cafe run by my old friends. Techno music blared and I was given a chillum to light (the traditional conical pipe of clay); puffing smoke sideways out of my cupped hands, to blur the faces of freaks from all corners of the Earth. I was given a bed in the chill-out room next door.

The next day, I was taken into the house of my old friends who ran the cafe. By giving the odd shiatsu massage treatment and by the generosity of other freaks who enjoyed my story, I passed a happy two and a half weeks in the mountains.

I'd expected everything to be boarded up and closed for the winter. But the season hadn't ended yet and there were more parties and jam sessions to be had yet, before most people fled to warmer climates. The fortnight brought many bright reunions–some more awkward than others as heavy charas smokers often have shaky memories–but if that's true, then they're also equally ready to welcome and accept friends again. Relations generally moved with ease in the community of Westerners buzzing around the various garden cafes and rooftops.

There was an inevitable conflict thrown up by the clique-iness of the long-term resident freaks and the first-time India travellers, who often got the vibe that they weren't so welcome amongst this alternative family. But there were enough people with broad enough natures to bridge the gap that occurs in any scene between the established and the new.

The focus of conversations ranged from LSD encounters with

aliens, to forthcoming travel plans in India and Asia. This was a place for consolidation of the learning in the furnace of the plains and stood as a shanti-shelf on a spectacular valley, where apples were-a-growing, chillums-glowing and minds-a-blowing. There were the modern merchants who sold silver on the streets of South Korea; the electronic wizards who could fix a sound system in the pouring rain at a party, whilst on ten hits of acid; there were also straight English couples who lived extended holidays of moving all day from cafe to cafe, eating four times a day and smoking as much as they liked; and there were travellers who had settled down with houses of their own, living on a budget not much more than the richer of the villagers.

Of course, there was still a world of difference between any localized Westerner and an Indian as every one of us had the potential to leave the country and earn comparative fortunes. The villagers were of a conservative and religious frame of mind with complex rules and traditions that were being blown apart by the culture invasion that follows on the footprints of the freaks.

The pattern is always the same—the first Westerners arrive looking for the real India and the quiet, unspoilt life. They're welcomed for the break in monotony they represent and the extra rupees they bring in. Gradually, the place wins a reputation as an easy-going resthole for travellers and more arrive, bringing with them an appetite for Coca-Cola, mineral water in plastic bottles and other non-degradable entities, never before to have entered the simple dimension. The more travellers come to an area the more it is tamed, thus giving it wider appeal until it makes the pages of the popular guidebooks. Then it's doomed. A one-two-three step formula for destroying in a few years what took thousands of years to develop—not *destroy* exactly but throw enough salt into the cauldron of stew and it becomes inedible or at the best, foul-tasting.

This village had already changed a lot in the year and a half since I'd last come and there were now quite a few concrete guesthouses up, as demand grew for accommodation. But what to do? Just to hope the road to Delhi is washed out more often and make the most of the special times that still exist. Which is what we did; trying to ignore the traffic chaos in the only road in the village, as taxied Indian tourists from Delhi, the Punjab and Bengal drove right up to the temple in the centre. It was necessary to employ a kind of alchemy to extract the magical essence of the encounters that could still be had with locals and other freaks.

It was still a special place with Nature never more than a few minutes walk away, cows trampling hay, chickens hopping around and far-out glaciers at either end of the North-South valley. The local temple had free public baths, full of the steaming-hot sulphur water that ran out of the mountain. Nothing beat a 3am bath on a full-moon night, then hurrying out to get warm by the *dhuni*, the fire kept going by the *babas*. These resident sadhus cooked a couple of meals a day that anyone could come and share.

The *baba*/sadhu game is often said to be India's answer to a social security system as in temples and *dhunis* across the lands, many thousands of men in loincloths sit around their sacred fires, relying upon donations from the locals of the odd sack of rice, *dal* and chapatti flour. Let's hear it now: 'No chillum, no chai,

No charas, no cry!'

This was a particularly friendly *baba*-circle and there wasn't too much emphasis on the kind of etiquette that can make a newcomer feel nervous–Walk clockwise around the fire but pass the chillum to your right! Never touch anything with your left hand! Salute Shiva before inhaling on the chillum! And so on.

In fact, every traveller who's smoked chillums in India knows that it's more often the Italian 'chillum fascists' who give you grief for some minor transgression of the code. These people come fleeing from their own spiritual vacuum and swallow aspects of the Hindu culture like feeders upon carrion. The joke is, of course, that no foreigner can become a Hindu and so they are theoretically outcastes, the lowest of the low just like the rest of us whiteys. My venom might be better understood by the experience of a friend of mine who had gone walking in the Parvati Valley, way up to the hot springs of Kiergange where Shiva is supposed to have sat for ten thousand years in meditation.

She had only been in India for ten days and didn't know better than to draw out in front of an Italian guy in loincloth a lump of charas she'd bought in another valley.

"Where, did you get this… piece?" he asked with squinting eyes.

"Oh, someone sold it to me in Manali!"she answered cheerfully. Upon which the Italian flew into a rage and raised his arms to the sky in disbelief.

"You bring *Manali* charas to *Parvati*? You insult the Gods!"

Where was I? Oh yeah, here in this village the vibe was a lot more relaxed and the head *baba* who was in charge of the meal preparations took pains to ensure that everyone felt comfortable. There was pretty much free license to say or do what you liked and we sat idly around the smoking logs and passing the odd fuming chillum.

In reality there was not so much difference between these guys and a bunch of drinkers ordering rounds, as the same contests of bull-shitting and piss-taking still went on–though one would hope that the *baba*s were more conscious of all that was happening. But I'm out of my depth (again!) and shouldn't make sweeping conclusions about *babas* as the quality of the *dhuni* varies depending upon the exposure to tourism. This was not the genuine article for most of the sadhus here were not much more than charas dealers. I could only guess at which of them were genuine because I had no conversational grasp on Hindi. Generally I left them to their thing, not wanting to have to prove myself to anyone any more.

In truth, I was tired of who I'd become as my whole trip had backfired on me–though I knew it might only be for a few months, I'd genuinely renounced my former life, taken farewell of my friends and even changed my name, as I cast myself naked into the cooking pot of experience to see what might happen. But no one walks without clothes for long and rather than killing my identity to be left in harmonious egolessness I had, in fact, weaved a very neat raiment around myself as the Mysterious Wanderer, the Hitchhiking Sadhu fresh from a transcendental, transcontinental journey that marked me way and above all the rest–if only shown by the *humility* with which I told my tale! So whilst erasing my former identity on a surface level, a scourging great shadow of a new ego had crept up behind me!

Of course, it was useful to have an impressive tale to tell as a means to getting meals bought for me but that too highlighted the other problem. I had learned to be an effective scrounger. Blag, scam, scavenge–any way I could find an honest route to filling my greedy belly. I had unconsciously developed the look of a hungry dog as I sat in the cafes making other people feel uncomfortable at eating food in front of me. I'm maybe exaggerating a little but it became my natural tendency to size people up as to what they might be able to provide for me.

It sounds pretty base and it was. But it was also part of a transition process I had to fully traverse when I eventually came to Goa, as the Hand-To-Mouth journeying is a different thing to the resident Poor Man story and different rules apply. When you're on the move people don't mind helping you along. But when you stay in an area you have to hustle like everyone else and it's not cool to just sit back on your reputation.

Nevertheless, the king never wants to give up his crown and even now, when I enter a new town I instinctively look for a good place to sleep. Even if I were a millionaire, I'm sure that I'd still cast a wistful eye at the remains left behind on unfinished plates. There's even a kind of pride involved that you can live cheaper and with less than everyone else. When the other travellers played anally-retentive games of stressing what a low budget they were on and how terribly soon their money would run out, I took a grim satisfaction in knowing that the money that they had would last me ten times as long.

But that was actually quite untrue for whenever I receive a little more money I'd start to treat myself to the extra milkshake or piece of cake, more deluxe drugs or comfortable clothes and room–big fucking deal if I could live on wood-shavings for half a year! The richest person would seem to be the one who thinks about money the least.

However, I was still fucking poor and that became apparent when six weeks too early, it began to snow. That is, it began and didn't end for a full two days. Even within a few hours, it lay half a foot deep on the ground. Huge flakes of white came floating down and we all gazed upwards at the sky falling upon our heads. The village looked beautiful and virgin once again and the electricity immediately went off for four days (which the Power Board do as a kind of precaution, in case the lines should break!).

Predictably, we all whooped and had epic snowball fights until we realised that we had no effective way of getting warm and dry again. Some other travellers kindly sorted me out with a duvet jacket and extra pair of socks. I was lent the odd extra jumper and got through okay.

An old India hand taught me the trick of tying plastic bags on the feet between the socks and shoes, relating how once she'd known a sadhu who had made himself a complete suit of plastic bags when winter caught him unawares!

The snow marked the end of the season and it was clear that it was too cold for any more outdoor techno parties, for which this area has a deservedly good reputation. The police sometimes make matters difficult as they do for the party scene in so many places in the world but they can rarely be bothered to climb to the heights at which the raves are held. As a natural stage setting, the Himalayas are unbeatable—it's even good that you sometimes have to walk for a couple of hours to reach the party. It gives a sense of accomplishment before the action even begins and it weeds out the fringe freaks, leaving just a solid hardcore of partyers.

The first party I ever went to took place in the Kulu Valley and I discovered the freedom of movement that could be attained on LSD. This elixir acted as the lubricant to suddenly understanding what techno music was all about. Previously it had all just sounded like a messy collaboration of drum beats, sound effects and corny samples of people saying, 'wow, this must be heaven!' Only when suitably high did I tune in to the wavelength where techno finally made sense. I learnt that a good DJ takes his dancers on a voyage of discovery, setting the entire backdrop for the partyers to spin off.

And spin we did. Every time I surfaced from the dancefloor, the donor of my dose would gently push me back in, saying:

"Go on! It's good for you!" And I was happy to take his word for it.

The parties are positive and funky events and represent a remarkable expressive movement of alternative modern culture, the turned-on gathering to expand their consciousnesses and celebrate life together, combining the grounding of Nature with state-of-the-art sounds and producing something quite original. But aside from the physical debris left behind by the irresponsible, there are some for whom the entire occasion can be simply too much; the revelations a little too bright, the truths a little too vivid and close for comfort and many are the acid casualties who suffer sudden identity collapse on the dancefloor and have nowhere to turn.

The party casualties weren't limited to Westerners. The village had a good handful of lost-its who had altogether forgotten the plot, wandering around smoking too much charas with imbecilic grins on their faces that betrayed the underlying sadness, gnawing at their hearts. They lived in psychological limbo, being too weird for the locals, too gauche and dumb for the freaks. Their presence was so irritating that all sympathy for them was choked by the dark shadow they cast over any situation. I'm sure I came dangerously close to incurring violent retribution for my stridency in throwing them out of our hang-out spaces.

Corrupted though much of the original culture may be, it's all just part of the inevitable modernisation of an India that is joining the 20th century and lapping up the ideals of the West in the process.

Only in the less-exposed areas do traditional values thrive. I met an English couple who lived in a small village further down the valley and I was told about how the girl had been increasingly aware of someone watching her, when she went outside the house in the mornings. She told her boyfriend and when he followed her at a distance the next morning, he came across a young Indian guy who'd been masturbating in the bushes a few metres away. They kicked up a huge fuss and furore in the street, until they finally got to have a meeting with the leader of the village. With the help of a French guy who spoke good Hindi, he told them:

"I want this matter to be finished by sunset. If that means beating up the offender–we will help you! But after that, it must be finished."

" If this was England," my friend told him, with a stern face, "We would kill this man! Just like that!"

"Yes, yes, the English are very barbarous!" The French translator agreed.

"No, no, no! " The village leader cried. "This is *India,* not *England!"* They ended up with an agreement that if the young pervert ever came within sight of the house, they'd have licence to beat him up with full community support.

For in the mountains the torch of Hinduism still burns strong and with a typically charming glow. In the couple of weeks that I spent up there, there were two 'god-feasts' when householders invited the local gods to their houses and provided an eight-course meal for all-comers. A grand and costly *'puja'* to win favour with the local deities (and of course, in the village itself!). The ceremonies went all day, the figure-head of the local god carried up the hillside on the shoulders of honoured attendants. The god was surrounded by an entourage of trumpet-blaring and horn-blowing heralds who emitted a screeching fanfare every two or three minutes, just to let everyone know that the god had arrived.

Then the meal sessions sat and each new crowd took their place around the edge of the allotted area and brahmins then came round with baskets full of rice, *dal* and six other types of beans and curry in what was a banquet for the whole village. A constant stream of young and old women could be seen scurrying back from the feast, with tiffins full of food for family members unable to attend the feast in person.

I walked down to Manali, resolved to leave before any more

snow could come and block the road down to Delhi. In town, I had a chance meeting with the French couple I'd met whilst waiting for a lift at Calais! We didn't have much to say to each other and it was strange to exchange our stories of how we escaped the port area. The details seemed bland and irrelevant, now.

Chapter 18

Pink robes on the road
(India, the Plains)

As usual, I was sad to leave the mountains. We really were high above the psychic dross of the rest of the world and going back to Delhi was in every way a descent. But seasons change and things move on. There was a beautiful beach waiting for me at the end of it all–so best thumb forward!

A ride with some kids in a car took me down to Kulu and from there I got a lift in another car, driven by some businessmen from the Punjab. Small shrines were to be seen at the side of the road, to mark the place where buses have gone over the edge in the past. After bashing my head on the roof a hundred times in the course of the downhill journey on the bumpy and pot-holed road, I was dropped off at the first major town at the foot of the mountains.

After a moment of standing around, trying to work out if there was enough daylight to make any more progress that day, the question was solved by an elderly Sikh guy who invited me for some chai. It seemed that it was always the Sikhs who were the first to help me out in North India. He played me some of the transporting Punjabi song that I'd heard in the Golden Temple and was so pleased at my evident enjoyment that he put me up for a night and gave me dinner, too.

In recording any adventure, it all sounds smooth and straight-forward but there are generally long and dull periods where you have nothing to do except think and wait. Even Jack Kerouac described himself as 'a strange, solitary, Catholic mystic' and that seems a weird description for a man who spearheaded the Beat generation in its full glory. Hoboes may blaze a trail of glory but the sparks are scattered over some bare and desolate ground. It was in these hours of introspection and endurance that I could feel the process of internal growth.

I still had a way to go and I was tired of it all. I had to complete my journey and only hoped that there might be a literal pot of gold waiting at the other end of the rainbow. I had to find a new plot for myself as this one was wearing thin. I had a celebrated arrival in Goa to look forward to and I wondered if my hand-to-mouth mentors might have some positive suggestions to make (Write a book, they said) **

So in the morning, I hitched on to Delhi in various trucks and cars, finally getting a lift for two hundred kilometres straight to Delhi, in an air-conditioned chauffeur-driven car hired by an ex-patriate Indian businessman on his trip to visit family.

I caught a bus to Pahar Ganj, one of the most insane streets in the world and I strolled up and down for an hour in nostalgia for the manic times I've had to spend in this place. Most people coming to India fly in and out of Delhi and if they're on a budget, they invariably stay on Pahar ganj—as does anyone travelling up to or back from the mountains and other destinations in the area. Consequently, it has a constant stream of travellers coming to stay for a couple of nights, before getting out of the pandemonium as fast as they can.

In this kind of metropolis I always feel like I have a limited time to get through and out before some mysterious predatory forces swoop down upon me and break my back right there in the gutter; beggars already scrambling my clothes; ants, rats and vultures licking their lips at the prospect of fresh carrion as I finally succumb to the inexorable pull towards the all-consuming rot and decay that hangs thick in the air, spawning mould upon the walls, disease in the blood of the cringing street dogs and a vicious desperation in the souls of all condemned to live in these concrete deserts.

Your face turns black with the pollution after a couple of hours and to walk the full-length of the street means to be hassled about twenty-five times on average, by a crew including Kashmiri travel agents trying to get you to reserve your place on a house-boat in Srinigar, beggars pointing to their deformed limbs, wallahs of incense, stickers and maps and guys wanting to give you black market currency exchange.

I was emotionally blackmailed, into giving away my thick

blanket to a persistent beggar-lady with a baby on her arm. I rued my carefreeness later that night as I went to the Sikh temple to sleep. I was so cold that the attendant eventually had to roll me up in the carpet so that I could get some warmth.

As I got ready to leave the next morning I bumped into a couple of friends from the mountains, which was no surprise as on Pahar Ganj, you always meet people you haven't seen for ages and it would not be so strange to see Elvis riding down there on a cycle rickshaw. We adjourned to a rooftop terrace for breakfast at their generous expense and I remembered how an amazing view could be had from up high.

If you were to take just a five metre section of street on camera the day's events would make a fascinating short story, as samosa wallahs fight with the cows that try to steal food from their wheelbarrow carts, travellers stumble through the chaos stoned and freaked and endless rickshaws make the world a noisier place to live in. From this vantage point the world of the rooftops was also exposed; every last inch of space was used for living and locals could be seen going through their protracted washing rituals, whilst below them in the street stank a whole variety of decaying vegetable matter, cow shit and general rubbish, that epitomised the contradictions of standards in India as a whole.

I didn't look in great condition but that seemed to be appropriate to my situation–if I wanted people to feed me then it was necessary that I looked as though I needed help–on the other hand, being scruffy meant that the more luxurious rides would never let me into their cars–Damned if you do! Damned if you don't!

I found my way to the highway and got a few lifts in cars with well-educated Indians. I used the opportunity to expand my pathetic Hindi vocabulary–as a hand-to-mouth traveller, it's useful to know how to say 'I'm hungry' and 'I need a place to sleep'!

Then I got the most terrifying ride of the whole trip. I clambered on board the back of a flat-top lorry with another Indian and we hung on to a few ropes as the truck thundered along at top speed, with nothing to stop us from sliding off the sides to a grisly meeting with the ground! We tensed to cling even tighter as each pothole bumped us a few centimetres into the air. My new friend didn't seem too worried by this and so I reassured myself that it wasn't as absurdly dangerous as it seemed. But by the time we stopped for chai at a roadside place, after an hour of this white-knuckle riding, I was drenched in sweat from all the effort. We met an Indian guy who now lived in Florida and was taking his family on a holiday to see his home country. As if sent by the angels, he gave me a woolen blanket and 60 rupees to help me on my way.

A few of the guys in the front got on board other trucks and there was now space to ride in the cabin. There followed an uncomfortable night of shunting on to various chai stops, trying to catch some sleep in the meantime. The morning brought us close to Pushkar in Rajasthan and I arrived at this much-talked about jewel of the desert about noon.

The big attraction about this place was the holy lake and I was taken down to the water's edge by a canny brahmin priest, who made me go through the whole '*puja*' (the act of 'pleasing' the gods) ritual. It was actually quite soothing to throw bits of rice and flowers into the lake, in accordance with the worship that has gone on for thousands of years in much the same way. It was also about money of course but he didn't mind that I only gave five rupees, once I explained that I was a hand-to-mouthing my way around.

It was now a tourist town beyond any doubt and the main bazaar was packed with shops selling the kind of artifacts and clothes that only a traveller would buy. This was sad as in every face could be seen the glow of greed and one look in the eyes of most of the people of the town, revealed that their vision only extended as far as the acquisition of the next rupee.

I walked round to the other side of the lake and was invited to sit by the *dhuni* of a wooden hut. There was a very weird vibe and the sadhus decided not to allow me to smoke with them, on the grounds that charas makes Westerners 'crazy'. It occurred to me that I didn't have to sit and listen to this kind of shit and so I walked on, meeting another sadhu who beckoned for me to sit in his little clay room. He became enraged when I didn't even have a cigarette to offer him and so I walked out with a very bad taste in my mouth.

Children approached me with cries of 'one rupee' and 'schoolpen', as the result of tourists having showered them with these handouts in the past and now the rest of us have to endure the endless requests. Sadhus begged persistently in the street and I was fed up of the whole thing. I climbed up to a temple on a high rock but was refused permission to sleep there on the grounds that it was only for 'Pushkar *babas*'. I said to hell with the lot of them and made my way out of town.

I slept the night in the train station of the adjacent town of Ajmer and got some really quality kip on a bench. The sweetness of the dawn made up for the sourness of the previous day and some chai shop guys gave me a breakfast of tea and biscuits. It took a while to get a ride this morning because not all of the trucks were permitted to enter the state of Madhya Pradesh that we bordered.

I finally got moving and spent the day adjusting my body to the continual jerky motion of the trucks that rolled along at about 30kmph on terrible roads. Progress was unbearably slow as the drivers were forever pulling over for cups of sickly sweet chai, or to wash at the assigned areas provided by the roadside cafes by pouring jugs of water over themselves in their underclothes. Otherwise they might pull over to check the condition of the huge tyres, by rapping a spanner on them and listening for the tell-tale clunk of punctured rubber–if there's one thing that India tries to teach me, it's patience.

The first palm trees started to appear, though not yet of the coconut-bearing variety and the bushes cherished perfect flowers of red and orange. I was cheered to see that some brightness could survive the relentless dust that rose in dull clouds as we trundled past. I counted the kilometres wearily and reflected that the days of drives in Mercedes-Benz on smooth autobahns were now a long way behind me.

I spent the next night in a train station too and had dinner with a few opium farmers who told me they had never seen a white guy before. Indian cities all seem the same to me although here I attracted a lot more attention for no tourists have cause to come through these parts.

A cold wind blew as I waited for a ride in the morning. It was hard to believe that I was in the middle of India. I waited for about four hours before a ride with a motorbike revealed the reason for my slow progress, as we passed sixty trucks all held up due to an accident. Then we scooted past another one hundred and twenty trucks going the other way, also stuck.

Everywhere people were working and I had to remind myself that, whatever else I might have to go through, at least I wasn't planting potatoes! The trucks that I travelled in represented an age that was a century ahead of the lives of the peasants working in the fields and I wondered what it all must mean to the furry caterpillars that took ten minutes to cross the road.

A Sikh chap (driving trucks is a respectable and popular profession for these folk) took me to Indore. In accordance with the typical kindness of his people he gave me twenty rupees for my food that day. I hopped out by a chai stall and spent three anxious minutes trying to find out where I could go and shit. I shouted 'Latrine! Latrine!' at them but had to give a mock demonstration until they finally got the idea. When I returned, I was handed some bananas and chai and was taken to the home of the grumpy stall-holder, where I was given dinner and a bed there. I tried to deafen myself to the shouting and sounds of violence in the other room and grimly recalled what a dark world most or many Indians live in.

I was given a breakfast of 'buoy' in the morning, which is a pleasant dish of fried potatoes, onion and garlic in turmeric, with lemon juice, coriander and pomegranate on top! Then they stopped a driver who agreed to take me on to the Narmada River and we were off. I didn't know much about the place I was going to, except that it was supposed to be very shanti and picturesque.

But with the barren scenery around, I couldn't visualize how that could be–until we turned a corner and thick forest began to flank us on both sides, continuing all the way to the small town whose main income is from pilgrimages to this site.

My destination marked the point where the two holy rivers converge and the island that is the site of their meeting, is accordingly considered a place of power–Shiva power. Shiva is probably the most popular of the Hindu gods and is a pretty scary character, all things considered. He is the ultimate wielder of all destruction and has the gall to make a dance out of the act! Shiva is the favoured deity of most sadhus and freaks, as he is representative of lots of cool things from the smoking of hashish, to primal male sexual energy–and how can you go wrong by worshipping a god with dreadlocks?

He's saluted when a fuming chillum goes around by the all-too-serious smokers in the circle who, by yelling out 'Bom Shankar' or 'Shumbo' before they inhale, are summoning Shiva to come and join them–never mind that he rides a bull, has a cobra wrapped around his neck and has four mighty arms, waving tridents with strident devastation!

I caught a boat across the two hundred metres to the island and felt like I'd stepped back a century into an untainted India. Stepped ghats ran down to the water and women scrubbed their laundry on the stone, next to pilgrims taking baths and making *puja* to please Shiva. I slipped quickly up the steps to avoid the brahmins who would undoubtably want to smear red paint on my forehead, in the hope of a few rupees and I walked through the noisy bazaar, until I found a place by the river where I could try and erase six days of dust from my travel-worn body.

That done, I started to make my way around this island and the atmosphere began to quieten as I walked. Small temples containing huge phallic lingams watched from the side of the rocky path and donation boxes stood by to receive baksheesh from pilgrims.

Up above the path I saw a mud hut that looked like a sadhu's residence. A woman with top-knotted dreadlocks beckoned me up. I scrambled the path that led to the shack and sat down for some chai with her and her husband. My pitiful Hindi was soon put to the test but it was easy to get along with this couple who, until ten years ago, were simple farmers! They were just a couple of country-folk potato-planters and one day they just jacked it all in to embark on the sadhu way of life!*

They invited me to stay with them and I and the husband slept outside under the light bamboo shelter; until the rain came and forced us to go inside and join his wife. We woke at 4am and the male sadhu went straight outside to shit and wash (of course, the woman had had to attend to these duties hours before, in accordance with Hindu 'propriety'), to purify himself for this magical hour of the day when all *babas* rise and shine. His wife busied herself with the morning chai, whilst he put on his glasses and recited out loud his mantras and Shiva salutations for the morning.

When daylight came, I followed the husband down to the convergence of the two rivers which is always considered a place of power in many cultures across the world.

The morning was strangely melancholy and though it was all very beautiful and traditional and all, I felt quite at a loss to know what to do. It seemed like I was trespassing on a world that had nothing to do with me and I considered that I should perhaps just get back on the road, back towards the homeground of Goa.

As I was mulling in this feeble melancholy, a French guy that I passed beside a chai shop invited me over for a glass. He was an excellent character called Jean-Pierre and he was interested to know why I wore the pink colours. I explained that it just made it easier with the Indians, to not have to explain why I had no money

* *I returned with a friend to visit them six months later and discovered that they seemed to do rather well out of their hospitality towards Westerners; their stick and mud hut now had a huge metal door hinged to the front (never mind that a chicken could have pecked its way in through the back). Then, whilst I was assuring my friend that there was no need to worry about the malaria 'because after all, the locals deal with it okay'—we turned to see the old sadhu erecting his new mosquito net! ***

all the time and he nodded in understanding.

"Ah good! I saw you and said to myself 'Is this guy on a duplicate sadhu-trip?'" He told me how he had done much the same journey twenty years ago but that he had continued this way of life for seven years—after that period of time he was jailed in Thailand for seven years. He saw it as a poetic balance of life-tides.

He explained to me that prison was not the cage that most people imagine and told me that time was just a concept of which we can be the master rather than the subject. He was a cool and collected cat who regretted nothing and did not look like he'd been on the road for twenty-five years. When I told him that I had felt like leaving the island at once, he smiled and said:

"Ah no! This is just the Shiva energy of the island working on you! The rivers here are different to that of the Ganga in Benares, which is much more *shanti* —tabla and flute drifting story—here the rivers are much more strong and like Shiva, you know? And people come here with much energy and they meet with what is here and bounce right off!"

He was right. Once I cooled off a bit and took things easy, it became a lot easier to hang about. I played jazz beside the river and smoked charas with some of the sadhus I met. But because I didn't speak the language properly, I was never able to penetrate the surface of life in India and so I didn't quite sink into the feel of this place.

The Indians who lived here were of a low-caste and conse-quently had very few pretensions or illusions about their lives. They were easy-going company and their daughters were unbearably beautiful—but I knew that they were well beyond my reach.

**There was quite a lot of malaria about and it was kind of eerie to know that locals were going through the fever just a few houses down. It made me look at mosquitoes with a different eye—but what to do? The malaria tablets are more or less useless (even if the locals could afford them) and can cause blindness and other nasty ailments if taken for more than a few months!

I should perhaps have spent more time here, absorbing the subtle riches of the area that take a little time to appreciate. But I was re-reading Kerouac's "On The Road" and I was being filled with the get-up-and-go energy that fuels mind-less expeditions. Riding in rackety old trucks at 30kmph along routes that seem more like river beds than roads, is hardly what any of the Beat generation had to contend with but the spirit of the thing was with me and I hungered for the sea.

Using half of the 100 rupees that Jean-Pierre had given me, I bought a load of groceries for my sadhu couple and tried not to get too upset by the cheek of the boy who hoped I'd forget my fifty rupees change. Back at the shack they were very appreciative of the food and the wife at once set about preparing a huge meal, insisting that I eat three times my fill. I felt like I was back in Iran.

I woke about 3am and left them my woolen blanket, slipping out of the mud hut without saying 'goodbye'. I played jazz by the river until the light came and then made my way back into town, where devotional music of 'Om namah Shivaya' could already be heard at full pitch though the sun had not yet risen.

I hitched a ride back into Indore and had to make a quick exit, when the drivers asked for money at the end. I realised that that was the accepted protocol around here and afterwards I made sure to always explain to the truck guys that I had no money to give them, before getting in. The folks around here had a mean and hungry look and it was many hours before I was able to get moving.

When I did get a ride, it was in a small pick-up truck and in the course of the journey into the state of Maharastra, we took on board four or five individuals who paid for their ride. We had to swerve to avoid many others who attempted to accost our vehicle in the most aggressive hitchhiking I'd ever seen. Most things are reduced to money in India but it seemed that people made an exception of me as a white man in grubby sadhu garb.

The hills here were high and green and as evening came we seemed to be moving onto new lands. I was let off at a truck stand, where I was given a meal and a rope bed to sleep on by the smiling chai-shop wallahs.

Chapter 19

Last Legs to Goa
(India, Goa)

Bright and early the next morning, a truck full of guys who'd come all the way from the Himalayas stopped for me and they were delighted to know that I'd spent some time in their home state. They left me with some rupees for lunch and by evening I had come to Pune–though only after the mind-numbing hassle in asking directions of a country without logic.

It was assumed by the locals that in my pink outfit, I must be one of the 'sunnyasins' of Osho's Ashram, the institution that put the name of this city on the map for millions across the world. Osho, otherwise known as Rajneesh, was an Indian vastly learned in the traditional scriptures who came to pronounce himself as a Realised Being. Whether he was a Buddha or a con-man seems to be a matter of the individual heart -for me, I wince when I hear his voice but his words themselves are undeniably brilliant. Some feel that he simply tapped into a profitable market of Westerners come to India in search of truth. Rajneesh gave them a package whereby they could combine their spirituality with drugs, sex and money-making. Nothing wrong with that in itself but it meant that thousands of people now mooch around professing to be holy without appearing to do very much in that direction. The phoney rhetoric of these dilettantes is perhaps what gains the Ashram a dubious reputation in some circles.

But there are many whom I respect and love who spent years at the feet of Rajneesh and who have no doubts that he had achieved the Final State. At the very least, it has to be admitted that he was an unparalelled success at bringing the mountain to him as devotees built ashrams around his feet and an entire organisation sprang up to disseminate his teachings. Maybe he was too successful at this as the Pune Ashram began to take the leading hand more and more, becoming bogged down in the politics of running a religion. Rajneesh died some years ago and now the Ashram has set his teachings of worldly transience into clay. But as I've been sternly told, I shouldn't speak too authoritively of these things without personal experience. I couldn't afford the entrance fee to the Ashram, which was a pity as I had heard they are sensational.

I had thoughts about trying to hitch through the night but these were soon soggy notions as a mighty thunderstorm let loose. Everyone was forced to retreat to the shelter of door ways and the odd bit of terracing or else face the punishment of truly angry rain.

When the torrents eased up, I scuttled along to the train station to see if I could travel some of the remaining distance through the night. A strange vibe was in the air and there were not too many smiles to be seen in one of India's most modern cities.

The rain had caused everyone at the station to huddle closer, away from the dampness that crept in at the exposed edges and which was brought in by each successive dripping arrival. People slept on laid-out pieces of cardboard on the concrete platforms. I didn't know if they were homeless or if they were just waiting for a train that, for them, looked like it might never arrive.

Others slept on the benches of the waiting areas until the police came along and rapped the metal benches with their batons, producing a harsh clatter that shook all the reclining awake with a shocked dizziness. It all seemed in accord with the dark mood of the night and I was glad to board my train going South.

I climbed into what used to be the third class compartment before such terminology was abolished and fought for a seat on the uncomfortable wooden benches with the other poor folk. Sleep came, more or less and I awoke at about two or three a.m. when ticket inspectors came in from each end of the carriage, blocking any route of escape. I was rehearsing my lines in Hindi to explain that I was a sadhu and was thus travelling for free–when the conductor stopped at the man in front of me: a poor man in peasant clothes, sitting on the floor. The conductor yelled at him:

"Paise nahin?("no money?") Then he clipped him roughly about the ear and stood back to let fly a huge punt into the small man's thigh as he cowered on the ground. He then turned to me and fortunately, I was too sleepy to be as afraid as I ought to have been.

I gave him my story in faltering Hindi. He replied in English:

"What are you doing in India?" And he began to walk past to check the next tickets as I replied:

"Oh, just living in temples and trying to stay alive really!" I suppose if I'd been a real defender of the people, I should have broken his ribs as the reward for his minor fascism–but sometimes the waves of evil just sweep over everything and everyone, over-whelming all that gets in the way. So I took the path of least resistance and hoped he'd get his just desserts sooner rather than later. Surely I could reply upon the laws of karma to function properly in India?

When I woke again, it was morning and we were coming into Kolhapur station. Some great change had occurred during the dark of the night and now the world seemed to be full of flowers and fresh smells. The sky shone with a bright blue that the North could never have known, as colours and sounds behaved with a new-born vibrance. It was a happy hitchhiker that bounced down the early morning streets to waste no time in flagging a lift out.

Since coming into Maharastra, the general wealth of the areas could be seen in contrast to the bleakness of Middle India and Kolhapur was no exception. The most striking thing was the middle classness of the people, who wore smart Western clothes and walked down streets that were alarmingly clean for India. The attitudes were of a predictable bent also as whenever I asked directions for the road to Goa, I was directed to the bus station. This would happen however I might phrase my question. The Indians I met were all so pleased with themselves for being able to direct me to the bus terminal that they couldn't consider that I might be asking them something else. When they finally did just listen to my actual words and understood that I was hitchhiking, they invariably answered:

"Oh! This is not possible, here!" I would then heatedly inform them that I had managed my first six thousand miles and I reckoned I could manage the remaining two hundred okay! Indians just love to make pronouncements on things whether they know anything about the subject or not.

I breathed deeply and counted to ten as I received this reaction again and again. I reminded myself that it would soon all be over. I laughed as I realised that I had not had this hassle in leaving a town since the times I would hitch out of London–I would stand in outer Streatham, waiting for a lift and almost invariably some black guy would come up to me saying:

"You've got no chance, mate! No one's gonna stop for you! You're gonna have to walk home!" Which is just what you need when you've been waiting in vain for three hours.

A truck going all the way across the continent to Pondicherry picked me up and I found myself chatting to George and James, two Indian Christians, who wanted me to come with them to the East coast! They bought me a South Indian breakfast of rice cakes and coconut chutney and shortly afterwards I got a motorbike ride into the outskirts of Goa. This was a welcome change from the stifling cabins of the trucks, though I bruised my coccyx on a winding trail through shadowy roads obscuring the holes in the road that threatened to dismount us.

The journey was coming to an end and in the twelve days since leaving the mountains, I'd been on the move so much that I'd not really considered what would happen when I arrived. Goa is the place where people go, to run away from India! It's cleaner, more ordered and is probably less challenging in a cultural context than any other place in India.

Until 1961 it was a Portugese colony and it's full of Latin archi-tecture and glorious white churches that prove that something can stay clean in India. After the Portugese left the Goans sat around wishing they'd come back, until the first few freaks arrived in 1965–one old Goan lady said at the time:

"Thank God you've come–now we have someone to talk to!" Not only did life become more entertaining for the locals, the Western drop-outs brought in welcome revenue as they began to rent rooms and buy fruit and fish to cook on the beaches that were almost completely empty. A beach is a pretty easy place to live on as most of the essentials of life are within reach. The natural beauty of the place was a perfect setting for the freaks to party and let all hang loose.

These beaches that were only of importance to the Goans for the good fishing and coconut trees that were the basis of their livelihood, soon became precious landholdings that families fought over. The natural panorama of the place was in many parts hideously marred as they built as many houses and hotels as they could. Now Goa draws over a million charter tourists a year as podgy beer-drinking European tourists arrive each winter to brave it in this tamed outlet of India. They sit in huge hotels with swimming pools that usurp much of the scarce water supply and bring the foreign currency that fuels the greed and ambition of the locals, polluting their peace of mind. The fishermen now have motorised boats instead of oars and every Goan family has televisions, radios and motorbikes that are good on acceleration, bad on brakes. They no longer smile very much.

If that has been the fate of the locals then a similar change has occurred amongst the freaks themselves, who are not any longer so freakish. Whereas they used to eat and live communally and regularly take acid to expand their minds to live each day a-fresh–now most sit back on their stories and whinge and complain about the decay of their paradise, like old folks anywhere in the world: 'Oh, it's not like it used to be!' they cry–and they're right.

In fact a while ago, it was even better. Techno music came to Goa in the 80's and added a new dimension to the traditional thriving scene where a few hundred people would take acid from a free punch and dance through the night on personal journeys, that all came together in the mornings. With the approach of daylight you could suddenly see just who you had been dancing with as colour returned to the world and it was delightful to be in amongst palm trees, a sparkling sea and unspoilt beaches. There existed something of a psychedelic community where everyone took care of each other's trip and there was a kind of support network of understanding, that made it easier for people to integrate their voyages into the unknown back into the continuity of day-to-day life.

I arrived at the tail-end of this as the whole scene became

corrupted by over-exposure, the greed of Goan and Indian business and all of the nasties that came with it. Parties still do happen but the police receive up to a thousand pounds baksheesh for each one for permission to be given and they're staged at locations centred around a bar serving alcohol rather than in remote idylls in Nature. It's no fun to be trying to hold your head together on acid and turn to find a beggar thrusting their poverty in your face–especially if they look like they're having a better time than you!

However, there survives a kind of precious beauty to the place and it holds a special magic of its own that may survive all the crassness that descends upon the area. There are still many, many interesting people who spend up to six months living here and there's still a kind of international village feeling, existing within certain strongholds of freakdom in hidden-away spots. It's not always immediately obvious to outsiders though: Onemorning, whilst sitting on the part of the beach where characters of twenty or thirty years standing hung out, three Brits on holiday turned up, a little lost and, after ordering three beers in the midday sun, asked me if I knew where the 'hippie camp' was!

McDonalds hasn't arrived yet and certain areas hold an ambience that can't be beat. It's quaint to stroll through dirt tracks in the shade of palm trees whilst pigs, chickens and cows roam about and there's the space to do your thing without interference from others. It gets harder and harder to maintain a peaceful space but for now its the best that I've found.

I arrived in Panaji on Saint Xavier's day and the Goans were in full festive mode. There were lots of guys in suits bombing around on their scooters and respectable Catholic girls who milled about in vaguely content crowds. I weaved my way through and stretched my memory by taking various backroads to avoid the traffic generated by the flea market.

It all got easier by the moment as I came across the little turnings and places that I knew so well. My final ride was in the back of a three-wheeled pick-up truck.

Standing like a proud charioteer, we rode into the sunset and I ran the final two hundred metres across the rice paddies and down to the sea.

The moon hung in three day-old virginity and glints of phosphorescence played at the water's edge.

The thump of techno resounded behind me and everyone had come out to play for as long as the stars held session.

I had come a long way. I still had my health, my sanity and thirty rupees in my pocket.

Did this mean that the journey was over?

It still wasn't going to be easy but is it ever?

I ambled down the beach, away from the music and lay down to gaze at the sky, with my head a few metres away from the sea's edge.

I listened to the lapping water and smiled as I heard each arriving wave bring the message, that there is no ending...